"The distinguishing marks ...odist

are not his opinions of any sort. His assenting

to this or that scheme of Religion, his embracing

any particular set of notions, his espousing

the judgment of one man or of another,

are all quite wide of the point."

John Wesley

THE METHODIST STORY

Volume 1 ▪ 1703-1791

by Donald W. Haynes

The Methodist Story
Volume 1 • 1703-1791
by Donald W. Haynes

In Praise of This Book

"Dr. Haynes' work is truly the work of a student of the faith. He has pulled together the thinking of many of the finest minds that have tackled the developing spirit of Wesley and put them into a masterful narrative. We all grow as Wesley did during his long life, and perhaps in the end we are a bit closer to understanding each other within the Wesleyan scheme."

Richard P. Heitzenrater
Retired William Kellon Quick Professor of Church History and Wesley Studies
The Divinity School, Duke University

"Donald Haynes was not alive for the first chapters of Methodist history about which he writes, but he should have been! He would have been at home equally with the theological debates and the innovative methods employed to reach new disciples. Few people have been shaped by more themes that make up the fabric of United Methodism's past and promise than this author. The story he tells is about history, but it also comes from the heart."

Lovett H. Weems, Jr.
Distinguished Professor of Church Leadership,
Wesley Theological Seminary, Washington, DC

"Engaging, lucid, readable, and grounded on pertinent scholarship, The Methodist Story is aptly titled, and guides the 'story' with frequent headers and bolded emphases, inviting in even the casual reader."

Russell E. Richey
William R. Cannon, Distinguished Professor Emeritus
The Divinity School, Duke University

"Donald Haynes continues to guide us toward the critical contribution of class meetings and covenant groups that build authentic community as a means of grace. The contribution and role of laity is once again offered as a reminder of the mutual fulfillment of our baptism, and the influence of the Church on a society in great need of trusting, spiritual communities."

Bishop Paul L. Leeland, Ed.D.
Resident Bishop
Western North Carolina Conference, The United Methodist Church

"In The Methodist Story, Volume I, Donald Haynes provides a lively and accessible overview of the origins of Methodism in eighteenth century England. Haynes, who has taught and researched in the field of Wesleyan Studies for decades, is a natural storyteller who has grounded his writing in the most important primary and secondary sources in the field. His text is a welcome addition to the library of any pastor, student, or lay person who wants to learn more about John Wesley and the founding principles and practices that comprised early Methodism."

Michael K. Turner, Ph.D.
Associate Professor of the History of Christianity and Wesleyan Studies
Memphis Theological Seminary

"Dr. Don Haynes has a brilliant way to present an important body of information in an interesting and persuasive manner. In this book, he shares the history of Methodism with clarity and accuracy. It is both informative and enjoyable."

Dr. Nido R. Qubein
President, High Point University

"Don Haynes has a sharp mind and passionate heart. Both come together brilliantly in this first volume of Methodism's story that does so much more than trace our Wesleyan roots, but also interprets our spiritual history for the missional challenge of our times. This is an outstanding resource for any Methodist who wants to get our story straight!"

Rob Fuquay
Senior Pastor, St. Luke's UMC, Indianapolis IN

Table of Contents

Acknowledgments

In a general but very profound way, I must acknowledge my debt to the unquenchable thirst for Methodist history and doctrine that was instilled in me by my mother and her two brothers, the Revs. John Cephas and Theemon Garrett Williams. Both of them began their ministries on horseback. From them at a very early age, I learned all the polity terms of The Methodist Church and what it meant to be doctrinally Arminian. The oldest of my two hundred and ninety-three books categorized by the Dewey Decimal System as "Methodist," and are from my uncles' libraries - hagiographic nineteenth century biographies of Wesley and histories of Methodism.

As a young pastor in the 1950's, I owe a debt to Dr. Wilson Nesbitt of the Rural Ministry staff of Duke Endowment for exposing me to the denominational Town and Country Movement which had faculty in almost every seminary in Methodism. I studied under most of them, learning especially from Earl D. C. Brewer at Candler School of Theology and Marvin Judy at Perkins School of Theology. With Dr. Brewer, I spent a summer "mapping" the history of Methodism in Southern Appalachia, first its phenomenal growth and then its precipitous decline. At that time, I was a pastor in Appalachia.

Studying one summer under Rupert Davies of Wesley College in England was a game changer. It was under his tutelage that I first "walked in the steps of Wesley," spending time in every major place of his childhood, Oxford Years, and ministry, learning from curators and Wesley collections and buildings in London, Bristol, and Epworth. After those experiences, I led tour groups, seminary students, clergy, and grandsons to study Wesley in the context of the eighteenth-century Enlightenment, his life long journey in "holy living" (pre and post Aldersgate), and the early, middle, and later times in his own journey. Concurrently, I was teaching classes in the local churches I served as pastor. I am grateful to Alpha Christian Tours for their allowing me to be the "color" person on their tours.

In 1977 Dr. Thomas Langford provided me a scholarship to study under a world-wide Methodist faculty at Lincoln College where we studied *Sanctification and Liberation* in the rooms where Wesley tutored. In formal lectures, informal conversations, and table talk, I learned from Ted Runyon, José Bonino, Rupert Davies, James Cone, Nancy Hardesty, Kwesi Dickson, and others. It was an experience after which one is "never the same again."

From my development of "Vision 2000," a paradigm for church growth, I was blessed to become friends with Len Sweet, Lovett Weems, Joe Harding, Ralph Mohney, Chuck Hunter, Jeff Spiller, Stan Copeland, and other leading voices of United Methodism in the late twentieth century. All of them contributed to my knowledge of our Methodist Story and message.

In 1991, I met Dr. Peter Graves, a superlative British Methodist minister, when both of us were teaching at the World Methodist Evangelism Congress at Candler School of Theology. I am deeply indebted to him for the many days we spent in England and America in his parishes and mine. He introduced many resources, provided a British perspective, and opened for me relationships with British leaders like Donald English when he was President of the British Conference. When Dr. Graves was Superintendent Minister at Westminster Central Hall which had a large African and English membership, he invited me to preach and to listen and take notes at the British Methodist Conference. Peter has read this present copy. To him, I am deeply grateful.

Upon retirement I taught at Hood Theological Seminary as Director of Wesleyan Studies for sixteen years. There I added a new journey with students and fellow faculty from African American expressions of Methodist history and Wesleyan doctrine. Friendship with present authors like Dr. Jason Vickers and Dr. Michael Turner were formed at Hood. Simultaneously through a professional mentor, I learned so much about the paradigm of feminist accents needed to flesh out our overlooked history and theological experience.

Dr. Randy Maddox of Duke Divinity School assembled in the 300th anniversary of Wesley's birth a number of persons who were teaching Wesleyan Studies in a variety of seminaries. Duke faculty leaders were Drs. Maddox, Richard Heitzenrater, Russell Richey, and Stephen Gunter. Those weeks I developed as personal friends Drs. Heitzenrater and Richey who are perhaps Methodism's preeminent scholars in Methodist history, per se. Both have been enormously helpful through their own superb writings, and their critique of some of my pedestrian work.

From my own library, I have compiled a mountain of notes from which I first drew my seminary lectures and their conversion to a book manuscript. Kevin Slimp of Market Square Books has been so helpful in his encouragement for me to write this two-volume account of *The Methodist Story* and for assigning the manuscript to his editorial staff in proofing and printing. Personally, I am indebted to Allen Holt of Asheboro, North Carolina for his help in formatting and Martha Webster of Lubbock, Texas for her incredible help and scores of hours in proofing. To my wife, Joan, I am deeply grateful for her being a "book widow" as I spent hundreds of hours over many years in the study, researching, chasing footnote sources, and writing. An English teacher, she then proofed each chapter.

Lastly, to those scholars who were gracious enough to praise this endeavor in words printed on the first page, I am so grateful. Most readers will take their endorsement over my name as author. As Montaigne wrote "I have gathered a bouquet of other men's flowers, and nothing but the thread that binds them is mine own."

Preview of Volume II
The Methodist Story in America

Volume II of *The Methodist Story* begins really in 1760 when the first Methodist missionaries came at their own initiative to America. It documents Methodism in the colonial era, the Revolutionary War, and the early days of both Methodism and the new Republic. Volume II continues through the General Conference of 2019.

The name or names, the polity or polities, the theology or pluralism, the definition of social justice positions, and the Trust Clause and ownership of church property will be determined by the action of the special General Conference in St. Louis February 23-26, 2019. The last chapter of Volume II of *The Methodist Story* will reflect the "way forward."

Prior to publication, you may preorder your copy of Volume II from MarketSquareBooks.com.

Preface

In one sense the story of Methodism is a much-plowed ground. Books far superior to this volume have been written on every phase and facet of John Wesley's life and ministry, on Methodist beginnings in Great Britain, and on American Methodism. No research, experience, or writing can equal the work of superlative historians and Wesley scholars like Richard Heitzenrater and Russell Richey. However, the 2016-2020 quadrennium has a heightened anxiety for United Methodism.

The "catholic spirit" has held us together through many divisive issues. "Through many dangers, toils, and snares, we have already come." In this current context, it seems appropriate to renew laity and clergy acquaintance with "the way it was," as we seek our "way forward." Our hope is to fulfill Mr. Wesley's admonition that "though we may not think alike, we can love alike." This is not an attempt to "white-wash" the many splendored story, nor to deny the vision, energy, and spirituality of our leaders and "foot soldiers." This version of *The Methodist Story* both applauds our noble past and is candid in recognizing the human frailty of our leaders in every generation.

In this first of two volumes, we review John Wesley and his family, and Methodism as a movement in England within the context of the eighteenth century. Volume I includes Mr. Wesley's eventual ordination of clergy to form a new American Church. It ends at an arbitrary date, John Wesley's death on March 2, 1791.

In Volume II, we shall document Methodist beginnings in America, the phenomenal early years, the nineteenth century when "Asburian" Methodism was a major shaper of American culture, the ecumenism, mergers, and eventual decline in the twentieth century, and the painful decline and divisiveness of United Methodism in America in the twenty-first century.

The content of this book is well documented from primary and superb secondary sources. It has been written, and re-written, over a fifteen-year period of teaching the history of "the people called Methodist" to seminary students at Hood Theological Seminary in Salisbury, North Carolina. Hood is the only African Methodist Episcopal Zion seminary in the United States. Therefore, *The Methodist Story* here includes Americans of African ethnicity.

My journey began in a small rural church in North Carolina, founded by my grandmother who wanted a Methodist Episcopal Church, South in her rural community. It was founded in 1904, always very small, and held together by the Sunday School teachers, nurturing me in Bible stories and Arminian theology.

The Methodist Discipline was on our meager bookshelves; I was reared on many quotations from Mr. Wesley. Two of my uncles from that little church became Methodist preachers in the 1920's. When I left for college, my mother said, "Son, as far back as we know, our people have been Methodists." The die was cast, I would live and I shall die a Methodist.

This proximity of two "MP" churches and our "MEC,S" church gave me a lifelong interest in the "Unification" of Methodism in 1939 which formed "The Methodist Church, healing breaches that had occurred in 1828 and 1844." I was appointed in 1954, ordained Deacon in 1956, Elder in 1958, and retired in 1999.

In my teen years, my own theology was forged by the holiness Methodist movement at John Wesley Holiness Camp Meeting with powerful preachers and evangelists. God used that context for my call to ordained ministry. My earliest invitations to preach were in a Nazarene Church, but I would be a Methodist preacher.

At High Point College, the faculty were excellent scholars of "19th century liberalism" but I remained a Fundamentalist who insisted on inerrant, verbally inspired biblical literalism. I later, on bended knee, had to apologize to Dr. William R. Locke for my rudeness.

At Duke Divinity School my rigid orthodoxy and unChristlike attitude were met by devout professors. I must name Dr. McMurry Richey in Christian Education, Dr. William Brownlee in Old Testament, Dr. James Price in New Testament, and Dr. H. Shelton Smith in American Protestant Thought as game changers. Duke at that time did not have a strong faculty in Wesleyan grace theology. I had one course in Methodism, taught by a Mennonite.

My conscience of social justice issues was shaped 1966-70 while I served First Methodist Church in Franklin, North Carolina. The "War on Poverty" staff from all over America came to Southern Appalachia. They introduced me to liberation theology.

Years later, I was on the faculty of St. Paul School of Theology in Kansas City when it was devoted to liberation theology. I never

became a disciple of liberation theology, but those personal relationships and their life commitments to social justice left an indelible impression on my own theology and my ministry.

In the early 1990's, utilizing insights and data of the emergent
Church Growth Movement, and, as "Director of Annual Conference Ministries" I developed "Vision 2000" for the Western North
Carolina Conference. The General Board of Discipleship later
launched it in three jurisdictions.

Upon retirement in 1999, I became the Director of Wesleyan
Studies at Hood Theological Seminary in Salisbury, North
Carolina. I owe much to my colleagues there for insight into the
perspective of African American Methodism and the encouragement of the students to develop class notes into a manuscript for
publication.

For eight years after retirement, I wrote a column called
"Wesleyan Wisdom" for The United Methodist Reporter. My previously published books have been *On the Threshold of Grace, Reading the Bible Again and Seeing It for the First Time,* and *A Digest of
Wesleyan Grace Theology.*

The second volume's last chapter on Methodism in America
will be written immediately after the adjournment of the special
session of General Conference. That chapter reflects the actions
and immediate reaction to the "Way Forward" which are adopted
or tabled in February, 2019.

Donald W. Haynes
Asheboro, North Carolina
2019

Introduction

Every schoolchild learned about the Pilgrims who came to the "stern and rockbound coast" of New England, landing at Plymouth Rock in 1620. As an historical curiosity, Wesley's home of Epworth in Lincolnshire is only fourteen miles from Scrooby, the village from which the Pilgrims left in 1605 to go to Holland and from which they left in 1620 to come to America. Halford Luccock and Webb Garrison wrote, "Though totally unrelated, from 'these two little dots on the map' religious movements were born -movements that had a 'blind date' with destiny. From these two small villages in northern England, a century apart in dates, the spiritual forces went out that became spiritual influences in the English-speaking world."[1]

Church historians and theologians for two centuries failed to understand the soul of Methodism. One term used to describe it was "popular religion" because of its origin among the English underclass. More accurately it must be described as "lived religion," according to the insightful work of David Hempton who was born in Ireland, studied in England, and teaches in Boston. He says of early Methodism, "It was a movement of discipline and sobriety, but also of ecstasy and enthusiasm."[2] Hempton then asks a most profound question, and one that needs to be revisited as United Methodism sinks further into membership decline, societal influence weakening, and possible schism. The question is, "What gave Methodism its competitive advantage over scores of other populist religious traditions, and why did it grow in some places, but not in others?"[3]

Methodism was not a product of the Enlightenment, but Wesley did adopt, adapt, and "tweak" the theory of knowledge developed by John Locke, "father" of British Enlightenment. Wesley was not a fire brand, but he developed, preached, and explicated his own version of religious enthusiasm, using the term "witness of the Spirit" as a special gift of God to the Methodists. Hempton also points out the rather disparate sources of Wesley's opposition:

---

[1] Garrison, Webb; Luccock, Halford, *Endless Line of Splendor,* United Methodist Communications, 1950, 12

[2] Hempton, David, *Methodism—Empire of the Spirit,* Yale, 2005, 7

[3] Ibid., 7

- The clergy of the Church of England, especially the diocesan bishops who detested Wesley's espousal of enthusiasm

- The Dissenters who saw Wesley as an "Oxford man" and Anglican priest

- Local law enforcement who saw Wesley's crowds as disturbing the peace

- Loyal Anglican parents who forbade their grown children to associate with the rabble who went out to hear Wesley

- Violent mobs, often spilling out of grog shops and simply looking for trouble.

The Industrial Revolution was enticing rural peasants to move to the cities and work in factories. Men, women, and children as young as five and six years of age were pressed by landlords to work in mines and factories twelve hours a day, six days a week. The streets were open sewers running with putrid water. The houses were but hovels thrown up by the owners of the mills and mines.

Methodism went where Anglicanism did not. Parish churches had been planted to serve a rural society. Almost no new churches were built to serve the new industrial areas. This meant an almost total chasm between the church and families. For the first time, many children were not baptized, and common law marriage replaced marriage by a priest. Both the sheriff and the parish priests were opposed to any populist movement that might threaten the status quo.

By the 1740's John Wesley's reputation as a preacher meant that when he appeared on horseback and stood on the steps of the monument at the village square or in front of a town center pub, large crowds gathered. The practice of Methodist Societies was to meet at night and on Sundays at an hour to avoid conflict with "church hours." However, meeting in the dark, and the practice of issuing tickets for admission to both women and men, gave rise to wild rumors and accusations of what went on behind locked doors!

The itinerant Methodist lay preachers were heckled, humiliated, and subjected to insulting forms of punishment: rolled in mud, doused in ponds, stripped of clothing, rocked, and sometimes literally "ridden out of town on a rail." Yet their perseverance,

their witness, their personal character, and the music all created
a new religious paradigm. It was said of Jesus, "The common
people heard him gladly for he spoke with authority, not as the
scribes." The Methodist lay preachers, exhorters, and stewards
likewise spoke with the authority of Christian witness, not with
the pedantry that characterized the 18th century Anglican pulpit.

Wesley was an enigma. He was a graduate of Christ Church
College, he was a fourth generation Oxonian, a "professor"
at Oxford's Lincoln College. He was a priest in the Church of
England. He was attracted to what was called the "pietist"
movement of Moravianism and relished the testimonials of new
converts who were called "enthusiasts." The Wesleyan revival
was nothing short of a religious phenomenon. David Hempton
described it as "a revolutionary religious movement coming of
age in an era of political revolutions across the North Atlantic
region."[4] There is no question that in the revival in England, and
the Second Great Awakening of America, the Wesleyan heritage
was definitely evangelistic in tone, content, and worship style.
Socio-economic gentrification and a modicum of worship liturgy
came later.

However, we must not revise Methodist history. There were
"fightings and fears within and without." By 1740, Wesley broke
fellowship with the Moravians who had midwifed him to his
assurance of salvation. By that time, he had serious theological
conflict with George Whitefield, who was a Calvinist. He had
serious conflict with his brothers, Samuel, Jr. and Charles over
administration of the sacraments and separation from the Anglican Church. He deeply resented Charles' breakup of his near
marriage relationship to Grace Murray. Also, by 1760, Wesley was
allowing women to preach, a practice forbidden by the Anglicans.
He parted ways with Thomas Maxfield and others about Christian perfection. His marriage in 1751 was a disaster; he and Molly
Vazeille never had a chapter of domestic peace or privacy. He lived
in a fish bowl and she never came to terms with his belonging to
the people.

He was a prolific writer and his writings were read widely;
his collected works in 1771 filled thirty-two volumes. Indeed, he
was wealthy in annual income. One year when he made £1400
from book sales, he allowed himself to keep only £30. He told his

---

⁴ Ibid., 99

sister Martha, "Money never stays with me."[5] He could have been one of the wealthier men of his times, but when he died at age eighty-eight, his major assets were his books, his horses, and one carriage. He willed everything to what he called "poor people," lay preachers, and his nephews and nieces. He insisted that "six poor men" carry his casket to his grave behind Wesley's Chapel: "no hearse, no coach, no escutcheon, no pomp except the tears of them that loved me and are following me to Abraham's bosom."[6]

Let's let the story unfold on its own.

---

[5] Tomkins, Stephen,. *John Wesley, A Biography*, Eerdmans, 2003, 167

[6] Heitzenrater, Richard, *The Elusive Mr. Wesley—John Wesley, his own biographer*, Abingdon, 1984, 220

CHAPTER ONE

The Times in Britain
During Wesley's Ministry

We too often have looked at the life of John Wesley in isolation from the incredible changes that occurred in the generation before him and the 18th century during which he lived as a British citizen. This we must not do; John Wesley was highly connected through family and education. The eighteenth century was one of great ideas, great men and women, and one of seismic paradigm shifts. "All human institutions were shaken to their foundations, all past authority was ignored or repudiated; the old system of society was crumbling into ruin."[7] He was a man of his own generation who did not live in a political and cultural vacuum.

While Wesley was planting Methodism,

- In 1707 Scotland and England merged to form Great Britain; the "UK" was still new.

- The Industrial Revolution was remaking the demographic map of Britain.

- Soldiers and sailors were being recruited and drafted to fight wars in Scotland, France, Germany, India, Canada, and the American Colonies.

- The "Enlightenment" was producing writings from some of history's most brilliant minds in the natural sciences, economics, political theory, and philosophy.

- The American War for Independence created a radically different political context for the Methodist missionaries

---

[7] Whiteley, J.H., *Wesley's England,* London: Epworth Press, 1954, 25

in America than Wesley and the Methodist lay preachers in
Britain were experiencing.

Industrial Revolution

Let us begin our journey by walking briefly into the eighteenth
century of "that island nation." Dickens described Wesley's as "the
best of times and the worst of times." No culture was so dramatically affected by inventions as Great Britain during the years that
John Wesley personified Methodism.

England and Scotland were literally the birthplace of the
Industrial Revolution. The word "manufacture" means "hand-
made." The Latin word "manu" means "by hand." The word
"factum" means "to make." The original location was not a
factory to which people went to work. Manufacturing was in the
home, therefore, often called "cottage industry." Then manufacturing was moved to factories. This forced workers to leave
their rural villages and move to one of the growing cities, to
leave their homes for ten or twelve hours a day, and to work with
former strangers rather than family members. These changes
created a new and radically changed psychological and physical
environment. One aspect of this change is insecurity, another is
a new genre of temptations. Both of these created the probability
of increased immorality and, paradoxically, an opportunity for
religious conversion. As we think about the impact on people's
livelihood and lives by the Industrial Revolution, let us realize
the impact of John Wesley's field preaching at mine shafts and
factory gates. He literally went where the people were, something
unthinkable in the Anglican Church.

When John Wesley was one-year-old, France had the most
powerful army in the world and had not lost a battle in fifty
years. In four major wars of the eighteenth century, world power
shifted to Britain. The English Duke of Marlborough, in one of the
incredible marches of history, had his army walk from Belgium
to near Munich and link up with small armies from Bavaria and
Savoy to fight and win the Battle of Blenheim. France and Austria
never recovered. Britain subsequently created a worldwide empire
"on which the sun never set." Military victory and a new source
of money were the matrix used to forge the worldwide British
Empire which brought the natural resources and foreign cultures
to the "island nation."

War always accelerates change. Military personnel leave the restraining influence of their families. Soldiers and sailors leave their own culture to fight in a foreign environment. Governments throw new money into research and development for inventions. War exploration and colonization created the "British Empire on which the sun never set" and brought the world to England's doorstep.

The global empire changed architecture, furniture, all manual arts, brought insights into other religions, and brought to Europe products like tea, sugar, tobacco, and ceramics which replaced wood mulch floors with mosaics. However, to create capital, the national debt was a new phenomenon, and it created the need for a new institution - the Bank of England.

Look briefly at the inventions that created an industrial revolution during Wesley's lifetime:

- William Harvey described accurately the circulatory system of the human body.

- James Watt invented the steam engine in Scotland. The steam driven piston engine revolutionized the power source for many tasks. It became a pump for water to run mills, and the dredging of canals.

- Canals were dug to connect many English cities and provide means for horse-drawn boats when cables were hooked to horses that walked the bank paths, moving barges laden with newly manufactured products. The canals created a maze of shipping lanes. There were 2000 miles of canals in little England. Robert Fulton invented the steam boat that eliminated many jobs by horsepower.

- Cotton manufacturing in factories following invention of the "spinning jenny," enabling a person to operate multiple spools of thread. By 1778 there were 20,000 spinning jennys operating in Great Britain. This created enormous demand for more cotton as people began wearing cotton clothes. Obviously, it also helped agriculture.

- A similar revolution occurred in wool when the power loom was invented. Factories employed 600 people, a third of whom were children under age fifteen.

- Coal was heated to a temperature that would smelt iron and make steel.

- The skill of making cast iron enabled revolutions from home cooking utensils to locomotives. Melting iron was enhanced by use of coke rather than charcoal. Metallurgy blossomed. Such common items as nails, belt buckles, and frying pans came into use. (Bishop Francis Asbury was an apprentice in making buckles.)

- In 1770, Josiah Wedgwood perfected porcelain glazed pottery for dinnerware.

- Macadam was made into a roadbed that reduced stage coach travel from Edinburgh to London from two weeks to two days.

- Sir Isaac Newton revolutionized the "laws" of physical science which had remained mistakenly the same since the days of Aristotle.

- George Hadley charted the latitude, a major breakthrough for shipping lanes. John Harrison and the "Commissioners of Longitude" did likewise with longitude.

- For Enlightenment philosophers and many Anglican preachers, Jesus was reduced to the role of teacher, not the Son of God.

Cultural changes that were a corollary of science and industry:

- Handel, Bach, Mozart, Haydn, and Beethoven were revolutionizing music.

- Giant libraries at Oxford and Cambridge had new knowledge brought from around the world by missionaries, soldiers, and explorers.

- Novels, ballads, newspapers, and diaries were popularized.

- A national postal service began delivering daily mail.

- Coffee, tea, and chocolate were imported and changed English life.

- Shipbuilding was revolutionized, providing passenger ships for trans-Atlantic voyages.

- The rising national debt caused the need to raise taxes which, by 1775, in turn brought resistance in the American colonies.

It was also the 'worst of times.' Two tragedies changed the physical face of London and the demographics of England. Less than a century before Wesley, the "Black Death" killed 70,000, and the Great Fire in London burned eighty-nine parish churches and old St. Paul's Cathedral.

In 1666, following the Great Fire, Sir Christopher Wren was the architect who virtually recast the skyline and construction accuracy of London. St. Paul's Cathedral, 365 feet in height including the spire, was located on the highest topographical point in the city.

Wesley brought a religious experience and a faith community to the people in a time when so much change was affecting family structure, daily lives, household and workplace products, facial makeup, clothing fashions, etc. He called Methodism "experimental divinity." When the American colonies won their War for Independence, Wesley recognized that the seismic plates of history had shifted.

When he was eighty-one years old, he reversed his position of opposing the independence of the American colonies and approved of a Methodist Church in America. He breached ecclesiastical tradition and Anglican canon law, and ordained two lay clergy.

Subsequently, The Methodist Episcopal Church in the United States was formally constituted at the "Christmas Conference" in Baltimore in 1784. Francis Asbury and Thomas Coke were elected bishops. They were the first American clergy to call on President George Washington in New York City and pledge the loyalty of the Methodists to the newly formed union.

The Enlightenment

We know Wesley's century philosophically as "The Enlightenment." It was coming of age in Scotland, England, and France as Wesley was in college and throughout his long ministry. He was well read in its theories and personally acquainted with most of its advocates.

During that pivotal time in history, John Wesley grew up, attended a secular prep school, studied, went to America and Germany, preached sixty-six years, wrote volumes, fell in love three times, married and separated once, and related to the political, literary, and military issues of his day. He was a prodigious reader with a bright mind who lived on the campus of Oxford University for ten years.

Few periods in human history have seen the "power of the pen" so vividly as the eighteenth century in England and France. Every phase and facet of life were affected by the Enlightenment. The "world of thought" was revolutionized as John Wesley was studying at Oxford and developing the new religious phenomenon of Methodism. Emerging ideas common to most of the Enlightenment philosophers were championing individual liberty, criticism of monarchies and popery, skepticism of traditional religious beliefs, and a Pollyanna view of "natural human nature." "It was a system of beliefs that spread like wildfire."[8] Alexander Pope euphemized the entire era of the Enlightenment with his doggerel:

> *"Nature and Nature's laws lay hidden in the night;*
> *God said, 'Let Newton be.' and all was light."*

Let us illustrate some of the Enlightenment's contribution to an explosion in knowledge:

- In 1751, **Denis Diderot of France** published *Encyclopédie.* His auspicious aim was to explain the universe. He was convinced, and his readers became convinced, that emergent explanations "for everything" would enhance knowledge and change the idiom of most faculties of learning. The *Encyclopédie* included the work of revolutionary political theorists like Voltaire, Montesquieu, and Rousseau, Newton's discovery of the physical laws of the universe, Swedish botanist Linnaeus' classification of the natural world into species, the early discoveries of the Industrial Revolution, and the "reign of Reason" in theology and philosophy.

---

[8] Fraser, Rebecca, *The Story of Britain,* Norton and Company, 2003, 450

- **John Locke of England** (1662-1704) developed a theory that all cognitive knowledge is perceived through the five physical senses plus reflection upon their sensations. This was highly influential on John Wesley. Locke's political science theory influenced James Madison in the conceptualization and writing of the United States Constitution.

- **Jacques Rousseau from France** (1712-1778) was literally a contemporary of Wesley and wrote the popular *Social Contract* that questioned the right of private property, individual rights, and equality that must replace the feudalistic class system. (He had more influence on the French Revolution than on the American.)

- **Adam Smith, Professor of Moral Philosophy at Glasgow,** inquired about *The Nature of the Wealth of Nations* (1776) and heralded the breakup of state licensed monopolies in trade. (He is considered the father of free enterprise economics, the secret of the young United States' meteoric rise from colonial vassalage to global wealth and might in contrast to Latin America which had the same natural resources).

- **Montesquieu in France** wrote *The Spirit of Laws* (1748), the book that had profound influence on James Madison as he wrote the United States Constitution. His theory destroyed the medieval theory of powers as monarchy, clergy, and military. He conceived a new paradigm of government with the balance of powers: executive, legislative, and judicial that was adopted with the ratification of a constitution and election of a president.

Most of the aforementioned philosophers and scientists were theological Deists. To oversimplify Deism, one can say that "there is a God but the preferred word is "Nature." (Jefferson used the term "Nature or Nature's God.") To Deism, the reasoning capacity of the human mind reigned and emotion was considered deranged. This "god" is revealed not through established religions like Judaism, Christianity, or Islam but by the study of common principles in nature and the intuitive reasoning capacity of the human mind. Every religious belief should be questioned, and if it were lacking in the light of Reason, it should be abandoned. This included the miracles recorded in the Bible and the divinity of Jesus.

The doctrine of original sin was abandoned in the university classrooms. Humankind was considered innately "reasonable," and therefore morally neutral. One dictum was "As a twig is bent; so grows the tree." According to Deism, God's providential influence "upon the affairs of men" is no more than the influence of a watchmaker on a fine watch. Once it is out of his shop, the watchmaker has no more contact with it. In the later social science of psychology, this meant that human behavior is shaped totally by environment, not heredity.

More than we ordinarily think, Wesley knew the giants and was comfortable in their company. He met with the bishops of the Church of England. Wesley often met with Alexander Pope, Jonathan Swift, Edmund Burke, and Samuel Johnson. Johnson, "arguably the most distinguished man of letters in English history," sought out both John and his sister, "Hetty" Wesley, as favorite conversationalists. All the more significant, then, is the observation of Sir Leslie Stephen, not a favorable critic of Wesley's, who wrote of the eighteenth century, "No such leader of men appeared anywhere as Wesley."

Of course, this is but a sampling of the exposure to and involvement in John Wesley's generation. We must see him as a fourth generation Oxonian, and an Anglican priest in an era known for the decadence of the established Church. He was a "bookworm" and read voluminously in English, Latin, and French. His "reading list" consisted of politics, economics, theology, and understanding of what we know now as sociology.

Let this all too brief reference be sufficient to illustrate that Methodism was born in a maelstrom of new ideas. Wesley's loyalty to the Church of England, his Tory politics, his oratory, his writing, his knowledge of secular literature, and his organizational skills were all reflections of his time in England's culture and history. It was into this intellectual context that Methodism was born.

We must see Samuel and Susanna Wesley, Wesley himself, and early Methodism in the context of a cultural reaction to the Puritan Commonwealth that legislated morality and orthodoxy from 1642-1662. Restoration of the monarchy, the transition from absolute to constitutional monarchy, (William and Mary), and the German Monarchs like George I, II, & III affected and infected politics, economics, and religion.

Fifteen years prior to Wesley's death, the English colonies won the War of Independence in what he called a "strange act of Providence." Because of the radically changing times in England, Wales, Scotland, Ireland, France, and Germany, one of the most massive population shifts in history brought thousands of immigrants to America. This phenomenon occupied much of Wesley's thought and leadership for the last thirty years of his life.

"John Locke Philosophy" - John Wesley's Adoption and Adaptation

Tennyson was right: "We are a part of all that we have met." Each of us, at least to some degree, is a person of our time who lives within the context of prevailing culture. First of all, before we see the Wesley family in the context of their times, let us reflect on the rather revolutionary philosophical shift from the middle ages and the theological gyrations of Anglican theology from Henry VIII to the German King George I.

Let us begin with the influence of John Locke upon John Wesley.

John Locke was the major English voice of Enlightenment philosophy. Challenging René Descartes, Locke determined that knowledge is perceived through the five physical senses. That is, we learn by what we see, what we hear, what we touch, what we smell, what we taste. Locke's theory of knowledge was called "Sensation followed by reflection."

Wesley adopted the Lockean formula with the pivotally important exception that Wesley insisted we have a sixth sense, a *spiritual sense*. This spiritual sense is one dimension of being created in the image of God (Genesis 1:27). For Wesley, it is a divine gift, "attuned to the level of reality that the physical senses cannot penetrate."[9] By God's grace, Wesley believed that we are all enlightened and enabled. Here is my paraphrase of Ted Runyon's four factors of *spiritual sense*:

1. "The Divine Source of religious experience. "God provided humans with *spiritual senses* to sense spiritual realities, in addition to Locke's accurate identification of our physical senses to sense empirical knowledge

---

[9] Runyon, Ted, IN Maddox, Randy, *Aldersgate Reconsidered*, Kingswood, 1990, 96

2. God's will and intent for every human being (accented by Arminian theology)

3. The transformation of sinners to celebrate the eradication of guilt and the mastery of self-willed spiritual discipline

4. The feelings that accompany religious experience, but with the ebb and flow of feelings, the confidence of trusting God's love and grace.[10]

Wesley, unlike Locke, believed in original sin and that our "original righteousness" was dulled by the Fall. Humankind has perpetually yielded to temptation as Charles Wesley wrote in a famous hymn, "prone to wander, Lord I feel it, prone to leave the God I love."[11] However, as Albert Outler suggested in his Fondren Lectures at SMU, "Wesley believed in depravity, but not in tee-total depravity." Wesley believed we can experience what he called, "inward impressions on the soul," "whispers to the heart," "spiritual sense," and the distant drumbeat of a "Holy Other."

We must be clear, however to insist that God is the initiator. Paul wrote to the Corinthians, "…so that your faith might rest not on human wisdom but on the power of God. What no eye has seen and no ear has heard, nor the human heart conceived, God has prepared for those who love him."[12] God provides this "spiritual sense" as a gift of grace.[13] This gift of a sixth or "spiritual sense" is intermittently reawakened by the Holy Spirit through what Wesley called "prevenient grace"— Christ's "knocking at the door of the human heart." This is fundamentally important.

Wesley agreed with Calvin that salvation must be initiated by God, but he differed from Calvin in that Wesley insisted that this "whisper to the heart" came to every human being. Wesley called this "spiritual sense," *prevenient grace.*" We learn about God through divinely imparted inner peace rather than through human engendered feelings. "In contrast to Deism, Wesley

---

[10] Ibid., 94

[11] Wesley, Charles, IN hymn, "Come, Thou Fount of Every Blessing."

[12] I Corinthians 2:5, 9 - 11

[13] Maddox, Randy, *Responsible Grace,* Kingswood, 1994, 28

assumed that the most definitive and important knowledge of God was not inherently acquired. It must be obtained directly from God."[14] *(Rex Matthews has traced this theology back to Origen (c. 185-254).)*[15]

We must remember that as an undergraduate student, Wesley mastered Greek and Latin classical literature, read deeply in logic, modern languages, and sciences, practiced oratory, and wrote poetry. Sarah Lancaster accurately reports, "Though he did not become a "scholar" in the technical sense, he did continue to engage in study throughout his life, and produced a large body of theological literature."[16] It is his adaptation of Locke to which Peter Bohler, the Moravian, was referring when he said to Wesley in the early spring of 1738, "My brother, my brother, the philosophy must be purged away." In point of fact, it never was purged. Wesley continued throughout his life to read the works of the Enlightenment philosophers. He did not confine his reading or his relationships to religion per se.

Wesley's Specific Adaptation of "Lockean" Theory of Knowledge

Perhaps more than any other denomination founder, John Wesley's lifestyle has been idolized as a model of regimented demands on Methodism's "traveling preachers." The story of his spiritual journey, ministry, and lifestyle are carefully documented by his own records, closely observed by his contemporaries, and voluminously editorialized by scholars in four centuries. He had more published pages than any writer of his time. He left behind more written documentation revealing his daily life and inmost feelings than almost any major historical figure. The man had hardly a single unwritten thought. Yet, he was for two centuries an enigma, excoriated by his critics and idolized by his followers. Not until the work of Richard Heitzenrater of Duke University did we

---

[14] Ibid., 31

[15] Runyon, Theodore, *"With the Eyes of Faith: Spiritual Experience and the Knowledge of God in the Theology of John Wesley,"* in *Wesleyan Theology Today,* ed. Theodore Runyon, Kingswood Books, 1985, 406-15.

[16] Lancaster, Sarah, *"Current Debates over Wesley's Legacy,"* IN Maddox,ed., *Aldersgate Reconsidered,* 299

begin to use the term, "the elusive Mr. Wesley."[17]

Defining the real John Wesley is no easy task. Richard Heitzenrater has documented this unquestionably in his two small volumes that he aptly entitled *The Elusive Mr. Wesley*. He points out that, "Wesley was an educated upper-class Oxford don who spent most of his life working among the poor and disadvantaged. He combined the preaching of the revivalist with the concerns and programs of a social worker. His theology was hammered out on the anvil of controversy. He was 'fighting in the trenches,' countering attacks from the theological and political left and right."[18]

Heitzenrater "emphasizes the necessity to view Wesley in the light of the whole of his life and thought. The private man must be considered along with the public; ...his views from any given period must stand the test of his own changing mind. We must look at the sources with a critical eye, noting whether they are early or late in his life, friendly or antagonistic, public or private, exaggerated or simplistic, firsthand or secondary accounts."[19]

Wesley was not primarily a student of philosophy that he called "speculative," but of soteriology (the study of salvation). This was his attraction to John Locke's theory of knowledge — how can we know that we are saved? There is a sense in which Wesley's whole life was a prelude to Aldersgate when he was thirty-five years old. Heitzenrater pointedly cites correspondence between Wesley and his mother while Wesley was in college more than a decade earlier. The twenty-two-year-old collegiate raised the question, "How do I *know* that I am a Christian? If we dwell in Christ and Christ in us...certainly we must be sensible of it.... If we can never have any certainty of our being in a state of salvation, good reason it is that every moment should be spent, not in joy, but fear and trembling." She wrote back that the goal, 'through grace' was Christian perfection which she defined as "sincerely endeavoring to plant each virtue in our minds that may through Christ render us pleasing to God."[20] Note that for

---

17 Heizenrater, Richard, *The Elusive Mr. Wesley—John Wesley, his own biographer; AND The Elusive Mr. Wesley—as seen by contemporaries and biographers,* Abingdon, 1984

18 Heitzenrater, Richard, *Mirror and Memory,* Kingswood, 55

19 Ibid. 59

20 Ibid. 53

Susanna, the burden of proof was not in feeling, but in sincerity and obedience.

Wesley worked through his mother's words and answered on July 29, 1776: "I am persuaded that we may know if we are now in a state of salvation, since that is expressly promised in the Holy Scriptures to our sincere endeavors, and we are surely able to judge of our own sincerity." He adopted the dictum that Thomas à Kempis adapted from Augustine's: "Do what lieth in thy power, and God will assist thy good will."[21]

Six years later, he responded to a similar question from a seeker that the solution to the dilemma of wondering about our faith is "a reliance upon sincerity." He wrote to Miss Ann Granville "to know our hope is sincerity, not perfection; not to do well, but to do our best." Frustrated with his lack of peace and joy in his soul, he repeatedly concluded that the most valid assurance of one's salvation is sincerity.

While at Oxford, his spiritual mentors were authors of books he devoured. That included contemporary works that became spiritual classics: Jeremy Taylor's *Rule and Exercises of Holy Living and Holy Dying*, and Thomas à Kempis' *Image of Christ*.

Later, in 1730, he devoured William Law's *Serious Call to a Devout and Holy Life*. "His lifestyle was extreme austerity, regular devotion to what he called 'the means of grace,' unremitting works of charity, ceaseless desire to preach the Gospel to the godless and the heathen."[22] All this was his quest for Christian perfection through "holiness of heart" and "holy living," but it was a journey of conflict as well as quest.[23] This remained Wesley's best answer to the "witness of the Spirit" until he met the Moravians in 1735. Under their influence he finally concluded that rigid spiritual discipline and sincerity were not the sufficient answers in our search for assurance of salvation. However, this "early Wesley" influence of Catholic and Anglican saints caused him to part ways with the Moravians, the final break coming on July 20, 1740.

---

[21] Heitzenrater, Richard, 1990, *"Great Expectations,"* IN *Aldersgate Reconsidered,* ed. Randy Maddox, Kingswood,

[22] Davies, Rupert, *Methodism,* Epworth, Press, 1985, 42-43

[23] Ibid. 43

John Wesley's Influence and Impact

Irish historian William Edward Lecky wrote *A History of England in the Eighteenth Century* - a secular, non-evangelical, evaluation of John Wesley. "Although the career of Prime Minister Pitt, the Elder, and England's splendid victories by land and sea form unquestionably the most dazzling episodes from 1727-60; they must yield, I think, in real importance to that religious revolution in England created by the preaching of the Wesleys and Whitefield."[24] *(Many twentieth century secular scholars questioned that.)* Later, Lecky continued, "The scene which took place in that humble meeting on Aldersgate Street unleashed one of the most powerful and active intellects in England. His genius and energy are the true source of English Methodism."[25] (*Very few* Methodist *scholars question that).*

In citing that passage a century later, S. Parkes Cadman of the great Central Congregational Church in Brooklyn, wrote,

"While a character such as John Wesley does infinitely more for the advancement of morals and religion than any abstract theory could ever accomplish, it also creates the difficulty of interpreting him adequately. He occasionally lapsed into sentimentalism, but was a great Christian whose piety was never divorced from either reason or ethics and whose persistent test for enthusiasm was practice. His nature was complex and his spirit accommodated many apparently contradictory elements. He shared sentiments common to variable schools of thought and displayed an admirable catholicity toward those who did not hold his opinions. He was dedicated to pragmatism and accepted paradoxical compromises and kept his ear to public opinion. He was fascinated and influenced by the mystical fervor of the Moravians, but moderated it by the Anglican insistence on degrees of faith and holy living. That is, he connected spiritual ecstasies to earthly affairs. He clung to the guarantees of historic Christianity, avoiding sensational and gratuitous changes, but adopting those dictated by his heart and work. Most attempts falter in attempting

---

[24] Lecky, W.E.H., *History of England in the Eighteenth Century,* Vol. III, p. 1

[25] Ibid., Vol. III., p. 48

to delineate the secret history of his rich and contagious spirituality." [26]

In the twentieth century, biographer J. H. Whitely exhorted,

"Wesley, like other great people of the past, now and then receives scurvy treatment at the hands of modern writers who would 'discount the great deed.' The excessive praise with which Wesleyan historiography surrounded the Founder of Methodism may have been the reason for contemporary and modern belittling sentiments. However, if it were only a legend that Wesley was a major contributor to a freer and better England that was spared revolution like France, it has been a powerful legend and one believed by eminent historians. More ordinary people have found his sermons and tracts resolute in conviction, sure in the progress of the argument, and reasonable in logic. Those who knew him found the man to be tender, sympathetic, wide and rich of vision."[27]

Only the carping cynic would discount the comprehensive contributions of the founder of the Methodist movement. Diarmaid MacCulloch, in his monumental *Christianity—the First Three Thousand Years,* gives this credit to Wesley:

The English Evangelicals sought to create a religion of the heart and of direct personal relationship with Jesus Christ.... The Evangelicals produced a new religious body that by accident rather than design found itself outside the established Church: Methodism. The leader in what became a world-wide movement was John Wesley, a man who made sure that his career was as well documented as any Pietist might desire, assuring that his own version of the story would get first hearing. Wesley's mission was set amid rapid economic transformation in Britain, and a great shift in population to new manufacturing centres as the industrial revolution gained momentum. Wesley relished organizing people, sending out itinerant lay preachers to establish societies from among the excited crowds. He had a charac-

---

[26] Cadman, S. Parkes, *The Three Religious Leaders of Oxford and Their Movements–Wycliffe, Wesley, and Newman,* Macmillan, 1916, p. 179

[27] Op. cit., Whiteley, 23

teristic Evangelical emphasis on Jesus' direct address to the individual, the Saviour's grace turned lovingly on the poorest wretch." MacCulloch calls "O For A Thousand Tongues to Sing" the universal anthem of Methodism."[28]

[28] MacCulloch, Diarmaid, *Christianity—The First Three Thousand Years*, Viking, 2010, 749-751

CHAPTER TWO

Geo-politics During Wesley's Ministry

Religion is always in the context of culture. Look at the secular culture in which God inspired the biblical writings. In the Old Testament, the history and religion of Israel was influenced, sometimes shaped, by the regional politics of the "Fertile Crescent" from Egypt to Persia. From Abraham to Joseph, the Hebrews' culture was influenced by Egypt's worship of the sun. Moses had to cope with the Canaanite tribes who were in the Jordan Valley. The days of the Judges were times when the Israelites had to take their broken iron tools to the Philistine blacksmiths. "Not a blacksmith could be found in the whole land of Israel...so all Israel went down to the Philistines to have their plowshares, mattocks, axes, and sickles sharpened" (I Samuel 13:19-22). In Isaiah's ministry, the Assyrians were at the gates of Jerusalem; in Jeremiah's ministry, Babylon captured and deported the Jews. Ezekiel, Daniel, Esther, and the anonymous Prophet of the Exile all reflected Jewish life not in Israel but in Babylon. Ezra and Nehemiah began in Persia but came back to Jerusalem as vassals of Cyrus. Jesus' ministry was in the context of Roman military occupation, Roman coinage, and Roman political rule. Paul's missionary ministry was in the context of Greek culture and language and Roman Pax.

As it was in biblical times, so it was in Wesley's time. Therefore, we err to ignore the geo-politics of Europe in John Wesley's day. Let's take a look.

English Politics and Religion Before and During Wesley's Life

For twelve years, from 1649 until 1660, Oliver Cromwell, a

Puritan, ruled England as the Lord Protector. Cromwell abolished all holy days, including Christmas, and forbade the use of organ music! He also forbade festivals of gaiety, theatrical performances, and horse racing. Both of John Wesley's grandparents were Puritans (also called "Dissenters" and "Cromwellians") who rose to considerable prestige and ecclesiastical power during the "Commonwealth" years of Cromwell.

The restoration of the monarchy brought to the throne King Charles II on May 29, 1660. The new king was immensely popular, but religion took a backseat. The lords followed the king's example in consorting with actresses who became mistresses who bore bastard children. Since King Charles II's wife was unable to conceive, he happily claimed all the children born to ladies of his own queen's court and made them dukes and duchesses. In 1662, the new king removed from their pulpits all dissenting non-Anglicans: Presbyterians, Baptists, Quakers, and Socinians *(who evolved into Unitarians)*. The fathers of both Samuel and Susanna Annesley Wesley were removed from their pulpits in 1662.

In 1685, King Charles II died at age fifty-eight of a stroke. Upon his death, word leaked out that a Catholic priest had been sneaked in to give him the last rites of the Catholic Church. The king, a first cousin of King Louis XIV of France, had been converted to Catholicism while in exile during the Cromwell years. Charles II's brother, the Duke of York, was brought from France and crowned King James II. The Latin name for James is "Jacob." Therefore, his followers were called "Jacobites" and Susanna Annesley Wesley was a Jacobite.

James II and his first wife had two children who, by Act of Parliament, would succeed him on the throne. Mary and Anne both of whom were secretly whisked to Holland and reared as Protestants. James II and his second wife, Mary of Modena, had one child. She was Catholic. The mother died in childbirth but the son survived and was baptized in France as "James Edward Stuart," a Catholic. "Jacobites" *(including Susanna Wesley in 1701)* considered him the rightful heir to the throne but Parliament thought otherwise.

The possibility of another Catholic king was unthinkable. Princess Anne wrote to her sister, Mary, in Holland, "Things come to pass now that if they go on much longer, I believe no Protestant will be able to live." Parliament moved quickly. On

June 30, 1688, Parliament sent a secret letter to William of Orange (Holland) and his wife, Mary, sister to both Anne and King James.

The letter asked William to invade England. When King James II learned of the conspiracy, he dispatched his queen and their new son to France, disguised himself as a fisherman, and tried to cross the channel, but was recognized by two fishermen and brought to London in disgrace. This was interpreted by Parliament as his abdication, which provided them a legal means of declaring his sister, Mary, as queen. William's army defeated the king's army, most of whom deserted before William reached London where he was welcomed by the people and Parliament.

The reign of William and Mary introduced to England a "constitutional monarchy" to replace the "absolute monarchy." Queen Mary developed smallpox and died in 1694, leaving William, a Dutchman, as the monarch. Meanwhile, the Prince of Wales, a Catholic, was in France and known as "the Jacobite Pretender" or simply "The Young Pretender." To prevent a Catholic from every being king, Parliament passed the "Act of Settlement" in 1701, requiring all future kings and queens to be members of the Church of England, a requirement that remains until this day. The argument in the Epworth rectory that caused a marital separation was one result of the "Act of Settlement." When William died in 1702, his sister in law, Anne became queen. It was in the second year of the reign of Queen Anne that John Wesley was born. She had seventeen children, none of whom reached adolescence. Upon Anne's death in 1714, Parliament called a German to be king. So it was that during John Wesley's entire life, there were three King George's. The German "House of Hanover" was renamed "Windsor" during World War I and still is the royal line.

Four years after John Wesley was born, the "Treaty of Union" created the nation called "Great Britain." England had gradually absorbed the political and economic independence of Wales in 1685, but it was 1707 when a deal was struck, without war, between Scotland and England. One demand of the Scots was to keep the Scottish Kirk, with its presbyterial governance, and not be subjected to the Archbishop of Canterbury who was appointed by the king and had jurisprudence over England and Wales. This geo-political reality in Scotland is a major reason why Methodism never took a deep root in the religious experience of the Scots.

The formation of the new nation of Great Britain occurred in 1707. During Wesley's lifetime there were three Hanoverian kings - George I (1714-27), George II (1727-60), and George III (1760-1820). George III was the first of the three to speak English. During their reigns, the office of "Prime Minister" evolved as the most power-ful person in the British government. That person is chosen by a political party, not by the reigning monarch. King George III was the hated British king just before and during the American Revo-lutionary War.

The "Treaty of Union" that united Scotland and England in 1707 was threatened in 1746 when the "Young Pretender", came from France to lead a "rising of the Scottish clans" and seek to be crowned king of an independent Scotland. Charles or "Bonnie Prince Charlie" was a descendent of James I. His ragtag army of Scottish clans was ignominiously defeated in a bloody battle on Culloden Moor just south of the Highlands in April, 1746. The English bayoneted to death every wounded Scot. The penalty for the survivors was that they could never again wear their tartan plaids. Bonnie Prince Charlie was not a fighter. He left Scotland dressed as a woman and ended up in Rome. Many left Scotland for Ireland and North Carolina in the colonies. Thousands of these misnamed "Scotch-Irish" would become Methodists, leaving their Presbyterian heritage because a Methodist circuit rider found their remote log cabins which were the forest counterpart of the rock huts in which they lived in Scotland, and the rail fences which were the forest counterpart of the mortar-less rock walls in Scotland.

The Seven Years War
(In America, called "French and Indian War")

For most of John Wesley's life, and during Methodism's birth, Great Britain was engaged in major wars. Since the time of Christopher Columbus, France, England, The Netherlands, and Spain had all tried to colonize the Western Hemisphere. The French and several Indian tribes controlled everything from Newfoundland through the Great Lakes and down the Mississippi River Basin to the Gulf of Mexico. The English controlled the Atlantic coast except for Florida which was claimed by Spain. Once the Dutch lost "New Amsterdam" to the English who named it "New York," Dutch imperialism in this hemisphere was limited to the West Indies.

Most Americans know about the so-called "French and Indian War" that here in America pitted Britain against France and a confederacy of Indian nations (1756-63). Actually, it was virtually a world war fought on five continents. It ended in a British victory and a great expansion of the British Empire, a monumental reduction of the French Empire, a long period of decay of the Austrian Empire, and a long rise in power of the Prussians that would eventually result in the nation of Germany. The "genius of war" who led to the greatest era of British expansion was William Pitt, the giant of eighteenth-century British politics. He said categorically, "I know I can save the country and that no one else can."[29] He not only saved Britain, he conquered India from the French and indigenous Indian Moguls, he colonized much of West Africa, and he drove the French militarily out of Canada and the Great Lakes (renaming Fort Duquesne "Pittsburgh"). He also built the British Navy into the dominant force of the seas of the world. That war reshaped the geo-political map of the world and had major religious ramifications.

The Seven Years' War ended with a British victory that transferred ownership, trade, and culture from French to British hegemony. Britain in the Treaty of Paris of 1763 became the worldwide empire "on which the sun never set." The Great Lakes area and the Ohio River Basin were finally English.

When the "Seven Years War" ended with great British victory, the English thought they were entering a long period of peace. However, the British American colonies had been affected very little by the war. Therefore, it was with both surprise and denial that England in 1775 was faced with rebellious colonies in North America.

One negative consequence of the Seven Years' War was a massive accumulation of national debt for Britain. The major way of servicing that debt was heavier taxation. Parliament, in the 1760's, passed a series of acts that imposed new taxes on the colonists - the Stamp Act, the tax on tea that resulted in the Boston Tea Party, the Townsend Acts, etc. These were the fuses that ignited the smoldering spirit of independence into open rebellion in the English colonies. Hence, the cry arose, "No taxation without representation" since the colonies did not have a voting member in Parliament. Speakers like Patrick Henry and

---

[29] Op. cit., 440

pamphleteers like Thomas Paine gave a "fighting spirit" to the ideas of Jefferson, Adams, Madison, and Franklin.

Fighting the French had depleted British manpower, money, and political capital from 1740 until the outbreak of revolution in the American colonies. Also, most British leadership did not imagine how thirteen colonies should be taken seriously when they had no central government, very little indigenous manufacturing, and a network of business and heritage ties with the country that most considered their "mother country."

In England, the seven years of war left other issues: food prices were painfully inflated, creating "bread riots" and mobs emerged in many places for most any imaginable issue. There was not much passion in Britain for fighting another war. Most English were like John Wesley. They could not imagine wanting to live outside the shadow of the Union Jack. The French did not have that kind of national loyalty.

The winds of war in the very colonies where John Wesley felt called of God to send evangelist missionaries produced a painful dilemma for Wesley. He was politically a conservative Tory who opposed the American Revolution, and ecclesiastically an Anglican "blueblood" who considered Methodism a reform movement, not a new denomination. His vision for the evangelizing of America was so much in conflict with his political philosophy. He could not imagine anyone's wanting to live outside the political security of the British crown.

In effect, the climate in England and the colonies had developed the proverbial "perfect storm" that leads to war. Britain's Parliament saw the productive colonies as a means of reducing the national debt by taxation at the very time when men of talent and political vision developed in the colonies. A new dream had arisen in the minds of colonial leaders—the dream of liberty. From the end of the "French and Indian War" in 1763 until the several stamp acts, the American colonists moved from resentment to resistance to open rebellion against Great Britain. Few in Britain saw the American War of Independence coming and when it came, few took it seriously. Britain was so weary of war that they hired Hessian soldiers from Germany as mercenaries for much of their infantry. The Hessians fought for pay, not passion, a factor that influenced the colonies' ability to win their independence.

On June 15, 1775, Wesley wrote to Lord North, the prime minister, urging a more conciliatory policy. He wrote, "I cannot avoid thinking...that these oppressed people ask for nothing more than their legal rights. Above all, force should not be employed against the colonists."

However, by October of that same year, he wrote to his brother, Charles, that he was "losing love" for the colonial position. It was then that he plagiarized a tract by Samuel Johnson and had it circularized in both England and among the Methodists in America. It was entitled *A Calm Address to Our American Colonies*, but it was anything but calm. He said that England had a right to tax the colonies and that their request for representation in Parliament was unreasonable. At this point politics and religion were at odds because all the lay Methodist preachers who had come to America were opposed to American independence. It made American patriots very suspicious of all Methodists and might have ended Methodism except for Francis Asbury.

Francis Asbury had only about a fourth-grade education and was from a poor family. He had responded to Wesley's call for missionaries to America and arrived here, penniless, in 1771. Four years later, he was a leader in American Methodism that was still a "movement," not a church. Asbury responded to Wesley's anti-war pamphlet, "I am truly sorry that the venerable man ever dipped into the politics of America."[30] Asbury added that Wesley simply revealed his loyalty to the land in which he lived. Then, Asbury added, "Had he been a subject of America, no doubt he would have been as zealous an advocate of the American cause."[31] Asbury had become, heart and soul, an American. Wesley retained his explicit anti-American stance. When lay preachers returned, he gave them appointments in the British itinerancy.

Wesley's British Ministry During American War

In 1775, Wesley wrote the fifth extract of his *Journal*. He once again wrote in the same language about his being "strangely warmed" on May 24, 1738, in a Moravian/Lutheran meeting on Aldersgate Street. However, he gave the experience a new inter-

---

[30] Ferguson, Charles, *Organizing to Beat the Devil (Methodists and the Making of America)*, Doubleday 1971, 16-17.

[31] Ibid. 17.

pretation that is important for every Christian to read. Immediately after Aldersgate, under intense Moravian influence, he wrote that he had not been a Christian before Aldersgate. Every Christian should follow what Richard Heitzenrater calls "Wesley's emendations."[32]

They are unusual in their public form of admission, but they are fully in keeping with Wesley's life-long habit of self-examination and reflection on his own spiritual condition." This is Heitzenrater's most helpful comparison of Wesley's earlier interpretation of the state of his soul, and the interpretation now that he was seventy-two years old:

- He wrote in his 1740 extract of the *Journal,* "I who went to America to convert others was never myself converted to God." He repeated the line in his 1775 extract, but wrote in a parenthesis, "I am not sure of this."

- He wrote in his earlier *Journal*, "I lack faith in Christ." In 1775 he wrote, "I (before Aldersgate) had even then the faith of a servant."

- Earlier he wrote, "I am child of wrath." In 1775 he wrote, "I believe not; …. I was persuaded that even then (1728-29) I was in a state of salvation." ("And I believe I was.")

- He had written earlier, "I had been all this time building on the sand," but in 1775, he wrote in the margin, "Not so; I was right, as far as I went."[33]

The societies grew by about sixteen hundred per year during the late "seventies." As the war raged in America and Wesley had to absorb the British lay preachers who were coming home, he increased the normative size of the class meetings to about thirty. As a septuagenarian, he wrote, "I can preach better than at twenty-three" and he congratulated himself that he exercised regularly in fresh air, slept easily, and had an evenness of temper.[34] He wrote in his diary, "I *feel* and *grieve*, but by the grace of God, I *fret*

---

[32] Heitzenrater, *People Called Methodists*, 262

[33] Ibid., 261-162

[34] Ibid., 265

at nothing." By the time that Thomas Jefferson was writing the American Declaration of Independence, Wesley's *Primitive Physick* was selling its seventeenth edition. He had added a suggestion that mouth-to-mouth resuscitation could revive a person from asphyxia or near drowning.

Also in 1776, Wesley's lease on the old Foundery complex was running out and he saw the need for a new facility. He purchased land in Moorfields across City Road from the Dissenter's graveyard, "Bunhill Fields." In April 1777, he laid the foundation for New Chapel with plans for a three-story house beside it for apartments and his own study. He used the occasion to preach on the history of the Methodist movement from 1729 at Oxford. Interestingly, he did not mention Aldersgate in that sermon. He repeated his oft-stated definition of Methodism, "the old religion of the Bible, the Primitive Church, and indeed of the Church of England." However, no one could then or can today deny that New Chapel on City Road was more than a preaching house; it was a Church. The sacraments would be administered there. One criticism by the lay preachers was that only ordained Anglican clergy could preach there, but he was becoming more aggressive in his attempts to obtain ordination for his preachers through proper channels.[35]

George Whitefield, who became a Calvinist Methodist, had been dead a quarter century, but what Wesley considered unbiblical doctrine continued to infiltrate his laity and lay preachers. He therefore in 1777 launched a new magazine, *the Arminian Magazine* which he published monthly for the rest of his life. It was what Heitzenrater calls a "handbook of the spiritual pilgrimage of holy living and holy dying." Every month featured articles on the universal atonement of Christ: "Let everyone be Jesus' guest...not one be left behind," as Charles has Methodists to sing to this very day. Wesley was convinced that ninety-nine of every hundred thinking persons rejects the doctrine of predestination.[36] By 1781, there were 44,461 Methodists in England, Ireland, and Wales. One of the growing circuits was Epworth where a new factory had brought a lot of rural families with children in Wesley's home village.[37]

---

[35] Ibid., 269

[36] Ibid., 268

[37] Ibid. 277

Meanwhile, In the American Revolution.

By 1779-80, the American Revolution was in its fourth year and British victory seemed assured. The colonists had really won only one battle—Saratoga, and it was followed by the infamous treason and execution of Benedict Arnold. By 1778 all the British born Methodist lay preachers had gone back to England except one, Francis Asbury.

Even Asbury was in hiding in Delaware in Judge White's home, barn, and swamp, depending on when the Patriots were about to locate him. He was using the time to learn Hebrew and Greek.

Providentially, with no leader, Methodism was growing in the war years. The new converts, a number of whom were called to preach, were all devoted to the cause of liberty and supporting independence from Great Britain. They are the foot soldiers, the unsung heroes who saved Methodism. They knew little about John Wesley and had never heard Francis Asbury preach. Many were slaves because the message of Methodism included them in the human beings for whom Jesus died. Without doubt, the growth of Methodism among the unlettered ranks of white people and the enslaved ranks of black people had an influence on John Wesley's calling the American victory a very "strange act of Providence."

This is not a narrative on the development of the Revolutionary War, militarily speaking. However, it is worthy of note that suddenly, in 1781, Lord Cornwallis won a Pyrrhic victory at the Greensboro, North Carolina "Battle of Guilford Courthouse" and realized that North Carolina was loyal to the Patriot cause. Therefore, Cornwallis headed for the Virginia Tidewater where he would have the protection of the British navy. However, upon arriving at Yorktown, the flags on the ships off shore were not British but French. Cornwallis rather suddenly surrendered, and the British colonies were on the road to becoming a new nation.

Just as political victory was gained, Wesley had to decide what to do about the Methodists who were all unordained and now had no relation to the Church of England. We shall see later what he did!

The overview of the 18th century geo-political context in which Methodism was born ends here. Though this secular backdrop was and is fundamentally important, we revert now to the history of Methodism per se, beginning with the Wesley family genealogy.

CHAPTER THREE

The Wesley Family and John Wesley

History cannot be written in neat, chronological order because it is multi-dimensional. In order to appreciate without cynical criticism or cultist adulation the man who brought Methodism into being, let us devote some space to the Westley/Wesley and Annesley genealogy. Without question, our DNA and our early childhood years have a lasting effect on our psychological makeup. In John Wesley's case, the dynamics of the Epworth rectory family had an effect on Methodism. Tennyson was correct in saying, "We are a part of all that we have met." John Wesley was a fourth generation Oxonian. He also was a member of a large family. He was a son to two brilliant but rigid and strong-willed parents, brother to two brothers who also became clergy, and brother to seven sisters who had sad lives and looked to their brother, Jack, for solace and support. The parental and sibling relationships were complex.

The Genealogy of John Wesley

In contrast to most church reformers, John Wesley's family tree was most impressive. His great, great grandfather was a man of distinction, Sir Herbert Westley of Dargan. Sir Herbert married an Irish woman, Elisabeth de Wellesley of Dangran, Ireland. Both were brilliant, well read, and acquainted with the leading ideas of their time. The third son born to that marriage was Bartholomew, baptized in 1600, three years before the death of Queen Elizabeth I.

Dubbed as "puny" because of his own small stature, Bartholomew attended Oxford and studied both medicine (physick) and divinity. He was caught up in the rising dissenter movement called "Puritanism" by mid-life and applauded the end of the British monarchy when Charles I abdicated in 1649. Bartholomew Westley was pastor of a church during the twelve years of Oliver Cromwell's "Commonwealth" when Britain had no king.

Upon the restoration of the monarchy in 1661, there was a virtual "reign of religious terror," during which a series of Acts made "dissenters' worship" impossible. King Charles II had Parliament pass the Act of Uniformity, which forbade the worship of God except by the order found in the *Book of Common Prayer*. The intent was to destroy Puritanism. Presbyterians, Quakers, and all other non-conformists were persecuted with vigor. At least 2000 clergy were driven from their churches because they "dissented" from the law of the land. One of these dissenters was Bartholomew Westley, John Wesley's great grandfather, who was removed from his parish. Having studied medicine as well as divinity, Bartholomew became a doctor.

In 1636, Bartholomew Westley fathered a son who was baptized "John." At a very young age, he entered Oxford and earned the M.A. degree during Cromwell's reign. In 1658, at age 22, he was given what was called in that day (and for many years to come) "a living." This meant he had a parish with stipend, a rectory, land and tenants; thus, a "living." However, being a Puritan, John Westley was never ordained by the Church of England. He remained a lay preacher with an evangelical theology. Both he and his wife were political Dissenters. Upon the Restoration of the Monarchy, he was imprisoned for months. Both he and his father, Bartholomew, were formally expelled from their pulpits on the same day–August 17, 1662. Four months after John's expulsion from his pulpit, his wife gave birth to a son who was baptized "Samuel." John Westley died in 1679 at age forty-three.

The genes in John Wesley's ancestry could not have had a more providential combination. Even though his parents were Anglican in religious faith, Dissenter theology ran thickly in their theological heritage. His father, a staunch Anglican, died with a "dissenter's testimony" on his lips.

Samuel Westley becomes Samuel Wesley – and an Anglican

Samuel Westley, John Wesley's father, was born in 1662. After his father's death, young Samuel lived with his mother and an aunt who nurtured him in "Dissenters' faith." At age fifteen, they sent him to the Dissenting Academy in London where his education was sponsored by wealthy Puritans. Indeed, he was a flaming tongue of angry opposition to the Church of England and the king. In 1683, when he was twenty-one, he was given an assignment to refute a tract that enunciated Anglican belief and liturgy. Instead of refuting it, he was convinced by the tract to embrace Anglicanism.[38] Soon afterward, he ran away from both home and Puritanism to enter Exeter College, Oxford. Walking every mile of the long journey, he introduced himself as an Anglican "convert." Perhaps to separate himself from his dissenter ancestors who had been Oxford students, he changed the spelling of his name from "Westley" to "Wesley."

At Oxford, he became a servitor, waiting on the wealthy students in the refectory, and helping write their papers in order to earn bread and make his way through university. Fatherless and friendless, he nevertheless finished Oxford in five years, receiving his B.A. the same year of the "Glorious Revolution" (1688) when Parliament invited William and Mary to come from Holland to be crowned - on Parliament's terms.

In the same month in 1688 that William and Mary came to the British throne, Samuel, the son of a dissenter pastor who had become an Anglican, married Susanna Annesley. She was the brilliant, beautiful, and strong-willed daughter of an eminent non-conformist pastor. However, like her husband, the independent-minded Susanna had become first a Socinian and then an Anglican. It is important to note that though both had, as teenagers, left their Puritan family nurture and become Anglicans, dissenter blood ran in their theological veins. Their politics was the source of perennial conflict. She was a "Jacobite" who believed that James, a Scot and Catholic, should be king because he was genealogically the next in line. On the other hand, Samuel embraced the new political era, and immediately announced his loyalty to King William and Queen Mary.

Samuel and Susanna's first parish had a mud hut as a rectory. He was twenty-eight and she was twenty-two when the first of nineteen children was born. The baby was baptized "Samuel, Jr." Almost every year thereafter, a new baby was born.

---

[38] Op. cit., 8-9

Samuel spent all day studying, reading, and writing for publication. From the beginning, he wrote prodigiously and scholarly. Hoping that his politics would enhance his parish appointment, Rev. Samuel Wesley was the first British citizen to write and publish a formal defense of the new monarchs. Samuel dedicated his new book on the life of Jesus to "Her most sacred majesty Queen Mary." As a reward from King William and Queen Mary, he received a new parish. He was promoted to "the living" at Epworth in Lincolnshire. His appointment to Epworth meant a raise in salary from 50 pounds per annum to 200 pounds, but even with the added income, he had to borrow money to move. The Wesleys moved to his permanent parish in 1695. The rectory was not a mud hut. It was a large, two-story brick house located on the "living" at Epworth in Lincolnshire. The parish church was St. Andrews.

Even in 1701, after ten children had been born to the Wesley marriage and eleven years after William and Mary were crowned, Susanna still considered William, the Dutchman, "illegitimate" as the King of England. She was still a Jacobite. Indeed, James was the next of kin.

Unbelievably, that political debate was the cause of a marital separation. One morning in 1701 when Samuel finished table grace in which he asked God's blessings on King William, he noted that Susanna did not join the chorus of "Amens" that was the family custom. He said, "Sukey, I note that you did not say, 'Amen.'" "Nor shall I," she retorted, "so long as the head of this house prays for a usurper on the throne of Britain." He replied, "Very well, if this house is to have two kings, it shall have two beds." However, according to Susanna's letters at the time, he did not stop at moving to another bedroom. He left home and went to London.

This is the point of Susanna Wesley's quarrel with her husband. A Jacobite, she considered William as a "usurper on the throne of England. She believed and said to her husband, "The monarch is determined by bloodline, not by Parliament notion, and William of Orange is not related by blood to the English throne. Young James is." To that, Samuel lost his temper and said infamously, "Very well, if this hourse is to have two kings, it shall have two beds."

She went to bed, but the next morning found a note on Samuel's desk along with three measly pounds of money. He was gone. Again, according to the research done by Stephen Tomkins, Susanna wrote, "Since I'm willing to let him quietly enjoy his opinions, he ought not deprive me of my little liberty of conscience."[39] Susanna held the parish together in his absence.

When Samuel left in March, Susanna was pregnant, as usual. Word came that day that King William had died following a fall from a horse. His wife's sister, Anne, a Protestant, would be queen. When in May, Susanna gave birth to her fourteenth child, she named her after the new queen - Anne.

Samuel returned from London twice. In July as she was walking in her garden, Sam appeared. She did not embrace him. After a bit of small talk, she asked, "Are you here to stay?" He answered, "That depends. Are you ready to submit your will to mine in every regard as a proper wife must?" An argument ensued. Then he said, "If I had a Bible in my hand, I'd wag it in your face. The finger of God points to you, Sukey! To you!" He left again.

During his second sojourn in London of over a year, he wrote a tome on the Book of Job that he dedicated to Queen Anne, but she would never see it until John delivered it after his father's death in 1735. When he came home again, the rectory had a second fire, burning half the house. That persuaded the rector to remain at home, be reconciled to his wife, and take care of his family and parish.

Less than a year later, on June 28, 1703, another child was born to Samuel and Susanna into this conflicted marriage and this political antipathy. They named him John Benjamin though he never would use his middle name. (*John Wesley wrote of this himself in the <u>Arminian Magazine</u> in 1784, p.606.*)

By today's criteria for paternal parenting, no one can give John Wesley's father high marks. Samuel's insistent demand to control his wife's politics and his daughters' choices of husbands was virtual cruelty. His insistence on being what he called "the head and master of the house" was the basis of his leaving his wife and family and living in London where he wrote his tome on the Book of Job. He was not a good money manager which meant that he was not a good provider. He lived above his means and was constantly in debt. His wife and daughters were perennially embarrassed that they could not pay for even the bread they

---

[39] Ibid., 11

bought at the local bakery. Yet, he hired a maid for the house and a garden keeper for the grounds. He spent most of his day in his study with a prevailing ambition to publish books that would be widely read.

Methodist history and lore have not smiled upon Samuel Wesley, Sr. However, we must, first of all, see Samuel Wesley in the context of the eighteenth century and the context of being a scholarly vicar who was trapped in Epworth. To see into that relationship, let us note the observation of Maldwyn Edwards, who was President of the British Methodist Conference. Samuel Wesley was his subject in the 1959 Quillian Lectures at Emory University.

- First, though their mother was an excellent "home school" teacher, their father gave all his children a love of books and access to his substantial library. That opportunity enabled all the girls to become qualified as governesses and the boys to go eventually to Oxford. Samuel was able to collate the Hebrew text of the Bible with the Greek Septuagint, and to compare versions in Syriac, Arabic, and Latin.[40] He regularly asked young John to collate the Hebrew text with Jerome's Latin Vulgate. When Samuel, Jr. was sixteen, his father ordered him to convert Bible verses to poetic meter. Charles' aptitude for poetry is common knowledge. There is a biblical echo in almost every line of each of Charles' hymns. We often do not recognize the obscure references because we don't have the mastery of Scripture that Charles had. John laced every sermon with scriptural references. Later, John's Explanatory Notes Upon the New Testament proved him a master interpreter of Greek texts. He wrote that "I made my notes as short and plain as possible, and declined to go deep into many difficulties lest the ordinary reader be left behind."[41] The bottom line is that the sons' immersion in Scripture came from their father's scholarship.

- Secondly, the age of the Enlightenment was dawning, and theological Deism was flourishing, and Samuel was conversant in the "new philosophy." The trend of the age was to reduce God to a "First Cause" who created the world

---

[40] Edwards, Maldwyn, *Sons to Samuel*, Epworth, 1961, 9

[41] Ibid., 11

perfectly, then had no further contact than a watchmaker does with a fine watch. Humankind had only the cold light of reason to sustain us in life, with its pains and earthly rewards, peril, and mystery. Indeed, Deism left no place for the Incarnation, the atonement, or the resurrection of Jesus. To Deists, human fate was to "rake through the world and then sink into nothingness."[42] J. H. Whitely, a jurist, wrote, "The century opened an age pregnant with dynastic changes and political revolutions; all past authority was ignored or repudiated; the old system of society was crumbling into ruin."[43] The Wesleys were conversant in the "new age philosophy," but Samuel and Susanna retained a lot of the Dissenter theology that they had been taught as children and youth. Their Puritan childhood was indelible!

- Thirdly, their father instilled in all three sons a love of the Anglican Church—its liturgy and its sacraments. He was a Tory to the core in his belief in the State Church and the authority of archbishops and bishops. This no doubt affected Wesley's control of the Methodist conferences. On his death bed, Samuel requested of his sons that we "drink once more the cup of blessing before we drink it new in the Kingdom of God. With desire, I want to eat this Passover with you before I die."[44] John Wesley considered as a fundamental means of grace that we "take frequent communion." As late as 1788, he re-published a 1732 sermon entitled, "Constant Communion."

- Fourthly, and somewhat paradoxically, Samuel was an evangelical Anglican in his doctrine and preaching.[45] So often, when frustrated, he would almost lash out at the resistance of his parishioners and all of England to a revival. He preached and wrote of Jesus' atonement on the cross, his miracles, and the work of the Holy Spirit to bring a sense of our sins being forgiven. He called his preaching "the fundamentals of the historic Creeds." He was firmly Arminian

---

[42] Ibid., 14

[43] Op. cit., Whitely, 25

[44] Op. cit., Edwards, 19

[45] Ibid., 9

in a day when most Anglicans who were not Deists were Calvinists.[46] Maldwyn Edwards summarized Samuel's theology this way, "God has offered the pardon of all sin and the right to life in Christ to all men without exception on the condition of believing and repenting."

Samuel's words on his death bed in April, 1735, to John are well known, but just before he spoke to John, he said to Charles, "Be steady. The Christian faith shall surely revive in this kingdom; you shall see it though I shall not." Then he laid a feeble hand on John and said, "The inward witness, son, the inward witness—this is the proof, the strongest proof of Christianity."[47]

Susanna Annesley Wesley

Susanna's maternal grandfather, John White, was a graduate of New College, Oxford University. He became a "progressive" Puritan minister in 1608 and served for forty years in Dorchester, a town in England's West Country faced with social problems like alcoholism, unemployment, overcrowding, and poverty. White began to dream of and plan a utopia in America. While largely ignored in Salem, Massachusetts because he never crossed the Atlantic, he inspired so many others to cross, that there is a monument to him in Dorchester, England, with the inscribed assurance that "his name and fame will live in unfading remembrance."[48] In reality, he "was one of the architects of another Puritan experiment—the Massachusetts Bay Colony."[49]

John White contended, in a House of Commons speech in 1641, that the office of "bishop" and "presbyter" was the same in the New Testament. He then served in the Puritan Parliament that voted to overthrow the king. One can imagine Wesley's mother sharing those stories with her children. John Wesley knew about his great-grandfather's famous speech in Parliament. Could that have been what convinced him, years later, to ordain preachers for American Methodism?

Susanna Annesley Wesley's father was Samuel Annesley, born

---

[46] Ibid., 15

[47] Op. cit., 43

[48] Internet, Wikipedia, *"John White Puritan English minister, 1575-1648"*

[49] Op. cit., Tomkins 8

in 1620. He was graduated from Oxford in 1644, and his ministry covered fifty-five of England's most tumultuous years. After his first wife's early death, he married Mary White with whom twenty-four more children were born. He preached before the House of Commons in 1648 when it was already heavily Puritan. In "The Great Ejection" in 1662, he, along with 2000 other clergy, were ejected from their pulpits and parsonages. He then was carefully watched and was in constant danger of being arrested, which would have left his wife and children destitute.

Annesley was allowed to return to a pulpit in 1672 and preached twice every day of the week. His youngest and twenty-fifth child, Susanna, was a prodigy with whom the Rev. Annesley shared his books. "She used the English language with precision and possessed a theological knowledge superior to that of many ministers of that day, or this. Her life was governed by a self-discipline that allowed not the least deviation from its principle and purpose."[50] Susanna's efficiency as a mother was without parallel, her kindness was self-evident, and her concern for her children cannot be questioned. However, by her own written opinion, she was not an affectionate mother. Expressing love was a problem for her.

Susanna Wesley was brilliant and self-educated from her prominent and scholarly father's library. By reading, reason, and personal independence, she became first a Socinian.[51] Then, to her father's heartache, an Anglican when she was only thirteen. This was virtually unheard of for a girl, and there is much reason to believe that her subsequent relationship with her parents was strained.[52]

She also had a strong will and was not affectionate with her children. She lived a very sad life. Of her nineteen children, born in a twenty-year period, only ten lived to maturity. Her husband's poverty was a perennial embarrassment. He was totally domineering, insisting always that he was right in every opinion. Her daughter, Emilia, once referred to her mother's "want of clothes

---

[50] Dallimore, Arnold, *Susanna Wesley,* Baker Book House, 1993, 15

[51] *Socinius embraced human freedom, rejected the substitutionary theory of the atonement and predestination, rejected all authority of the Church and found its source in Scripture.*

[52] Ibid. 17

or convenient meal." Susanna said of herself, "I have many years suffered much pain and great bodily infirmities." Like St. Paul, she was convinced that her sufferings had "promoted her spiritual and eternal good." She home schooled all her children. She and John wrote letters to each other at least weekly from the time he went to Charterhouse, a prep school, just before he turned twelve.

When her husband died in 1735, she was penniless and homeless. Thereafter, she lived from daughter to daughter for five years with no hope of any security. She worried that neither John nor Charles had a church or a job with a stipend. She and her son, Samuel, Jr., shared their misgivings about the new Methodist movement with all its emphasis on experience.

John's elder brother, Samuel, never accepted the doctrine nor the practice of Methodism. Deeply influenced (as were most Anglican clergy) by "the age of reason," Samuel could not understand what happened to John and Charles in May, 1738. Later, he could not accept the heresy of their preaching outside "a consecrated house of worship." He wrote to Susanna, "I am not afraid that the Church will excommunicate him (discipline is at too low an ebb); but that he will excommunicate the Church." When John moved their mother into the Foundery, Samuel wrote her of his "concern and grief that 'you have countenanced this spreading delusion so far as to be one of Jack's congregation. Is it not enough that I am bereft of both my brothers, but must my mother follow too?'" He died that same year and did not have to bear the sorrow that his mother chose not to be buried in an Anglican cemetery.

Susanna's two younger sons were certain that the warm heart was God's legacy for all God's children, not just the elite. This witness of the Spirit was the key-note of their ministry, the burden of their mission, the theme of their songs, and the secret of their success. The weary and heavy-laden, and there were multitudes of them, were offered rest for their souls. What their culture had denied in self-esteem, the Wesley's told them God would instill as "grace esteem." Converts were made quickly and in large numbers. They not only testified and shouted, they cleaned up their lives, stopped beating their children, brought home their meager earnings, and, like the Christians of the primitive church, "turned the world upside down."

In 1739 John showed her the dilapidated building in London that he had just leased from the Crown and was renovating. He told her that he was building her an apartment where she could spend the rest of her life. She was sixty-nine years old when she moved into the Foundery in 1740.

In 1742, Susanna reverted to the "Dissenter faith" of her childhood. In Foundery worship, Susanna was surrounded by "all that was Methodist," Charles' hymns and worship very different from Anglican liturgy. She loved hearing people's testimonies after their religious experiences, and tales from the trail when the lay preachers would come into their own rooms after weeks on the road in field preaching.

Finally, in her old age, she enjoyed conversations with three of her daughters who were also living at the Foundery, and occasional time with Jack (John). As her son-in-law was giving her communion, she had her own experience of personal assurance of salvation. She wrote about it this way: "When my son Hall was pronouncing those words in delivering the cup to me, 'The blood of our Lord Jesus Christ, which was given for thee,' the words struck through my heart, and I knew God for Christ's sake had forgiven me all my sins."

Following that experience she, for the first time, became a Methodist. "She began attending outdoor preaching, approving of extemporaneous prayers, applauding lay preachers, embracing Evangelical theology, and heralding revival evangelism."[53] It was during that time that she recommended that John Wesley allow Thomas Maxfield to preach. It was Susanna Wesley that we must thank for initiating the lay preacher phenomenon.

Even Susanna had for years been concerned that neither John nor Charles had a parish of his own. She urged them to ask a bishop for an appointment. Only after her own experience of the witness of the Spirit did she become convinced that they were within God's will. She had three wonderful years in her apartment at the Foundery with all her needs provided, but her health was gradually failing. Also, grief came again. She lost two more children—Samuel, Jr. in 1739 and Kezziah in 1741.

Emily spoke often to her brothers about their mother's suffering from pain. By the spring of 1742, Susanna seldom left

---

[53] Thomas, Arthur, *Profiles in Faith—Susanna Wesley,* C.S. Lewis Institute, 2002

her apartment, but the lay preachers on furlough from their circuits loved to drop by to engage her in conversation since she was so much more learned than they were. By July she was bedridden. Martha "Patty," Emilia "Emily", and Charles were there. She asked them to send for Anne "Nancy." Susannah "Sukey" and Mehetabel "Hetty" came. John was in Bristol but did arrive to "find her on the borders of eternity." Charles was unable to get back to London before she died. John recorded that her last full sentence was, "Please, my children, as soon as I am released, sing a psalm of praise to God."[54] They did. Unable to speak, she looked calm and serene. And then, without a struggle or even a sigh, her soul was set at liberty. The mother of Methodism was gone to join her parents, her husband, and twelve of her children. It was July 23, 1742. She was in her seventy-fourth year.

She was not buried beside her husband, nor in an Anglican cemetery. At her request, she was buried in the Dissenters' graveyard, "Bunhill Fields," across the street from New Chapel in London. Nearby were the graves of other Dissenters like John Bunyan, Isaac Watts, and Daniel Defoe.

Beside Wesley's Chapel, John had built Wesley House and placed his own study on the front with a window facing the site where he later placed his mother's grave.[55] Her epitaph reads, "The youngest and last surviving daughter of Dr. Samuel Annesley." John Wesley was in so many ways "his mother's son."

Rectory Family Life – a brief glimpse in retrospect

The Epworth Rectory is an imposing brick home, the nicest house in that Lincolnshire village surrounded by low lying farmland and pasture from which Samuel Wesley collected rents. The sheep still silently graze in the fields, tourists still walk on the grounds, and the house is still as it was in the 18th century. Northwest of the rectory, one can see St. Andrew's Church, standing on higher ground. Some of the village volunteers who serve as guides will share their knowledge about family life for the Wesleys.

According to Gary Best in a biography of Charles Wesley, the friction between Samuel and Susanna was constant. "Father

---

[54] Dallimore, Arnold, *Susanna Wesley,* Baker Book House, 1993, 165

[55] Op. cit., Thomas, 166

Samuel" was gone to London for long stretches of time, using as his excuse, Samuel, Jr.'s being in school there at Westminster, and later John at Charterhouse. In reality he felt bored with the people at Epworth and loved the conversations around London. He was very ambitious and always hoped to make a contact that would get him a larger and more sophisticated parish, but that never happened.

Susanna and Samuel had nineteen or twenty children in twenty years. Like most homes of that day, death stalked the nursery. Nine of the nineteen children did not survive infancy. Samuel was rigidly strict, displaying no compassion of record, even when his children desperately needed his forgiving love. Samuel was always in debt, but their status in the community as family of the vicar made them upper class in cultural decorum and expectations. The Wesley home was marked by strict discipline, academic excellence, marital conflict, and religious regimen.

To understand the lives of the Wesley children in any measure, we must recognize that the political and psychological make-up of Samuel and Susanna's difficult marital relationship had a profound impact on the children. Shapers of Methodist memory and guides to the "Old Rectory" in Epworth have tended to glorify the parents and siblings. Reality is that the Wesley home was not a happy home where children were cuddled and where each child grew up in the security of being loved.

When her husband was imprisoned for debt, Susanna sent him her wedding ring to sell, but he refused to accept it. He stayed in prison three months. Immediately upon being released, he resumed frequent and long stays in London. Susanna met with parishioners in the kitchen. It was during Samuel's first long stay in London that Anne was born, May, 1701.

There were two rectory fires, not one. The first was about harvest time, 1702, while Samuel was en route to London following a spat with his wife. He returned upon learning of the fire from a man who rode at breakneck speed to catch him. Nine months later, almost to the day of Samuel's return, John Benjamin Wesley was born, June 17, 1703. The second fire was in 1708 when John was five. It was that rescue that made his mother call him "a brand plucked from the burning."

The boys all left Epworth up in Lincolnshire and went to prep schools in London at about eleven years of age. This meant that Samuel, Jr. was gone before John and Charles were born. Then

John left when Charles was only six years old. As for the girls, Samuel would not approve of any boy that his daughters wanted to marry, so most ended up with very poor choices. Only Samuel, Jr., Charles, and Anne had happy marriages.

Thanks to outside financial support, all three Wesley boys were sent to prestigious "prep schools" in London, and then to Oxford. Samuel, Jr. was sent to Westminster School in London. John Wesley was sent when he was barely twelve years old to "Charterhouse," a boarding school in London of less prestige. Thanks to an uncle, Charles was enrolled at Westminster. All the boys were graduated from colleges at Oxford University, but the imprint and influence of their Epworth family was indelible.

Susanna organized the household and educated her seven girls equally to her three boys. She gave her girls the same opportunities for reading that her father had allowed her. The girls were therefore prepared to be governesses, to write exquisite poetry, and for some, to be sought after by famous men of the times like Samuel Johnson, England's most sought-after conversationalist. However, biographer Best reports that one of the girls wrote in her diary, "We of the female part of the family consequently are left to get our own bread or starve." Most of the girls were so proficient in English and other basics that they were hired as governesses. However, one had to resign the next day because she did not have sufficient wardrobe.

Only one of the girls had any modicum of marital happiness, and certainly John did not. The death of ten children left its mark, the separation of Samuel and Susanna left its mark, the political rancor left its mark, and the perennial indebtedness for a highly cultured family left its mark. More than these, the moral rigidity which lacked overt expressions of love left its mark. While we do not wish to enter the shadowy world of psycho-biography nor to be unkind to Samuel and Susanna Wesley or their three famous sons, we must admit candidly that they were taught to love God with all their heart more than they witnessed a "happy and enduring home."

Susanna's virtue and her concern were unquestioned. Her kindness is apparent, but she was not affectionate. Once when John signed a letter to his mother, "Your Affectionate Dutiful Son," she answered, "The conclusion of your letter is very kind, but it would be unjust of me to desire the love of anyone." How sad, and how revealing is this response. Susanna's brother, Samuel

Annesley, Jr., wrote in a letter that he was surprised she had put up with her husband's failure to provide for his family. She replied that she would be loyal to him whatever his faults, but her motive was expressed as "Christian duty," not love. In a letter to John, she wrote, "Tis an unhappiness almost peculiar to our family that your father and I seldom think alike."[56]

The Nineteen (or twenty?) Wesley Children[57]

Let us first give a cursory glance at all the children's birth and death dates, marriages, and progeny. From numerous sources, a more detailed summary of each child and her/his faith journey will follow.

- **Samuel Wesley, Jr.** was born in 1690 and died in 1739 at age 49. He was an Anglican minister who taught in a preparatory school in London. He was married and had two sons. He never supported John's and Charles' evangelical theology or itinerant ministry.

- **Susanna** lived two years, 1691-1693.

- **Emilia (Emily)** lived from 1692-1771. She was a governess and married Robert Harper who died in 1740. Her daughter died in infancy.

- **Annesley and Jedediah** were twins born in 1694. He lived two months. She lived fourteen months.

- **Susanna (Sukey)** – 1695-1764. Married to Richard Ellison, Sukey had four children.

- **Mary (Molly)** – 1696-1734. She married Rev. John Whitelamb. Mother and daughter died in childbirth.

- **Mehetabel (Hetty)** – 1697-1750. She became pregnant the night before her intended marriage to a barrister and was forced by her father to marry William Wright, a drunkard. All her children died at childbirth or soon after.

- **An unnamed infant** was still born in 1698.

[56] Wallace, Charles, *Susanna Wesley's Complete Writings,* Oxford University Press, 1997, 106

[57] Pellowe, Susan, ed., *A Wesley Family Book of Days,* Benard Productions, 1994, 3-4

- **John** was born 1699 and died soon after birth.

- **Benjamin** was born in 1700 and died soon after birth.

- **Unnamed twins** born in 1701, and both died soon after birth.

- **Anne (Nancy)** – 1702 – ?. She was happily married John Lambert. She had one son, John, born 1726.

- **John (Jacky, Jack)** – 1703 - 1791. He married Mrs. Mary Vazeille in 1751 and had no children.

- **Unnamed son** – 1705-1705. He was accidentally smothered by his nurse.

- **Martha (Patty)** – 1706-1791. She was married to Rev. Westley Hall, a womanizer. Of her ten children, all except one died in infancy. John taught her to write. She is buried in monument with John.

- **Charles** – 1707-1788. He married Sarah Gwynne in 1726. They had eight children, three of whom survived infancy.

- **Kezziah (Kezzy)** – 1709-1741. (unnamed twin?) Kezzy had physically handicapping condition due to childhood accident when dropped by nurse. Never married.

Biographical Summaries of the Ten Children Who Became Adults

Samuel, Jr. - 1690-1639

One year after the birth of their first child, Samuel and Susanna moved from their "mud hut" when he was appointed to South Ormsby as a bona fide rector. The baby boy was baptized "Samuel, Jr." "It is sometimes forgotten," wrote Gary Best in his biography of Charles Wesley, "that it was Samuel who was viewed as the model son by his parents."[58] He attended Westminster School in London, a much more prestigious school than Charterhouse where John attended. At Christ Church, Oxford, Samuel "gained a reputation beyond most of his contemporaries, being

---

[58] Best, Gary, *Charles Wesley,* Epworth, 2006, 21

thoroughly skilled in the learned languages, and master of Classics to a degree of perfections, perhaps not very common."[59] His friends included a number of persons who came to future fame, including the poet Alexander Pope. Samuel was graduated from Christ Church College, Oxford University and was ordained.

His was a teaching ministry back at his alma mater, Westminster, where he first attained a position as "subordinate faculty." It was at that time in British culture called an "usher." One of his friends was Joseph Addison. In 1715, he married one of the daughters of Rev. John Berry who boarded some of the students of Westminster, and it is probable that he arranged for his younger brother, Charles, to board with the Berry family some. Later, Samuel became headmaster of another school, Tiverton, where he was "head of school" when he died.

He was very generous with his younger siblings since his father never got out of debt. He spent much of his meager income on helping his younger brothers, his sisters, and his mother. Charles, also a student at Westminster, was largely raised by Samuel and his wife. They had six children, four of whom died in infancy and are buried in Westminster Abbey. Two became adults: a daughter nicknamed "Phil," and a son, Samuel, who died in his teens.

As early as 1731, Samuel became concerned that his younger brother, John, was "taking his religion to unnecessary extremes." The pursuit of holiness was commendable but was he laying excessive burdens on himself that were liable to injure his health? Being prone to consumption, should Jack not sit by the fire and refrain from exposing himself to the elements? The older brother continued that John should get his hair cut and questioned, "Is long hair scriptural anyway?" John responded that the money he saved on haircuts he gave to those in need and, "Was that not more biblical than any hairstyle?"[60] Samuel strongly advised Charles not to fall under the influence of John's monastic lifestyle. One bit of his persuasive advice Charles followed - to remain faithful to the Church of England and never become a Dissenter.

Even as John and Charles became well known as leaders of the Methodist movement, Samuel, Jr., a traditional Anglican,

---

[59] Clarke, Adam, Memories of the Wesley Family, Charle Kelly, 1823, 374

[60] Op. cit., Tomkins, 36

never approved of John's and Charles' theology or their itinerant ministry. He strongly objected to his brothers' preaching "outside the church walls." Indeed, he wrote to their mother, chastising her for "countenancing a spreading delusion so far as to be one of Jack's congregation." He added, "For my own part, I had much rather have them picking straws within the walls (of Bedlam) than preaching out of doors in the area of Moorfields."[61] Telford wrote, "In the seclusion of his school life, he was quite unable to understand the constraint which led his younger brothers to go into the highways to declare the Gospel to the perishing." [62] Samuel, Jr. died November 6, 1739, at age forty-nine after a brief illness.

An appreciative Wesley family had the following inscription engraved on his tombstone:

"A man known for his uncommon wit and learning, for the benevolence of his temper, and simplicity of manners. Deservedly beloved and esteemed by all; an excellent Preacher; but whose best sermon was the constant example of an edifying life, so continually and zealously employed in acts of beneficence and charity, that he truly followed his blessed Master's example in going about doing good. Of such unscrupulous integrity that he declined occasions for advancement in the world...and avoided the usual ways to preferment as studiously as many others seek them."[63]

Considering the financial status of most of the family, John probably paid for the marker and its message. It could well be that John's famous statement, "Though we cannot think alike, can we not love alike?" came from his relationship with his brother Samuel.

John Benjamin—1703-1791

As we have written, Samuel Wesley left home before Easter, 1702. When Susanna, during evening prayers, had not said "Amen" after Samuel prayed for King William, he ended the prayer, went to his study, and summoned her to come. They had

---

[61] Telford, John, *The Life of John Wesley,* Charles Kelly, London, c. 1906, 130

[62] Ibid. 130

[63] Op. cit., Clarke, 465

lived together for twelve years and there was no doubt that Samuel knew of her Jacobite politics and did not believe William, a Dutchman, to be a legitimate monarch. She told him so and he dropped to his knees and swore to God that he would never touch her nor share a bed with her as long as he lived. Then, the week before Easter, he left for London and applied to be the chaplain on a ship and to live at sea. Furthermore, he threatened to report her to the Bishop in London for treason against the Crown.

Susanna wrote a highly sophisticated letter to the Suffragan Bishop who sympathized with her by return mail. His opinion was that instead of her being guilty of treason, Samuel was guilty of perjury for breaking his marriage vows. Samuel returned in July, the argument resumed and Samuel left, swearing to never return. Before he arrived at the edge of the village of Epworth, he was told that his house was on fire. It was. He returned, considered the fire to be "the finger of God," and remained at home, though with many future long visits to London at a cost of about £50 each while he was deeply in debt. Susanna subsequently set up a school in her home for the children with three hours of home schooling in the morning and three in the afternoon.

John Wesley was born ten months after Samuel's return in 1702. The Gregorian calendar was adopted in Great Britain in 1752. This created a change of eleven days in all dates. John Benjamin was born on June 17, 1703, but after the adoption of the Gregorian calendar, his birth-date was June 28. He was the only child with a double name. Perhaps this was because two of his deceased brothers were named "John" and "Benjamin."

Any casual knowledge of John Wesley leaves in one's memory the "Old Rectory" fire when little Jacky was five years old. Apparently set by belligerent parishioners on February 9, 1709, the thatch roofed house was quickly a torch. Five were sleeping in one bed in the nursery. The nurse grabbed Charles, then two, and instructed the others to follow her down the steep, winding stairs. When the children were counted in the back garden, Jacky was missing. His father approached the hot flames but the staircase was falling. John was standing on a chest, confused and crying, his head silhouetted against the blazing fire that filled the room. Samuel knelt to commit his burning child to God, but charitable neighbors formed a human ladder and lifted him from the upstairs window just as the roof caved in.

Samuel, Sr. wrote afterwards that all his books were lost, including the finished three longhand copies of manuscript, *The Life of Christ*. Concerning Jacky he wrote, "When poor Jacky was saved, I could not believe it until I had kissed him two or three times. He said that he did not know Susanna because 'her lips were black.'"[64]

Susanna told her family that story many times, always with the ending with a word to Jacky, "God spared your life, as a brand plucked from the burning, for some great purpose." In her own diary entry for "Evening, May 17th, 1711," she noted, "I do intend to be particularly careful of the soul of this child that I may instill in his mind the principles of true religion and virtue. Lord, give me grace to do it sincerely and prudently and bless my attempts with good success." [65] Without a fire in their home, he would never have been conceived, and without a miracle, the second rectory fire would have burned him alive. John, in a special way, was his mother's son!

History certainly confirms that her prayer was answered! Many of us know that instances in our lives which our parents believed to be providential can leave us with both some sense of manifest destiny, but also with a lot of guilt if we live even our teen years as "normal" kids do. John Wesley, as others of us, felt both the blessing and the pressure of being "God's chosen."

His parents sent him to Charterhouse, a London boarding school, in 1714. From age eleven to twenty-one, John's spiritual life was a slow downward spiral. (Today we would probably call this the adolescent period when he was "finding himself.") He was young and very small for his age. At Charterhouse, he was first exposed to the sins of young boys: harassment, practical jokes, vulgarity, some discussion and myriad references to human sexuality. He later wrote, "From ten to fourteen I had little but bread to eat and not plenty of that. I believe this was so far from hurting me that it laid the foundation of lasting health."[66]

After Charterhouse, he entered Oxford at age seventeen. There is no evidence that he felt either a call or desire to become

---

[64] McTyeire, Holland, *History of Methodism,* Southern MPH, 1886, p. 46

[65] Ibid. p. 46

[66] Op. cit., 37

ordained. In his first year, like most other students, he received
the sacraments three times a year as the extent of his worship![67]
He is described as "gay, sprightly, full of wit and humor."[68] "With
his auburn hair, his quick wit, and his excellent dancing, he
was invited to parties and confesses to "enjoying the company
of women more than the company of God."[69] Edward Gibbon
describes the typical Oxonian of Wesley's day as "a man who
remembered he had a salary to receive, but forgot he had a duty
to perform." Gibbon noted sarcastically that "perhaps I should
have embraced the lucrative pursuits of the law ... or the fat
slumber of the Church."

His correspondence with his mother is amazing, both in its
volume and its revelation of her influence. At Christ College,
the moment he hinted that he was struggling with a call to "holy
orders," Susanna urges him by return post, "to greater application to the study of practical divinity, which, of all other studies,
I humbly conceive to be the best for candidates for orders."[70]
She concludes with the exhortation, "And now, in good earnest,
resolve to make religion the business of your life, for after all,
that is the one thing which, strictly speaking, is necessary...I
heartily wish that you would now enter upon a strict examination of yourself, that you may know whether you have a reasonable hope of salvation by Jesus Christ."[71] He did seek holy orders
and was ordained Deacon in 1726 and Elder in 1729.

John Wesley loved women, but never gave himself permission to live out his affections. Perhaps an interesting anecdote
will explain this conflict. As one visits the "Old Rectory" in
Epworth, England, the Methodist lay volunteers point out the
bed on which John Wesley was born. Atop the bed is a beautiful,
hand-stitched quilt. On one occasion in visiting Epworth, there
were only two of us and, with a twinkle in his eye, the guide told
us the real story of that quilt. It was not there when little Jacky

---

[67] Ibid. p.46

[68] Tyerman, L. *Life and Times of John Wesley, Founder of the Methodists,* Hodder &
Stoughton, 1882, MDCCCLXX, Vol. I, p. 24

[69] Op. cit., Telford, 33

[70] Op. cit., McTyeire50

[71] Ibid., 50

was born. Rather, it was a gift to him from the Kirkman sisters
who lived near Oxford.

His sister Martha sheds more light on this through her letters.
Two days after he was elected to the Lincoln faculty, "Jack" went to
the Kirkman sisters' father's home where he enjoyed fox-hunting,
dancing quadrilles, and playing cards. Martha also records that
"Jack loved to play the flute." It was a refined, literary, challenging
group and he had a good time. His auburn hair was shoulder length
and he "cut a romantic figure." He had attended their home at
Christmas time, 1725, and enjoyed himself. He fell in love with Sally,
but she was determined to be married and he could not support her
just then. He watched his precious Sally marry the local schoolmas-
ter on December 28, 1725. Back at Lincoln, he recorded in his diary
the steps of a new dance and copied this verse:

> "Belinda has such wondrous charms, tis heaven to lie
> within her arms;
>
> And she's so charitably given, she wishes all mankind in
> heaven."

Martha indicates that "Belinda" is Sally Kirkman.[72] Later,
when he was his father's assistant at Wroote parish, he wrote
much in his diary about a young woman in the parish named
Kitty Hargreaves. Samuel had her father send her away, "in suspi-
cion of my courting her," according to John's diary. Later on, he
fell in love but could not bring himself to marry young Sophia
Hopkey in Georgia. He loved Grace Murray, but did not marry her
in official ceremony. In 1751, he made the sad mistake of marrying
Madame Molly Vazeille when he was fifty-one years old.

It is only fair to say that the founder of Methodism struggled
into his old age with an inner conflict between sexual expression
and spiritual vitality. Importantly, John Wesley's bumbling efforts
at love were typically followed by re-doubled energies for his
ministry. Each time he lost a girlfriend, he vowed never to touch
or love another woman! His belated decision in 1751 to marry
proved disastrous. No wonder he preferred that the "traveling
preachers" remain single. Francis Asbury in America did the same.

---

[72] Wilder, Franklin, *The Remarkable World of John Wesley*, Exposition Press, 1978, p.
25. (Dr. Wilder, a physician from Little Rock, Arkansas, also quotes, without foot-
noting the pages, from an older book : Green, Vivian H.H., *The Young Mr. Wesley
and Oxford.*)

"Wrap" on John Wesley, the man

This book is a history of Methodism, not a biography of John Wesley. We do need to know that, on the one hand, he was reared with the manners and education as a son of the upper class. But being the child of a family always in financial straits gave him insight into what it means to be poor. It was a paradoxical combination.

Randy Maddox has done a "wrap" on Wesley on which we have elaborated, but he has stated so succinctly and accurately for anyone needing a synopsis:

"His grandfathers on both sides – John Westley (c. 1636-70) and Samuel Annesley (c. 1620-96) were Puritan clergy expelled from the Established Church when Charles II was recalled. Yet both of John's parents opted as young adults to return to the Established Church.... Thus John imbibed classic Anglican sensibilities in his youth, including the deep appreciation for early Church doctrine championed by the Nonjurors. These commitments were reinforced by his Oxford training, which privilege the writings of the {King Charles era) divines. But Wesley was also exposed to the currents of Enlightenment thought in his academic work. And on his trip to Georgia he made contact with the emerging evangelical movement in Moravian form. This contact led to Wesley's spiritual renewal in 1738 and the beginnings of the Methodist Revival."[73]

John Wesley would not have been a good pastor! He once wrote that when a person complained to him, it was like tearing the flesh from his bones. He frustrated his sisters. He often responded to them with lectures which reflected St. Paul's stoicism: "I have learned whatever state I am in; therewith to be content." But, as any missioner, John Wesley had to choose between his family role and his Kingdom role. To the chagrin of his sisters, and like Jesus when Mary sent for him to come home, Wesley had no choice but to follow his vision.

However, John did help each of his sisters financially. Also, each of the girls became a Methodist before she died which is

---

[73] Maddox, Randy, ed., *The Works of John Wesley, Doctrinal and Controversial Treatises*, Vol. 12, Abingdon, 2012, 15-16

quite a tribute to their faith in their two brothers' faith, integrity, and eventual emotional support.

David Hempton, a Britisher now on the Harvard Divinity School faculty, sums up Wesley's "various capabilities" this way:

"Son and brother, fourth generation Oxford graduate, Anglican priest, university fellow, missionary, itinerant evangelist, Methodist founder, authoritarian leader, unsuccessful in romance and marriage, prickly controversialist, energetic educator, creator of ministries for the poor, facilitator of female leadership, relentless activist, and connexional disciplinarian").[74]

Diarmaid MacCulloch, a secular historian, summarizes Wesley in these words:

"He built headquarters in London and Bristol; his societies put up preaching houses for themselves all over the country. This posed questions of identity—much as Wesley tried to avoid the issue by labeling his movement not a Church but a "Connexion," even writing a pamphlet in 1758, Reasons Against a Separation from the Church of England. Finally, in 1784, it was American Methodism that he took it upon himself to ordain, but he was furious when the American "superintendents" called themselves "bishops." He lived and died a member of the Church of England. In truth 'he was an Anglican and he was not.' Hard work was allied with strict morality; if ever there was anything resembling the 'Protestant work ethic,' it came out of Methodism and the Evangelical Revival rather than the sixteenth-century Reformation. The effect did not wear off until the 1960's."[75]

MacCulloch's observations cannot be denied or ignored if one is to interpret authentically the history of Methodism. John Wesley was a man whose work, high-Anglican heritage, and evangelical spirituality brought phenomenal growth of Christianity to world religious history.

---

[74] Hempton, David, *"Wesley In Context,"* IN *The Cambridge Companion to John Wesley,,* Randy Maddox, Jason Vickers, eds., Cambridge University Press, 2010, 61

[75] Op. cit., 152-154

Charles Wesley - 1707-1788

Though never recorded, many who knew the politics of the Wesley family thought that Charles was named for the martyred monarch, Charles, II. He was born two months prematurely and for weeks he did not cry or open his eyes. Trying to replicate life in the womb, Susanna kept him wrapped without a diaper in soft wool until the date of his expected birth. He was only eighteen months old when the famous rectory fire occurred. His life was saved by a maid who carried him from the burning building.

Charles was a pupil in Susanna's home school. He was but seven when his brother John was sent away to Charterhouse, a London school associated with almshouses for the poor though John was a paying student because of a scholarship from the Duke of Buckinghamshire. His departure meant that Charles was left in an essentially female household for the next two years. In April, 1716, he went to the prestigious Westminster School because his brother, Samuel, was on the faculty and Charles boarded with him and his wife. What a shock, from being home schooled with his mother and sisters to being a nine-year-old in a school of over four hundred boys, most of them from less religious and more wealthy homes. In some verse, he called it "the public school of sin where troops of young corrupters tried in wickedness to excel, lewdness their vile delight and pride their boasted principle." He also wrote of the practice of "destroying the innocence of others."[76] This is probably a thinly veiled reference to homosexual behavior as a norm at the Westminster School.

Charles' brother, Samuel, was deeply influential. From his modest income, he repeatedly sent money to his sisters and parents in their need. He also contributed to both of his younger brother's educational costs. His influence also embedded a love for Anglicanism deeply in Charles' psyche. Charles was known as a "fighter" when classmates were being bullied. One such boy, a Scot, later became Lord Chief Justice and helped Charles when he was ridiculed because of his Methodism.

From Oxford days, he and John were very close and their evangelical theology developed in sync. Charles wrote lines of verse from his early years. Contrary to popular opinion, he did not compose any music; rather he wrote lyrics that could be

---

[76] Op. cit., Best, 22

sung by familiar tunes. In so doing, he virtually was a pioneer in making congregational singing a major component of public worship. Since Methodist worship was never in a church, there was little liturgy used, as most of the service was "preaching and singing."

Charles joined his brother as a missionary to Georgia only four months after their father died in 1735. However, General Oglethorpe made Charles his personal secretary and took him along to Frederica, the southern edge of English territory. Indeed, a military garrison was stationed there in the event of a Spanish invasion from Florida. "Frederica was little more than a place on the map, a wretched outpost of Empire, consisting of a fort, huts and tent, with a storeroom used as a church. Beyond stretched the American hinterland, as yet wild and undeveloped."[77]

As secretary, his days were spent drawing contracts, trading bonds, keeping notes in magistrate's court, and writing Oglethorpe's correspondence. Oglethorpe treated him harshly from day one, and Charles was really in the middle when Mrs. Hawkins accused General Oglethorpe of seducing her. Charles hated the job and went back to England. On July 25, seven months after his arrival, he wrote his letter of resignation to Oglethorpe, who accepted it. His ship went first up the coast to Boston, a town which Charles loved and in which he stayed a month, awaiting the next boat to England. He was invited to preach in Anglican Churches, was guest of the Governor, and dined in the homes of leading Boston families.

Charles had chronic pulmonary issues. He was frequently ill in Georgia and the "consumption" returned while he was in Boston. A physician treated him without fee, but to little avail. "I vomited, purged, bled, sweated, and took laudanum." He became depressed, an emotional condition that recurred often in his life, resulting in many hymns that reflected his gloomy moods. He was delighted, after stormy seas and constant sickness, to see the English coast, and was soon in London.

Back in England, three men became Charles' mentors: William Law, the same author who had deeply influenced John five years earlier, Count Zinzendorf, a Moravian who happened to be in England, and Peter Böhler, a young Moravian missionary

---

[77] Gill, Frederick, *Charles Wesley, The First Methodist*, Lutterworth, 1964, 52

in London who was en route to Georgia. He also visited his sister, "Kezzy," and led her through a conversion, an experience during which he wrote one of his greatest hymns:

> **"Love divine, all loves excelling,**
> **joy of heaven to earth come down;**
> **Fix in us thy humble dwelling,**
> **all thy faithful mercies crown.**
> **Come, Almighty, to deliver, let us all Thy grace receive...**
> **Finish then thy new creation, pure and spotless let us be."**

He went on to Oxford and developed pleurisy. John had come back to London in January, 1738. Charles was often sick and thought he would die, but survived. Charles was led by Peter Bohler and John Bray, "a lowly brazier," to an experience of salvation on the eve of Pentecost, May 21, 1738. (*Mr. Bray's house is marked today by a plaque.*)

After John's Aldersgate experience on May 24, they remained a part of the Moravian fellowship until July 20, 1740, when both Wesley brothers left the Moravian Fetters Lane Society. The Wesleys could not forsake their Anglican belief that faith leads to holy living, not to meditative "stillness." Then, in 1741, the rupture came between the Wesleys, who were Arminians, and George Whitefield's converts who were Calvinists. The entire decade was one of riots, rockings, and profane abuse in town after town. In 1744, John preached at St. Mary's Chapel of Oxford and was never invited again though he remained technically on faculty at Lincoln College until 1751, when he married. Added to these doctrinal divisions, their mother, Susanna, died July 23, 1742. It was not a time without hardship and heartache.

Great happiness came to Charles when he fell in love155

with Sally Gwynne from Wales. Her family was wealthy and at first opposed the marriage because Charles' only income was from the sale of hymns for which he had a contract for £200. John intervened since he still drew a salary as a Fellow of Lincoln College and declared his own net worth at £2500. Since the brothers were both leaders in Methodism, he promised to pay Charles a regular salary. His offer was accepted and Charles and Sally were married April 8, 1749. Incredibly, while at Garth house on their honeymoon, Charles wrote, "Jesus Lover of My Soul, let me to thy bosom fly!"

Charles and Sally bought a nice brick home in Bristol. Though money was tight, he hired a servant for Sally who birthed eight children in sixteen years though only three survived infancy: Jacky (1752), Martha Maria (1755), Charles (1757), Sally (1759), Susanna (1761), Selina (1764), Samuel (1766), and John James (1768). In 1771, a Mrs. Gumley left them her house in Marylebone, London. It was well furnished, and his only expense would be maintenance and grounds keeping. "For the rest of his life, the commodious house ... was his home."[78]

The brothers were always very close in their ministry and brotherly love, but they had several important disagreements.

- First of all, Charles married a beautiful and wealthy Welsh girl, was happily married, and, unlike John, was a father.

- Secondly, and possibly because he was happily married to a woman of family means, he bought a lovely brick home in Bristol in his earlier years and then in the Marylebone section of London, the parish where he was buried. Consequently, he refused to travel like John did.

- Thirdly, he was totally opposed to John's several romantic relationships and literally blocked John's marriage to Grace Murray with a scurrilous interference.

- Fourthly, Charles was vehemently opposed to John's ordaining men for America and any other step toward separation from the Church of England.

- Lastly, John was very disappointed that Charles refused to be buried behind Wesley's Chapel. Charles was buried in an Anglican church graveyard in Marylebone, London.

One biographer of Charles Wesley, who subtitled his book, *The First Methodist*, insisted,

"Nothing could be further from the truth than that Charles was a pale shadow of his brother or that he stands in the background of his brother's work. Though less dynamic, his genius in other directions was marked. And, if he never occupied, like John, the centre of the stage, it was because

---

[78] Ibid., 177-178

he deliberately chose not to. He never liked the limelight ... but when God called, he never failed, no matter how reluctant to respond with the result that he, no less than John, established Methodism. ... John organized; Charles provided the impulse. John was the head; Charles was the heart."[79]

"Charles was patient yet impulsive, retiring yet resolute, frail yet a fighter, controversial and hot tempered yet gentle and forgiving; a rigid conformist yet a bold pioneer; a strict Churchman yet an ardent Methodist."[80]

It is doubtful whether Methodism would have survived without his hymns. In singing, the people's souls were awakened and they heard the whisper of God's voice. In singing, they were encouraged in their sorrows and their victories in Jesus were given voice. His hymns gave Methodism a memory that was hummed, whistled, and sung as miners slogged their way to work, as factory workers slaved in sweatshops, as mothers rocked sick babies, and as grieving families buried their young and saw their old suffer. His lyrics give voice to every theological affirmation of the Christian faith and give voice to every emotion of the human psyche.

"Methodism has never given him the place he merits," wrote Frederick Gill. "The work of the brothers was complementary. Each supplied what the other lacked. Their diversity and strong differences in opinion was lived out in the context of their love, and remains a marked feature of Methodism when we experience our finest hours.

John admonished Charles regularly to get out into the air, walk in the park, and even travel some. Often John referred to money, writing, "Do not die to save charges. You certainly need not want for anything so long as I live." And, on another occasion he wrote, "Never mind the expense; I will take care of that." Yet, in 1788, Charles grew weaker. He called to his bedside his son Samuel whose conversion to Catholicism broke Charles' heart. He said to his son, "I shall bless God to all eternity that ever you was born." When his daughter read a letter from Uncle John saying

---

[79] Ibid., 231

[80] Ibid., 232

he would be a father to them, Charles replied weakly, "He will be kind to you when I am gone. I am certain your uncle will be kind to all of you."[81] To a friend who sat with him in his last days, he said, "I am a mere sinner, saved by the grace of God." Then, he composed a hymn with that message. When asked near the last if he wanted anything, he answered, "Nothing but Christ."

His beloved Sally pressed his hand on his last night and asked him to press her hand if he knew her. He did and whispered, "Thanks, love, blessings." Then, "Lord—my heart—my God." He drew a short breath and, as he had prayed for in one of his last hymns, "dropped into Eternity." It was March 29, 1788. He was in his eighty-first year.

The letter to John telling him of his brother's death was not delivered for a week. Therefore, he did not attend Charles' funeral. That night, preaching in Bolton, John tried to sing the popular, "Come, O Thou Traveler Unknown." Normally John did not display emotions, but broke down when coming to the words, "My company before is gone and I am left alone with Thee." Later, in his own will, John left "to Sally Gywnne Wesley £85 per year for life. "

Outside the New Room in Bristol, the statue of Charles stands in one courtyard, and the statue of John in the other. Rooted in catholic spirit and impassioned in evangelical appeal second only to Whitefield as a preacher, his recurring theme is etched in stone at the foot of Charles' statue:

"O let me commend my Saviour to you."

Biographical Summaries of the Seven Daughters

Of Samuel and Susanna's nineteen children, ten lived to be adults: three sons and seven daughters. Many of their letters reveal excellent minds. There are numerous paintings and engravings of the three sons, but no facial record of the daughters except Martha. There is a painting of her talking with Samuel Johnson, the famous lexicographer of the 18th century!

Most women bore many children throughout history before the twentieth century. Much of that was due to the absence of

---

[81] Ibid., 224

any form of birth control, but a lot was due to infant mortality. Methodists have many written sources for the seven girls and three boys who reached adulthood, but to reveal the true life of Susanna Wesley, one must see the physical, emotional, and financial hardship that accompanied her giving birth to nineteen children between 1690 and 1709. Seven were born before Samuel was appointed to St. Andrews Parish in Epworth in Lincolnshire.

Let's look at the girls who reached maturity. Like the boys, they also grew up at Susanna's knee, all learning the alphabet in a day except Anne ("Nancy") whom her mother chastised as being "slow of mind!" The three-story brick rectory of the St. Andrew Parish in Epworth of Lincolnshire served as home, schoolhouse, rector's study, and "prayer meeting" place. The seven sisters who survived infancy were nicknamed "Emily," "Sukey," "Molly," "Hetty," "Nancy," "Patty," and "Kezzy." The girls all had sad lives and looked to their three brothers for both emotional and financial support. One historian has called the lives of the seven sisters "a matter of tears."

Like all great public figures, when John Wesley is seen from the vantage point of family, we see a different picture. "Jack" was one sibling in a large, intelligent, and strong-willed family with his own feet of clay. We see this especially in his lack of sensitivity regarding his seven sisters at difficult times in their lives. The girls' troubles could not have come at a worse time for John and Charles. They were first pre-occupied with their university lives including "The "Holy Club." Then for the better part of two years, they were on their missionary venture in Georgia.

Upon his return, John was so obsessed with the Moravians that he spent the summer of 1738 in Herrnhut, Germany. After their life-changing experiences of grace in the spring of 1738, both became involved in itinerant ministries and were "on the road." Perhaps every Methodist and other students of Wesley need to know this conflict of interests in John Wesley, the public leader, and Jack, the brother. Most of us have failed to match his Christ-likeness in personal discipline, but we might have surpassed him as a person relating to his family. Listen now to John Wesley from his sisters' points of view.

Emilia ("Emily") was born on the last day of 1692. Unhappily married to Robert Harper, Emily ran a school and was living in Gainsborough in poverty when John went to Germany against the wishes of his family. He had already left for Georgia only four months after their father's death and remained there nearly two years, returning in February, 1738, and leaving for Germany in June. The girls felt that they needed his counsel, financial support, and emotional strength. As important as this was in Wesley's spiritual journey immediately following Aldersgate in May, we who struggle between our soul search and our personal obligations can take heed. While he journeyed, first to Georgia and then to Germany, John Wesley had a widowed mother, two brothers, and seven sisters.

His sister Emily was married to a lazy bum, and was going through a very difficult time, emotionally and financially when he had left to be with the Moravians. He did not visit her in Gainsborough prior to departing, nor did he give his mother or sisters in distress any money. (Actually, his only income was his stipend from Oxford where he remained on faculty). Upon returning from Germany, two months later, he wrote Emily, not about her burdens, but about the state of the Moravians in Germany!

Emily's letter in response scorched the mailbox. She writes,

"For God's sake, tell me how a distressed woman, who expects daily to have the very bed taken from under her for lack of rent, can consider the state of the churches in Germany. I have sold many of my beautiful clothes for bread; is not that calamity? Sam and Charles, God bless them, kept me from destitution last summer. Had you the same, nay a quarter, of the love for me I have for you, long since you would have been with me; it was in your power—you who could go to Germany but could not reach Gainsborough. And, brother, had my soul been lost to self-murder, my damnation would have been at your door."

Her complaint doubtless hurt but did not deter him from his mission.

Emily obviously forgave John his negligence. She became a Methodist and died in 1771 after living at the Foundery and the "rooms" at Wesley's Chapel on City Road for twenty-five years.

Susanna ("Sukey") was pretty and is described as "bringing laughter as the sun brings warmth." After the rectory fire, she went to London to live with her mother's brother, Uncle Annesley. She married Richard Ellison, a wealthy man who became an alcoholic and abused her. They had four children. She finally left him, and John supported her emotionally and financially. Ellison later was converted and died a Methodist. Charles conducted his funeral in 1760. Sukey lived serially among her four children. Prior to her death, she was speechless for five days. Then she aroused to say, "Jesus is come! Heaven is here!" She died in 1764 as a Methodist.

Mary ("Molly") was born in South Ormsby about 1696. She was seriously injured either by being dropped by a careless nurse or in a childhood accident. She had a physically handicapping condition for life and was treated terribly by village children. She was beautiful. She wrote exquisite verse and wonderful letters.

She married Johnny Whitelamb who had lived in the Epworth rectory and assisted Samuel at the Wroote parish, apparently without pay. He was fourteen years younger than she. He went to Oxford, but was so poor that John and Samuel, Jr. had to pay the bursar for his university bills. He was ordained in 1733. While at Oxford, Johnny was guilty of some moral turpitude, but Mary married him in December, 1734.

Upon Samuel's request, Johnny Whitelamb was appointed to the Wroote Parish. They were deeply in love. Sadness came soon. Mary died in childbirth in October, 1735, only eleven months after their wedding. Whitelamb never remarried. He invited John Wesley to preach at Wroote, but later lost his enthusiasm for Methodism and became a Deist. He died in 1769. None of the Wesleys went to his funeral.

Mehetabel "Hetty" was born in 1697. Some called her the prettiest of the Wesley girls. She fell in love with a young lawyer while she was serving as a governess in London. Upon telling her father while at home in Epworth, Samuel categorically forbade the marriage, even though Hetty was in her late twenties. She eloped to London and spent the night with her fiancé. After making love during the night before their wedding, he refused to marry her the next morning. Rejected and dejected, she went home to Epworth, fearful she was pregnant, which she was. To protect her father's reputation as a cleric, she promised her father to marry anyone who would have her. Probably as punishment for her sin, Samuel picked an illiterate plumber – uncouth, boorish, and later, a drunkard – to marry his bright, educated, and desperate daughter. No member of the family attended the simple ceremony on October 13, 1725.

John felt his family was wrong. Therefore, on August 26, 1726, he preached a "grace-filled" sermon at Wroote parish entitled, "Universal Charity - charity due to wicked persons."[82] Samuel and Susanna were both present and were highly offended. Samuel wrote to Charles, "Every day you hear how he contradicts me and takes your sister's part before my face; nay, he disputes me, and preaches at me from my own pulpit." The little baby died in December. None of the Wesleys attended the funeral. So far as any personal letters indicate, Hetty's father never saw her again until his death.

Basically, Susanna defended her husband. After one visit to Hetty, she wrote that "I am returned home to Epworth, neither pleased with her or myself." Meanwhile, poor Hetty suffered from her husband's verbal drunken abuse, alcoholism, and from severe beatings.

Obsessed with seeking her father's forgiveness, she believed, after the death of her third child, that God's anger was directed at her because of her father's refusal to intercede for her. She wrote her father, "My brothers (Samuel, John, and Charles) will report to you what they have seen of my life and my daily struggle to redeem the past. I have come to the point where I desperately feel your forgiveness to be necessary to me. I beseech you then not to withhold it." But withhold it he did. Samuel Wesley died at Epworth April 25, 1735. Apparently and understandably, she did not go to his funeral.

Only after Samuel's death did Susanna re-establish a relationship with her broken-hearted daughter. Hetty became an active Methodist. Mrs. Nolan B. Harmon, in writing about the Wesley sisters, came to the conclusion that, had it not been for her husband, Susanna would have given emotional support to Hetty across the years. John, Charles, and Hetty's sisters did support her.

Following her mother's death, Hetty worked for a while with the Methodists in Bristol where she reported that the Methodist bands surrounded her with a love and friendship she had never known before. Her health broken, she returned to London where

---

[82] Op. cit., Edwards, 29 *(sermon referenced in many places, but this is full title.)*

she died in 1750. Charles recorded her having said to him, "I have long ardently wished for death because, you know, we Methodists always die in a transport of joy."

None of the Wesleys, except Charles and possibly Anne married happily, but Hetty married most tragically and suffered most from Samuel's judgment. She wrote her own sad epitaph:

> **"Destined while living to sustain an equal share of grief and pain,**
> **All various ills of human race within this breast had once a place.**
> **Without complaint she learn'd to bear a living death, a long despair;**
> **Till hard opress'd by adverse fate, o'ercharged, she sunk beneath the weight**
> **And to this peaceful tomb retired so much esteem'd, so long desir'd.**
> **The painful, mortal conflict's o'er; a broken heart can bleed no more."[83]**

We must note that the 18th century was the Age of Reason where emotions were repressed and the Puritan influence on Christian expression was right behavior, not forgiving love. Hetty did what few others dared to do; she got in touch with her feelings.

Perhaps Hetty's plight, and the similar sad stories of the other six Wesley sisters, mellowed John and Charles as they shaped, through hymns and sermons, the "grace theology" and the "catholic spirit" for which Methodism has been known.

Anne (nicknamed "Nancy") was born in 1701 and had a twin brother who had the baptismal name, "John Benjamin." Her twin died as a small child. She was educated by her mother and became a governess. Then, she married John Lambert, a land surveyor in 1725 and they were happily married. Her husband was wealthy but "drank it up." John often wrote to Nancy, was her son's godfather, visited them, and spent the night during his ministry and, as late as 1726, wrote that he danced! Anne loved her husband very much and apparently, they were happy. John Lambert did drink and did have a religious experience which included a covenant of abstinence but according to Charles' diary, John Lambert fell off the

---

[83] Op. cit., Pellows, (March 22)

wagon. On July 19, 1738, he repented and again promised to stop drinking. He then became an active Methodist.

In December 1741 while either living or visiting at the Foundery, Lambert became ill. He died at the Foundery in early 1742. We hear of Anne only once more. She was at her mother's bedside when Susanna died in July, 1742. Anne therefore lost her husband and her mother the same year. Anne was forty-one years old. (Strangely we do not know when, where, and under what circumstances Anne lived the rest of her life nor anything about her death.)

Martha was born in 1706, three years after "Jacky" and one year before Charles. "Patty" was taught to write by her brother John and their handwritings were almost identical! She became a governess in London where she matched wits with some of England's greatest minds. Martha's long friendship with Samuel Johnson is well documented. They "disputed theology and moral philosophy" and he invited her to live under his roof. She then fell for the charms of and married the Rev. Westley Hall, a former member of John's "Holy Club" who was first engaged to Kezzy Wesley! The Halls were happy for a few years, but his charms were not limited to the two Wesley sisters. Philandering was but one of his perennial failings. A spiritual vagabond (Anglican, Moravian, Independent), he took his parish in Salisbury out of the Anglican Church. Then he left Martha and went to the West Indies where he lived with a concubine and returned in disgrace. Martha was an active Methodist, died at age eighty-four, the oldest of the sisters. She is buried in the tomb with her brother, John, behind Wesley's Chapel on City Road, London.

Kezziah ("Kezzy"), the nineteenth child, was born in 1709 or 1710, when her mother was forty. Kezzy had a physically handicapping condition. Jilted by Rev. Westley Hall when he married Martha, Kezzy never married and died at thirty-two years of age. She was as close to Charles as Martha was to John. Kezzy, who had been quiet in her desperation, also died a Methodist.

*Much of the material about Wesley's sisters is drawn from an excellent volume, *Seven Sisters in Search of Love*, by Frederick Maser.[84]

---

[84] Maser, Frederick, *Seven Sisters In Search of Love*, Academy Books, 1988

CHAPTER FOUR

Oxford: The First Rise
of Methodism

In 1714, Samuel Wesley took diminutive eleven-year old Jacky to London to Charterhouse, a boarding school near where his older brother Samuel was an upperclassman at the more prestigious Westminster School. His £40 per annum allowance was provided by a nobleman who was a friend of Samuel Wesley's. Little Jacky certainly "saw sin" at Charterhouse! It was a "survival of the fittest" social environment, and he often got little to eat as larger boys emptied the serving trays.

Perhaps necessity introduced him to the vegetarianism that he practiced all his life! He was bullied and probably abused by larger boys, but the ruffian crowd also probably gave him an understanding of the more uncouth people in his ministry. He remained there until he was seventeen when he was accepted at Christ Church College in July, 1720. Christ Church was the largest in enrollment and campus acreage, and one of the most prestigious colleges of Oxford. As a graduate of Charterhouse, he had a scholarship of £40 per year for three years and £100 for his fourth year. However, he was chronically in debt. His mother wrote a note of sympathy, adding, "notwithstanding all, we shall pick up a few crumbs for you before the end of the year."[85]

Wesley – an undergraduate at Christ Church College, Oxford

John Wesley did not go to Oxford with the intention of being ordained. He studied the classics: Plato, Aristotle, Homer, Virgil, the Stoics, Chaucer, Spenser, Shakespeare, and Milton. Promiscuity was much a part of Oxford culture between college men

---

[85] Baker, Frank, *JWW, J & L,* Vol. 25, 148 (letter from Susanna Wesley, August 19, 1724)

74

and town girls, but considering his later tendency to exaggerate his sins, the only logical assumption is that John Wesley practiced "celibacy in singleness." However, he was not a prude. He occasionally attended theatre. He was invited to lots of parties on campus and in the homes of colleagues on weekends. At these, his wit, charm, and shoulder length auburn hair parted in the middle, made him rather popular.

His acumen in card games, backgammon, billiards, chess, tennis, rowing on the river, and love for dancing quadrilles made him "in" with a wide range of personality types, and girls. Indeed, the girls loved their brothers bringing him home for the holidays.

In spite of his "enjoying life as a typical collegiate," elements of seriousness in the area of religion were present even in those early college days. "The influence of Epworth - Puritan life style, self-discipline, principle of character - all evoked in Wesley an ardent desire for exacting moral rectitude in his personal life."[86] Indeed, his older brother, Samuel, Jr., admonished him in a letter about his intensity of discipline and religion, "Your soul is too great for your body."[87]

During Lent of 1725, his fourth year as an undergraduate student, Wesley began to struggle with the decision of ordination. During this struggle, he wrote both his father and his mother and both encouraged him to "take holy orders." By this point in Wesley's life, Dr. Richard Heitzenrater identifies three stages of spiritual development:

- First of all, Wesley's childhood with Samuel and Susanna Annesley Wesley as precocious parents was intellectually challenging. He was also taught to be rigidly self-disciplined. His father was one of the earliest parish priests to organize a chapter of the recently founded SPCK (Society for Promoting of Christian Knowledge). In that society, Jacky recorded that he learned two things about theology:

    a. to avoid too much stress on outward works as the "Papists" did; and

---

[86] Collins, Kenneth, *John Wesley: A Theological Journey,* Abingdon, 2003, 27-28

[87] Ibid., 28

b. to avoid too much emphasis on a faith without works as the radical Protestants did.

This provided an affinity for "inward religion." The latter led him to deeds of mercy, acts of kindness, and other works of charity. Thus, even in childhood, the rudiments were embedded for Wesley's famous *via media* or "middle way" between high-Anglican holy living and Lutheran/Moravian *sola fide* (only faith).

• Secondly, at Oxford, even as a college student, he was reading and conversing about theology. "I fell among some Lutherans and Calvinists authors, whose confused and undigested accounts magnified <u>faith</u> to such an amazing degree that it quite hid all the rest of the commandments."[88] He described the consequences of this for his developing theology. "In this labyrinth I was utterly lost ... not being able to reconcile this uncouth hypothesis either with Scripture or common sense."[89]

• Thirdly, by his senior year in undergraduate school, he had devoured books by the pietists of the "holy living tradition." He first read Thomas á Kempis' *Imitation of Christ*, and wrote, "I was angry at Kempis for being too strict ... but I began to alter the whole form of my conversation, and to set in earnest upon a new life. I set apart an hour or two a day for religious retirement."[90] Years later, when he was fifty-eight years old, he considered à Kempis' book second only to the Holy Bible!

• On his mother's recommendation, he read Bishop Jeremy Taylor's *Rules of Holy Living and Holy Dying*. Wesley wrote, "In reading this book, I was exceedingly affected; the part in particular which relates to the purity of intention. Instantly I resolved to dedicate all my life to God – my thoughts,

---

[88] Heitzenrater, Op. cit., 35

[89] Ward, Reginald; Heitzenrater, Richard, *JWW*, J & D, Vol. 18, 212

[90] Ibid. p. 50

words, and actions."[91] But he disagreed with the Bishop
in a way that would profoundly affect Methodist theology.
Taylor, in common with most theologians of his day, denied
that Christians can "know" God's acceptance of us. Wesley
commented, "If we can never have any certainty of our
being in a state of salvation ...; then, undoubtedly, in this
life we are of all men most miserable."[92] He is "feeling after"
the doctrine of assurance which would be the cardinal influence of Methodism on Christian thought.

What did Taylor mean? John wrote Mom! Susanna answered,
"If Taylor means such a certainty of pardon as cannot possibly
admit of the least doubt or scruple, he is infallibly in the right;
for such an absolute certainty we can never have till we come to
heaven. But if he forbids a reasonable persuasion of the forgiveness of sin which a true penitent feels when he reflects on the
evidence of his sincerity, he (Taylor) is certainly in the wrong, for
such a persuasion is actually enjoyed in this life."[93] Aha! Mother
and son are struggling already with that which would haunt him
for more than a decade.

Halford Luccock in *The Story of Methodism*, describes quite
well Wesley's remaining college years once he decided on holy
orders. "He was going to be a minister. He was still at Oxford.
What would he therefore do? He would read every book, hunt out
every mind ... do whatever it was humanly possible to do to make
himself in every respect a first-class member of his profession."[94]
British-American scholar David Hempton, provides an important
insight into Wesley's breadth and depth of academic mastery:

"In coming to terms with the Methodist message, it is obviously important to have a grasp of Wesley's own biography,
his patterns of thought, and the breadth of his theological
influences. He read and was influenced by a bewildering
array of Christian traditions: the church fathers, monastic
pietists, continental mystics, Byzantine theologians like
Gregory of Nyssa, English and Scottish divines, his mother

---

[91] Ibid. p. 51

[92] Ibid. p. 51

[93] Ibid. p. 51

[94] Op. Citl, Luccock, Hutchinson, & Goodloe,. 54

and through her to Pascal, classics of devotional literature, and Anglican canon writers especially from the days of the Edwardian Homilies. Any attempt to boil Wesley's theology down to a simple formula like the much-peddled quadrilateral of Scripture, reason, tradition, and experience spectacularly misses the point. Any precise, geometric approach to Wesley's theology is the one least likely to capture its essence. For instance, any model that lacks his dynamic movement toward holiness and its growth within individuals ... is clearly inadequate."[95]

In his journey toward "holy living" per se, it is noteworthy that by the time he finished Oxford and stood for ordination as a Deacon, he had read à Kempis, a Catholic, and Anglican Bishop Taylor. Not surprisingly, with those readings, Wesley wrote later, "I began to alter the whole form of my conversation and to set in earnest upon *a new life.*"[96] Those who insist that Wesley was not converted until 1738 at Aldersgate would have to ignore Wesley's later recollection of his spiritual life in 1725: "I doubted not but that I was a good Christian."[97]

Following the position of Anglican Bishop Jeremy Taylor, neither John Wesley nor his mother were assured of their salvation through what John later called "witness of the Spirit." The only dimension of assurance that he could claim was his sincerity. Witness of the Spirit will have to come later, through the Moravian influence in the mid-1730's.

Ordination and Arminianism

Wesley knew that at the time of his ordination, he would be questioned on every facet of his and the Church's theological positions. This would include predestination, a prevailing theological position in that era of Anglicanism. Even as a widely read academician, he turned to his mother for guidance:

---

[95] Op. cit., Hempton, 57

[96] Op. cit., Davies, 44

[97] Ibid., 44

"I do not think it possible, without perjury, to swear I believe anything unless I have reasonable grounds for my persuasion. What then shall I say to predestination? How is this consistent with either divine justice or mercy? Is it merciful to ordain a creature to everlasting misery? That God should be the author of sin and injustice, which must, I think, be the consequence of maintaining this opinion, is a contradiction to the clearest ideas we have of the divine nature and perfection."

Susanna answered, "The doctrine of predestination, as maintained by the rigid Calvinists, is very shocking, and ought to be abhorred, because it directly charges the Most High with being the author of sin. I think you reason well and justly against it." In a later paragraph, she concludes, "God's foreknowledge does not enforce predestination. Our knowledge that the sun will rise in the morning does not constitute the cause of the sun's rising." [98]

Wesley Commits to Arminianism

So, one theological die is cast. Not only would John Wesley eventually find his spiritual mentor in Jacob Arminius of Holland, Wesley would be the person through whom Arminius' teachings would be adopted by Methodism in England and America. This position of Arminianism underlines that God's grace is sufficient and equally applied to everyone. God wills that all be saved. Human response, not divine initiative, is the determining factor in who embraces God's love and who rejects it.

We are saved by grace by accepting that grace as each person makes free will decisions, not the foreordained providence of God. We individually choose to respond negatively or positively to God's grace. Therefore, we owe to Susanna Wesley a lot of credit for our doctrinal emphasis.

At that time, the Church of England did not require a Bachelor of Divinity degree for ordination. The Church required only an undergraduate degree and examination by a bishop for both the order of Deacon and the order of Presbyter (or priest). John Wesley was ordained Deacon, September 19, 1725. He began preaching in surrounding parish churches.

---

[98] Op. cit., McTyeire, 51. McTyeire credits older authors without specificity.

Fellow at Lincoln College

John's literary excellence was now known at Oxford University beyond the campus of Christ Church College. In 1726, he applied for, and was granted a fellowship at Lincoln College where, at age twenty-three, he became an instructor in Greek. His parents were ecstatic. His father wrote, "His income is ready for him on stated days, and all he has to do is to count it and carry it home." Then he wrote to his son a letter saying he would not and could not send him any more money, and probably could not afford to send Charles to the university, but closed with the sentence, "What will be my own fate, God only knows, but whatever I am, my Jack is a fellow of Lincoln."[99] The founding sponsors of Lincoln College were from Lincolnshire, the shire in which Epworth was located. "The atmosphere of the college was more congenial to Wesley's intentions than Christ Church had been. The men of Lincoln College were well-natured."[100]

His father was correct. The fellowship enabled him to teach and to complete his Master of Arts degree on February 14, 1727. (*In eighteenth century England, a university fellowship included a stipend, free rooms, and free meals while the fellow was in residence. Faculty dinners were settings for the matching of wits. Unless asked by the Dean to tutor or teach, the Fellow was free solely to study. He was never again invited to return to campus to teach, but one continued to receive the dividend from the patronage of the fellowship even if he left Oxford, unless he married. Therefore, John Wesley drew his annual stipend from Oxford while in Georgia and during his itinerancy as an ordained Anglican priest and traveling evangelist without a parish until 1751 when he married.*)

Being ordained a priest at Oxford, he was not accountable to any geographic diocese of the Church of England. Therefore, no bishop had specific control over him. This freedom from episcopal authority was later to prove infinitely beneficial when the Bishop of Bristol ordered Wesley to cease from preaching in that diocese. Wesley responded, "The world is my parish." Most scholars conclude that the bishop immediately knew the technicality to which Wesley referred. In other words, his having been ordained at Oxford enabled him to use his credentials anywhere

---

[99] Ibid., 54

[100] Op. cit., Telford, 43-44

the Anglican Church had ministries, which to Wesley was "anywhere in the world." John Wesley always had printed on the title page of his writings the words, "Fellow of Lincoln College." That was a quiet reminder to the Anglican episcopacy of his having been ordained at Oxford, not in a geographic diocese.

Unhappy Years as a Parish Minister

In the summer of 1727, his father, now age sixty-five, decided that he did not want his son to remain permanently in academia, but to be the curate of a congregation. He had a plan that might entice John away from Oxford and prepare him to be his father's successor. Samuel wrote that the swampy Lincolnshire village of Wroote had been added to his parish and he now had a "two-point circuit" which increased his "living" by several pounds – money he direly needed for his perennial debt. But his health was poor, the roads were little more than swamp trails, and Samuel implored his son to come home and help out.

John obediently complied. He assumed primary pastoral responsibilities at the little church in Wroote, and lived once again in the Epworth rectory with his parents for two years that are often overlooked in Wesley biographies. Initially he wrote to Charles that he was "settled for life – at least for years."[101] He returned to Oxford only once during those two years, to be ordained as Presbyter (priest) on September 22, 1728.

It was in the summer of 1727 that he preached a sermon at Wroote that created a breach between him and his father, and to some extent with his mother. The sermon title was *Universal Charity: or the charity due to wicked persons*. In the last paragraph of his sermon, he added that the way his father treated his daughter, Hetty, was not the way a Christian should "have charity toward a person who had done wickedly." Susanna wrote him, "You writ this sermon for Hetty; the rest was ... for the sake of the last paragraph."[102]

Also, the Wroote congregation was non-responsive to his entire ministry. Wesley wrote of his one parish experience, "I preached much but saw no fruits from my labour. Indeed, it could not be that I should; for I neither laid the foundation of repentance, nor of believing the Gospel; taking it for granted that all to

---

[101] Op. cit., Heitzenrater, *People Called Methodists*, 38

[102] Op. cit., 29

whom I preached were believers and that many of them needed no repentance."[103]

Samuel gave the Wroote parish to John Whitelamb, whom John befriended at Oxford. He also gave to Whitelamb the hand of his daughter Mary ("Molly") in marriage. She died in childbirth soon thereafter.[104] Johnny Whitelamb served on for years and never remarried.

Rise of Oxford Methodism

Upon receiving a letter from Charles who was a student at Oxford, John went to visit his brother, on Charles' birthday, June 17, 1729. Upon arriving, John discovered that Charles, William Morgan, and Bob Kirkman were meeting as a "band of brothers" living a basically monastic life style. On weekday evenings, they studied the classics. On Sunday mornings the foursome attended university worship or preached in rural parishes. On Sunday evenings they studied the contemporary "divines." When John, a faculty member, arrived he soon thereafter became the leader. It was the beginning of what Heitzenrater calls "Oxford Methodism" and less careful writers call the "Holy Club."

At the end of the summer, the two Wesley brothers headed home for Epworth and Wroote. In October, 1729, a letter came from "the head of college" at Lincoln. He wrote Wesley that his tutoring duties were needed. So it was that John Wesley's parish ministry in England ended forever. "Within days, owning no horses, he and Charles began the walk south, detouring by London in order to visit their brother Samuel, Jr. From there they walked the forty-three miles to Oxford, arriving on November 22, 1729.[105] Charles resumed his role as a student at Christ Church College.

"Their arrival back to Oxford incurred no visible alteration in the schedule"[106] of the Oxford Methodists than it had been before John's and Charles' absence. This we know; John resumed his role as leader. The "curriculum" was broadened to include religious conversation, frequent communion, and the discipline

---

[103] Op. cit., Telford, 53

[104] Op Cit., Best, 51

[105] Op. cit., Heitzenrater, People Called Methodists, 39

[106] Op. cit., Heitzenrater, 39

of writing daily diaries. The four friends met to study together the classics and works of divinity by writers like John Milton, Marquis de Renty, and others. John, now a Lincoln Fellow as well as an ordained Anglican priest, was invited to preach in country parish churches in Oxfordshire. That pattern, not noticed on campus, continued until the summer of 1730.

John Wesley was twenty-six years old. He again wore the academic robe and settled into the professor's lifestyle for six years. He taught both Greek and New Testament and loved both academia and the personal lifestyle with which he felt so comfortable. Known only to God, these years were the seedbed in which the future of Methodism germinated. One is reminded of I Corinthians 2:9, "Eye hath not seen, nor ear heard, neither have entered into the heart of man, the things which God hath prepared for them that love him!"

Wesley despised the term "Holy Club" which other students began mockingly calling his small band. Other derisive terms were used, among them, "Bible Moths," and "Enthusiasts." The eternally jousting mentality of collegiates produced this doggerel:

> "By rule they eat, by rule they drink,
>   do all things else by rule, but think–
> Accuse their priests of loose behavior,
>   to get more in the laymen's favor.
> Method alone must guide 'em all, whence
>   'Methodists' themselves they call."

This "appellation" was not a new name in Anglican history. It had been used "for those who stood up for God," but the campus hecklers did not use the term as a compliment. Wesley cited a group of Greek doctors who called patients "Methodist" if they followed a regimen of good diet and regular exercise. Dr. Richard Heitzenrater is a stickler for historical accuracy and notes it would be two years before the term "Methodist" would be applied to them.[107] "The first published attack on the Wesleyans at Oxford came in the fall of 1732 at a time when the term "Methodists" was especially associated with the group. The letter to the editor printed in *Fog's Weekly Journal* had been written on November 6 and included a reference to 'this sect call'd Methodists.' Wesley's

---

[107] Ibid., 42

diary notes that upon the appearance in Oxford of that edition of *Fog's* on 11 December, the talk in the Lincoln common room turned to the subject of 'the Methodists'—the first use of that term in Wesley's diary."[108] After that time, the word was never questioned.

Many years later, upon the laying of the cornerstone of Wesley's Chapel in London, he said of just four collegiates in 1729, "The name was new and quaint; it clave to them immediately and from that time all that had any connection with them were thus distinguished."

Upon advice from his mother, John read William Law's *Serious Call to Devout and Holy Life* in 1730, a book that had been published just a year or so earlier. Every serious biographer of Wesley notes the influence of William Law that "convinced him further of the 'exceeding height and breadth and depth of the law of God, inward and outward.'"[109] Indeed, upon reading William Law, Wesley wrote in 1730, "The light flowed in so mightily upon my soul, that everything appeared in a new view. I cried to God for help, and resolved not to prolong the time of obeying him as I had never done before. ...I was persuaded that I was even then in a state of salvation."[110]

From 1725-1730, Thomas à Kempis, Jeremy Taylor, and William Law convinced him that holiness was an inner reality, or in his words, "that true religion was seated in the heart and that God's law extends to all our thoughts and actions."[111] Typically, Wesley "took his spiritual temperature" at this time and concluded, "I doubted not but I was a good Christian."[112] Thereafter he epitomized the lifestyle called for in Law's spiritual regimen. British historian, Rupert Davies, put it this way, "Though the term "conversion" does not meet this time in Wesley's life, the period gave him a new aim in life. He became aware of the necessity for 'holiness' if a man is to be in the favour of God. It gave

---

[108] Op. cit., Heitzenrater, *Mirror and Memory,* 31

[109] Op. cit., Ward & Heitzerater, *JWW,* J & D, Vol. 18, 245

[110] Ibid. 244

[111] Op. cit., Heitzenrater, 36

[112] Op. cit., Ward and Heitzenrater, eds. *JWW, J & D,* Abingdon, Vol. 18:244

him a 'fixed intention' to give himself up to God."[113]

John Gambold, who later became a bishop in the Moravian Church, began meeting with the group. He wrote of being most impressed by both Wesley brothers, and then said of the group:

> It was their custom to meet most evenings either at his (John's) chamber or one of the other['s], where after some prayer (the chief object of which was charity), they ate their supper together and John read from some book. But the chief business was to review what each had done that day in pursuance of their common design, and to consult what steps were to be taken on the next day. Their under-takings were to converse with young students, to visit the prisons, to instruct some poor families, and to take care of a school and a parish work-house. They took great pains to protect younger students from bad company and to encourage in them a sober, studious life. He also read from the New Testament, and after each passage, having heard the conjectures of others, he made his observations on the phrase, design, and difficult places. He laid much stress on self-examination. He persisted against all discouragements, urging each to overlook his own disagreeable qualities, spiritual delusions, and to resist all temptations. He encour-aged all to lead in extemporaneous prayers. The last portion of time he devoted to silent meditation. His knowledge of the world and his insight into physic ("illnesses") were often of use to us.[114]

John imposed on himself the daily regimen of rising early to pray and to read the daily office and the Bible. He became convinced that "holiness of heart" meant that God would have him reject "all harmless conversations, so called, because they dampen all my good resolutions." One of these resolutions was not to attend any more parties, not to dance, and not to enjoy "the company of women more than the company of God." He did not keep that vow. Actually, John Wesley enjoyed the company of women all his life, and always struggled with the boundaries between spiritual counsel and romantic feelings.

---

[113] Davies, Rupert, *Methodism,* Epworth:1963, p. 42

[114] Op. cit., McTyeire, 57-58

William Morgan, an Irishman, made a rather happenstance visit to the "Castle Prison" (so named because it was surrounded by a moat). He persuaded them to add to their "acts of kindness and deeds of mercy," a daily visit to Castle Prison and the North Gate Prison to deliver warm bread to the debtors and felons incarcerated there. They were granted permission to talk with the prisoners. Upon their first visit to a man's cell, they would "after professions of good will, inquire of his circumstances back home. This questioning often led the young men to open up their heart." On the second visit, they moved to inquire if he regretted his actions and would repent. They also purchased and delivered books on physick (*sic)* and other necessaries.

On campus, they often took young students to breakfast "in an effort to rescue them from bad company." By mid-morning, they were engaged in their professional duties. Later, Wesley wrote the words he first embraced and began to live during the Lincoln College years, "There is no holiness without social holiness." In the town, they "took upon themselves poor families" whom they engaged by reading, asking them to desist from their vices, and taught their children to read - an unusual step for Oxford dons! [115]

Then, at the urging of Morgan, they expanded this ministry to the "work-house" and the "poor house for the aged" and read to them! John Gambold wrote that John would pay the schoolmistress from his own earnings and "clothed some, if not all, of the children.

In June, 1733, John Wesley turned thirty years of age. His ministry was not going well. William Morgan, who had been virtually a co-leader, first became emotionally ill and then died. The rumor spread like wildfire that the austerity Wesley imposed on the group was responsible for young Morgan's death. Wesley's letter to Morgan's father was a splendid defense that might have saved the movement. "The Morgan letter, used by Wesley as the standard defense of Oxford Methodism in 1732, has also become the standard account of its rise and design. ...The letter's wide circulation, as well as the popularization of the term 'Methodist' was due in part to an anonymous author ... describing Wesley and his group, *The Oxford Methodists (1733)."*[116]

---

[115] Ibid., 40

[116] Op. Cit., Heitzenrater, 64

In 1733, they were joined also by George Whitefield, who waited tables at Pembroke College to work for his tuition. Importantly, a very different personality type, young Whitefield had come to Oxford as a servitor who admired the Methodists but felt inferior to the likes of John Wesley, a faculty member! But as Whitefield began referring prisoners to the Methodists, Charles identified him and he was invited to join.

Let us not underestimate the importance of George Whitefield to Methodism. William Cowper was right, "God moves in a mysterious way, His wonders to perform ... behind a frowning providence, He hides a smiling face."[117] We must ask, "Had it not been for his friendship with Whitefield, would John Wesley, in 1739, ever have resorted to preaching in the open air? Had Wesley not preached in open air in and around Bristol, would there ever have been a Methodism?" Later, Benjamin Franklin would name George Whitefield as the most powerful orator in all the colonies, in the pulpit or the public square.

Wesley remained in this "Oxford" mode until 1735. The personal and social dimensions of holiness that Wesley attained were just that – attained. He was driven to a model of holy living which to John Wesley was a mighty effort to fill a vacuum. He was not a man at peace with himself.

Wesley's Oxford years were rich in spiritual formation. With each devotional classic from the Anglo/Catholic divines, he added to his life style of holy living. Already living a life of *outward* goodness, he began to strive for *inward* holiness:

- Rules and regulations prohibited much of the fun and frivolity he had enjoyed

- Means of grace helped him to keep his intended rules; meditation "implanted" virtue

- His self-examination was almost masochistic as he chastised himself for the slightest breach of discipline in thought, word, or deed

- A daily diary recorded hourly dispositions of mind and soul

---

[117] Cowper, William, "Table Talk," John Sharpe, Picadilly, 1782, lines 16,17

• Sincerity became the confirmation of his commitment to holiness of heart.[118]

Interpreting the Oxford Methodist chapter of Wesley's life, Heitzenrater notes that "some twentieth-century authors have seen this as a real conversion, by most definitions of the term."[119] Another evaluation comes from British Methodist author, Rupert Davies. Davies' assessment of this period in Wesley's spirituality development is, "He was a Christian all his life, and from 1725 he was a zealous and earnest Christian, but he was not a Christian at peace with God and with himself"[120] *(until Aldersgate).* His chief concern was to live a devout and holy life, but he did not find any particular joy or freedom in doing so. He was a good man, but not a happy man.

Unquestionably, John Wesley was the leader of Oxford Methodism and his life epitomized the word "Methodist." His life style was literally monastic. He lived frugally, dressed neatly but plainly, led the group, intervened with the justice system on behalf of prisoners, received the sacraments, was loyal to the Church of England, and tried in every way to attain peace within himself and with God.

However, like Luther in the Augustinian monastery and University of Wittenberg at the turn of the 16th century, Wesley could not find what he sought from so many sources. "It was an Arminian theology spelled out in a complex pattern of rules and expectations."[121]

It was three years later before John wrote to the Bishop, "I cannot therefore doubt that the Spirit of God bore an inward witness with his (my father's) spirit that he was a child of God." Another "prologue" factor in 1735 was a letter on May 5 from George Whitefield that he had experienced saving grace with its accompanying assurance of salvation. [122] Hence, for young Whitefield, before Wesley, holy living was being seen as lacking the assurance of amazing grace. As we bring our reflection of

---

[118] Op. Ct. Heitzenrater, *Mirror and Memory,* 1989 (format changed)

[119] Ibid., 43

[120] Op. cit., Davies, 43

[121] Op. cit., Heitzenrater, *People Called Methodists,* 45

[122] Pollock, John, *John Wesley, the Preacher,* Kingsway, 1989, p. 64

the "Holy Club" to a close, we cannot avoid noting the wisdom provided by Halford Luccock in the 1926 *The Story of Methodism:*

> "Colleges tend to turn out machine-made goods—folks who dress alike, think alike, talk alike, act alike, and all on a dead level of mediocrity. But, every so often there come men and women who refuse to 'wear the clothes,' either physical or mental, that are the mode of the moment."[123]

The paradigm of discipleship during the Oxford years did not survive into nineteenth century Methodism! Dr. Davies demonstrates that with this critique of Oxford Methodism:

> "It cannot be too strongly stressed that this was not Methodism as it later emerged in England. The name is the same and it is the ground out of which Methodism grew. Methodism took over some of the habits and customs and much of the idiom of the group. However, for instance, the doctrine of holiness suffered a sea-change. For the men of Oxford, the desire for personal holiness occupied the centre of the picture."[124]

Wesley's Struggles between Parish and Oxford

December 1734 brought a "very pressing letter" from his father, asking him to come home. The venerable old rector of Epworth was dying when he wrote John, asking him to become his successor at St. Andrew's Church in Epworth. Samuel, Jr. joined their father in trying to persuade John to take over the family living at Epworth and return to the parish. His brother raised an issue not strange to Methodist clergy to this very day, "is not the parish the front line of work for which one is ordained?"

John, though, went to his bishop! The bishop's reply was remarkable, "It doth not seem to me that at your ordination you engaged yourself to undertake the cure of any parish, provided you can as a clergyman better serve God and his Church in your present or some other station."[125]

---

[123] Op. cit., Luccock, 58

[124] Op. cit., Davies, 1985, 44

[125] Urlin, R. Denny, *The Churchman's Life of John Wesley,* London: SPCK, 20

To Samuel's chagrin, his son Jack followed the bishop's counsel and chose to remain at Lincoln College. His answer was a letter twenty-six paragraphs long, in which he said that he valued time for study, and those very frequent opportunities for worship which Oxford ever afforded. "At Oxford I am screened from all the frivolous importunities of the world, and here I have a better chance of becoming holy. I could not do any good to those boorish people, and I should probably fall back into habits of irregularity and indulgence."[126] He goes on to explain that within the "shadow of these walls, the fields are white unto harvest" and he thought that he might be a "fertilizing river in the schools of the prophets."[127] Clearly, John Wesley's paramount concern was not about task, but spiritual formation. Oxford was the best place "to promote his own, and therefore others' holiness."[128]

When his son declined, Samuel feared it was because of John's yen for the solitary life and the security of the university campus. So, he wrote, "I cannot allow austerity, or fasting, considered by themselves, to be proper acts of holiness, nor am I for the solitary life. God made us for a social life; we are not to bury our talent; we are to let our light shine before men, and that not merely through the chinks of a bushel for fear the wind will blow it out."[129]

Richard Heitzenrater quotes John's brother, Samuel, Jr., as writing, "It is not a college, not a university, it is the order of the Church according to which you were called."[130] John still pondered, prayed, studied, and reconsidered his decision. By February he was "almost convinced of duty to go to Epworth."[131]

Samuel's Death

By April, 1735, John was in Epworth and his father was dying. Years later, in controversial correspondence with Bishop Secker (1748), John resorts to telling of his father's last words. The dying

---

[126] Opt. cit., Davies, . 45

[127] Ibid. 20

[128] Op. cit., Heitzenrater, *People Called Methodists*, 55

[129] Winchester, C. T, *Life of Wesley,* McMillan, 1906. 39

[130] Op. cit., Heitzenrater p, *People*....54

[131] Ibid. p. 55

father, rigid Anglican that he was, laid his hands on Charles and said, "Be steady. The Christian faith shall surely revive in this kingdom; you shall see it, though I shall not."[132] To his son John the old man said, "The inward witness, son, the inward witness— this is the proof, the strongest proof of Christianity."[133] Samuel's dying words, in concert with Susanna's growing return to her father's evangelical mode, constituted an important prologue to Aldersgate. With John back in the Epworth parish, the "Holy Club" members left Oxford one by one, each going his own way.

Samuel Wesley died April 25, 1735. According to Richard Heitzenrater's research, John remained in Epworth for two months, preaching at St. Andrew Parish Church. According to a somewhat less careful biographer, Stephen Tomkins, "John finally agreed to apply for the post as rector, but it was too late."[134] Tomkins also writes that "Wesley spent the summer putting the finishing touches to the vast, learned commentary on Job to which his father had devoted the last ten years of his life."[135] In his last sermon he spoke of "pursuing one end in our life, in all our words and actions, that is the renewal of the *image of God* in our fallen state."

The culture and collegiality of Oxford had been the primary locus and focus of John Wesley's life from 1720 until 1735. The personal and social dimensions of holiness that Wesley attained were a combination of his devout obedience to God and his indefatigable work ethic. He was driven to a model of holy living trying to fill an inner vacuum. He still lacked the inner peace of God. However, Heitzenrater has documented that by 1735, perhaps pondering his father's dying words, Wesley began to see salvation not only as *outward goodness*, but also as *inward holiness*. He began to view true religion as seated in the heart. "God's law extends to all thoughts as well as words and actions."[136] Kenneth Collins is "spot on" when he quotes from Wesley's letter to his

---

132 Op. cit., Tomkins, Stephen, 41

133 Op. cit., Luccock, Halford; Hutchinson, Paul; Goodloe, Robert, , 43

134 Op. cit., Tomkins, 41

135 Ibid., 41-42

136 Heitzenrater, Op. cit., "Great Expectations," *Aldersgate Reconsidered,* Kingswood, 1990, 91

father just four months before the old vicar's death, "God deliver me from {being} a half Christian."[137] Wesley also used the term "almost Christian," which in Sermon #2, "The Almost Christian," he associated with the adage, "The road to hell is paved with good intentions."[138]

Bishop Holland McTyeire, writing in 1886, borrowed one of Wesley's own terms, calling these Oxford years, "the first rise of student Methodism."[139] (He points to an early historian, George Smith.) Richard Heitzenrater also used the term, "rise" in his book, *Wesley and the People Called Methodists,* written in 1995.[140]

In 1735, three chapters of John Wesley's life closed:

- his longstanding relationship with his father

- his English parish ministry

- his intensive leadership of the "Holy Club."

On October 12, 1735, John Wesley brought final closure to his father's business. He went to London, and, in the company of General Oglethorpe, he presented to Queen Caroline, a bound copy of his father's tome on Job. He reported later that she received it, commented on its pretty binding and laid it, unopened on a window ledge.[141] "After many good words and smiles," she dismissed him from his only audience with a reigning monarch of his beloved Britannia.

John's intention was to finish his father's business affairs, go back to Oxford, and remain there. In fact, he would never make his beloved Oxford his domicile again. He was about to enter a radically new chapter of life, vocationally and spiritually.

---

[137] Op. cit., Collins, 53

[138] Op. cit., Outler, ed., *JWW, Sermons,* Abingdon, Vol. 1, 140

[139] Op. cit., McTyeire, 177

[140] Op. cit., Heitzenrater, *People Called Methodists,* 33

[141] Ibid. p. 66

CHAPTER FIVE

Georgia: The Second Rise of Methodism

Providentially or coincidentally, while in London en route to Oxford in 1735, the Wesley brothers were consulted by a Dr. John Burton of Oxford's Corpus Christi College who worked with S.P.C.K (Society for Promoting Christian Knowledge). Burton had been asked by General Oglethorpe to secure a pastor for the Anglican Church in Savannah, Georgia, who would also serve as missionary to the Indians. Either he inquired also about Charles, or John suggested that they also consider his younger brother. Charles was recruited as Oglethorpe's personal secretary.

Missionary work was in the Wesley's veins. The John Westley of 1662 longed to go to Maryland! Samuel, Sr., languishing in the fenland of Lincolnshire, had wanted to go to the East, and even with nine living children, considered joining the Navy as a chaplain! If John could not fulfill his father's dream of having his son succeed him at Epworth, going to Georgia would enable him to live out his father's unfulfilled dream of being a missionary. Nothing in the service of God exceeded the sacrifice and heroism of a missionary. Just before his death, he had admonished John to "let his light shine" and not remain cloistered in Lincoln College, Oxford for life. He did not live to see it, but would have been delighted that his sons, John and Charles, were invited to go to Georgia, and that they accepted.

But how could two sons leave their mother so soon after her husband's death, particularly since Samuel Wesley died without estate? That was the question that Charles and John posed to their mother. Her response was that of a devout Christian mother, "Had I twenty sons, I should rejoice that they were all so employed, though I should never see them more."[142] And so it was that both Charles and John Wesley accepted.

Georgia. Their minds raced at what it would be to bring, in their idiom, "the heathen Indians to Christ." Furthermore, in that faraway land, surely the Anglicans would be more God fearing than in merry ole England. Georgia was so new, so virgin, so unravished by the sins of Europe. In 1732, King George II had grabbed up the only sliver of Atlantic shoreline still unclaimed. General James Oglethorpe, a member of Parliament, asked the King for a charter which would live out Oglethorpe's social justice conscience regarding the plight of the men placed in prison for being poor. He was also deeply opposed to slavery, and during his lifetime, slavery was not allowed in Georgia. King George appointed Oglethorpe and "21 trustees" to establish his namesake colony for the crown as a "trust for the poor." "The poor" were often prisoners whose only crime was being in debt because they were poor. Over four thousand citizens were imprisoned each year in England alone because they could not pay their debts, creating a "Catch 22" situation since imprisonment prohibited their making the money to pay their debts. Hundreds were sent to the gallows for petty theft when they were hungry. Their families wallowed in destitution. In going to Georgia, they would have the opportunity for a new lease on life.

Parliament released thousands through the Georgia Trustees into Oglethorpe's care, allowing them to be reunited with their families for the voyage. These were the same lot, mostly from London environs as the prisoners whom the "Methodists" of Oxford had visited, counseled, and fed. Therefore, John and Charles knew their prison circumstances. Protestant England also sympathized with persecuted Protestants in Catholic countries on the continent. Any refugees such as the Moravian and Bavarian Protestants, French Huguenots and Palatinates, Italian Protestants, and Portuguese Jews were offered asylum in Great Britain. In Georgia, only the Anglicans, French Huguenots, and Moravians had their own clergy. The rest were served by John.

The first settlers had arrived in Georgia in February, 1733, three years earlier. Since it was a British colony, the language was English, the currency was English, and the civil law was English. For those formerly imprisoned, there was free passage and a new

---

[142] Moore, Henry, *The Life of the Rev. John Wesley,* London: Kershaw, 1824, Vol. 1, p. 234

lease option on fifty acres of land, five in town or forty-five in the country provided you lived on it. Well-to-do men who could pay their own passage were promised 500 acres of free land in Georgia. Thus, began the Commonwealth of Georgia as an experiment in amnesty for prisoners, ethnic and linguistic diversity, religious pluralism, absence of slavery, and British imperialism.

Among the English was Thomas Causton, age 40, with his wife Martha, and her niece Sophia Hopkey, heir to a small fortune. Sophia's late father had a very prosperous business in England that traded in calico, the new "cloth of fashion" in that time. The Caustons were Sophia's legal guardians and therefore had access to her inheritance.

The Voyage to America – Autumn, 1735

It was Wesley's first time ever at sea. One hundred and twenty-four men, women, and children boarded the ship *Simmonds* on October 14, 1735. On board ship, General Oglethorpe was in command, but he had placed John Wesley, Fellow of Lincoln, as the religious head of the passengers and crew. Wesley already spoke French fluently, but he discovered quickly that they had twenty-six Germans on board, and since he was the ship's chaplain, he felt compelled to learn to read the Bible and preach in German. Three days after he boarded ship, John's diary shows that he began "to learn the German tongue." When ten days later, the Moravian Bishop began learning English, Wesley wrote, "O may we be not only of one tongue, but of one mind and of one heart."[143] Even this early we hear overtones of a catholic spirit. Due to nautical complications, they did not clear the English territorial waters until December 10. By that time, the Oxford don could converse in German.

The Moravians were going to Georgia for religious reasons. These were spiritual descendants of John Hus (burned at the stake in 1415 and patron saint of the Czech Republic to this day). From their homeland in Bohemia, they had migrated to Saxony where a Count Zinzendorf of Herrnhut gave them asylum. The Moravians were the first Protestants to "revive the duty of the Church to present the Gospel to all Nations."[144] Parliament's benevolence

---

[143] Op. cit., Ward and Heitzenrater, *JWW*, J & D, Vol 18. 137

[144] Cadman, Op. cit., p. 208

opened the door for the Moravians to go to Georgia.

Wesley dutifully records a spiritually masochistic rationale for going to Georgia. The leader of the "Holy Club" who was living a very disciplined life of spiritual purity wrote upon leaving:

"My chief motive is the hope of saving my own soul. I hope to learn the true sense of the Gospel by preaching it to the heathen. A right faith will, I trust, result in right practice; especially since most of those temptations are removed which so easily beset me. I cannot obtain the same degree of holiness here which I may there."[145]

His image of Georgia as a Utopia could not have been more wrong. The "temptations that so easily beset me" were not removed in the new world.

In addition to the Wesley brothers, Benjamin Ingham from the Oxford "Holy Club" and Charles Delamotte became the third and fourth missionaries. "The four young men adopted a regimented daily routine. They rose early, prayed for an hour, studied the Bible and German, had breakfast and studied the rest of the morning. At noon and mid-afternoon, they led public worship. The rest of the afternoons they mingled with the passengers."[146] Thomas Jackson's early biography of Charles Wesley entitled, *Life of C. Wesley,* is most likely on target as he notes, "According to the brothers, true holiness is attained principally through sufferings— mental and bodily. Holiness of heart and life they sought, not by faith, but by works and personal austerity. Their views, as they were later to learn, were not only defective, but erroneous."

The story of the voyage is oft told and well known in Methodist lore. It was the "beginning of the end" of Wesley's journey to find peace through spiritual disciplines and holiness of heart. The third storm at sea became violent. Wesley had been observing the Moravians daily, noting their "performing servile offices for the other passengers which none of the English would undertake, and for which they would receive no pay, saying that "their loving Saviour had done more for them."

Then, he wrote that during the storm, "I went to the Germans.

---

[145] Op. cit., Baker, Frank, ed., *JWW,* J & D, Vol. 25:439)

[146] Op. cit., Best, 59

In the midst of the psalm ... the sea broke over, split the mainsail in pieces, covered the ship, and poured in between the decks as if the great deep had already swallowed us up. A terrible screaming began among the English. The Germans calmly sang on. I asked one of them afterward, 'Was you not afraid?' He answered, 'I thank God, no.' I persisted, 'But were not your women and children afraid?' He replied mildly, 'No; our women and children are not afraid to die.'"[147] So it was that Wesley caught a glimpse of a religious experience that keeps the mind at peace under all circumstances and "vanquishes that feeling which a formal and defective religion may lull to temporary sleep but cannot eradicate – fear."

Wesley now had seen in the Moravians what his father referred to on his death bed – the inward witness. The "witness of the Spirit" would become the central focus of his spiritual journey, and, subsequently, the major tenet of Methodist doctrine, with an Anglican accent.

John's Georgia Ministry

The demographics of Georgia's early settlement, the setting for Wesley's ill-fated ministry, is often misunderstood. The Wesleys' ship arrived in the New World on February 6, 1736, as the third group to colonize Georgia. Oglethorpe wanted the presence of the Anglican Church and a parish priest. The first one died, and the second had to return to England when he seduced one of his parishioners. John was pastor and principal missionary. Charles, newly ordained, was Oglethorpe's secretary. There were about four hundred "generic" Anglicans in Savannah but, according to Wesley, less than half that number were actual communicants in the parish church.

He was impressed by many Christian attributes of some Scot Highlanders near Savannah, but was appalled at their extemporaneous prayers. Little did he know that the movement he would later "turn loose" in America would have his spiritual progeny like Peter Cartwright speaking critically of liturgical or written prayers.

In Georgia, as at Oxford, Wesley remained a prodigious reader. Indeed, in Georgia he read the biography of Mohammad

---

[147] Op. Cit, Heitzerater, *JWW*, J&D, 18:143)

and Machiavelli's *The Prince*. (His commentary on the latter was, "should a prince form himself by the maxims of this book ... Nero would be an angel of light compared to that man.")[148]

John Wesley's parishioners themselves were hardly the "cream" of English society. Rupert Davies, a careful British Methodist writer, describes them as "the ragtag and bobtail of the London debtor prisons whom the Wesleys treated as if they were pious undergraduates."[149] The "Mrs. Hawkins" and "Mrs. Welch" with whom John spent so much time in spiritual counsel on board ship were what Davies calls *betes noires* who were dubiously moral and undoubtedly scurrilous women ... ."[150] Three of the missionaries had a concern for Wesley's naiveté as these two women flattered John with solicitous attention and would bring him much grief and their names would show up often in Georgia; Beata Hawkins, wife of the ship's surgeon and her pregnant friend, Anne Welch, wife of a carpenter. Gary Best's research shows that the other missionary men thought, "John was blind to the fact that their flirtatious attention had less than honorable motives."[151]

Many of the men who were vestrymen in Savannah would have been marginalized in any English parish church. As we shall see later, this was especially true of Thomas Causton, the uncle of Sophia Hopkey, who, ironically was also chief magistrate.

Little did Oglethorpe know that his new priest would minister not only to the Anglicans, but also to the Portuguese Jews, the Protestant French Huguenots, the Italian Catholics, and the German Palatinates, each in their native tongues and religious liturgies. Primarily though, John's job and his relationships were to serve the Christ Anglican Church in an American colony and to convert the Indians. Wesley wrote, "I entered my ministry in Savannah by preaching on the Epistle for the day, being the thirteenth chapter of First Corinthians." The Gospel Lesson was the words of Jesus in Luke 18 that "when we leave house and friends ... for the Kingdom, we receive manifold more in return."[152] In his

---

148 Ibid., 466

149 Op. cit., Davis, 48

150 Ibid. p. 48

151 Op. cit., Best, 60

152 Ward and Heizenrater, eds., Vol 18, 153

sermon, Wesley told of his own father's death-bed witness that the essence of Christianity is the "inward witness" or the assurance of salvation, something that Wesley himself still lacked. He also told them how strictly he would require the rules of the Church in a most rigorous way. This was from the influence of John Clayton and others in the "Holy Club" back at Oxford and would come home to haunt him. For the time being though, in spite of his being much more puritanical than their custom was, church attendance actually improved and remained strong through the fall of 1737.

Bishop Holland McTyeire wrote in 1886, "The second rise of Methodism was in April 1736 when twenty or thirty persons began to meet in Wesley's house at Savannah."[153] Wesley himself refers to Savannah as the site of the "second rise" of Methodism. His conversations and theological exchanges which began on ship with "the Germans" continued. To the Moravians in Georgia must be given credit for enhancing the continuing work of the Holy Spirit in the life and theology of the frustrated Anglican who had for so long sought God through the discipline of holy living, rather than the grace of divine love. Not only did the Moravian, August Spangenberg, mentor him in things spiritual, he also counseled Wesley in romance. His caution to choose God over women might have been pivotal in Wesley's hesitancy to propose marriage to the young woman with whom he was literally obsessed and whom he thought he loved.

On July 31, 1737, he wrote, "Having long been in doubt concerning the principles of the Moravian Brethren, at Mr. Spangenberg's desire, I proposed to them the following queries ...." Then follows, in typical Wesley "Q & A" format, thirty-one questions, beginning with, "What do you mean by conversion?"[154] He rather desperately sought the Moravian experience of God's grace, replete with their assurance which Wesley later would call "witness of the spirit" and would still later cause him to break fellowship with the Moravians back in London on July 20, 1740.

What was happening in Wesley's heart was not manifest in his ministry. Impressed as he was by the Moravians, he remained a rigid Anglican! The particular "brand" of Anglicanism that he

---

[153] Op. cit., 177

[154] OOp. cit., Ward, Reginald; Heitzenrater, Richard, Vol. 18. 531

imposed on his congregation and attempted with the Indians was more like that of his puritanical father: strict and demanding. He remained a "high Anglican." He was too strict for a parish far from England.

He was following the 1549 Edwardian-era *Book of Common Prayer* which called for the trine immersion of infants even in mid-winter (unless in a weakened condition). The mothers were mortified. He also refused to acknowledge any baptism that was not an episcopal baptism done by a priest in apostolic succession. Therefore, he re-baptized Presbyterians, Huguenots, and Moravians. He also announced his first Sunday that he would "divide the morning prayer service" by reading the lessons and prayers at 5:45 a.m. without a sermon and deliver a sermon at 11:00 without all the liturgy of the *Book of Common Prayer*. (This "division" would be one of the charges against him in August, 1737.) Lastly, and perhaps most consequentially, he read from the Edwardian Homilies that if a communicant wished to receive the Eucharist on Sunday but had been habitually absent from worship, he or she must meet with the priest prior to communing. (It was this that became an inflamed issue when he denied "the Cup" to Sophia Hopkey Williamson in August, 1737.)

Early in his ministry, William Horton said to Wesley, "I like nothing you do. All your sermons are satires on particular persons. All the people are of my mind. We won't hear ourselves so abused ... they cannot tell what religion you are of. They never heard of such a religion before; they know not what to make of it. And then, your private behavior – all the quarrels that have been here since you came have been 'long of you.' Indeed there is neither a man nor woman in the town who minds a word you say. And so, you may preach long enough; but nobody will come to hear you."[155] Wesley writes, "He was too warm for an answer. So I had nothing to do but to thank him for his openness and walk away."[156] We must be fair, however, with the eventual result of this oft-printed quote. Mr. Horton said those caustic words on June 22, 1736, three months after Wesley arrived, but he later became reconciled to his pastor and remained in church.

John Wesley, the methodical keeper of records, religiously

---

[155] Op. cit., Ward & Heitzenrater, Vol. 18:162

[156] Ibid., 18:162

reported attendance in his diary at the three Sunday services (5:00, 11:00, and 2:45) and all three combined often equaled a hundred. He also provided services to the Savannah citizens from France, Germany, and Italy in their native tongues!

His Sunday schedule soon looked like this:

5:00-6:30	Morning Prayers (English)
9:00-10:00	Italian Prayers
10:30-12:30	Sermon and Sacraments (lots of baptisms are recorded)
1:00-2:00	French Prayers
2:00-3:00	Catechism for the children
3:00-4:00	Evening Prayers (English)
6:30	"with the Germans" (i.e. Moravians)
8:00-9:30	A small group at the rectory for "holy conversation"

Wesley noted that, "I have often observed that I scarce ever visited any persons, in health or sickness, but they attended Public Prayer for some time after. This increased my desire of seeing not only those who were sick, but all my parishioners as soon as possible at their own houses. Accordingly, I begun to visit them in order from house to house."[157]

(It is from this lesson in Savannah that the question, "Will you visit from house to house?" showed up later in all subsequent Methodist volumes of *The Book of Discipline*.)

He counseled daily, but the same names recur over and over, a perennial problem for pastors who give a high priority to counseling in their study. He organized catechism classes and was careful to follow every rubric of the *Edwardian Homilies,* including the requirement to meet with the priest before being served The Lord's Supper if you have been habitually absent. Failure to have this preliminary counsel resulted in being denied the cup.

Another dimension of Wesley's ministry both on St. Simon's Island (Frederica) and in Savannah was the Sunday evening meeting. This was at the parsonage and was a small group whom Wesley and Ingham tutored in theology of William Law, Jeremy

---

[157] Ibid., *JWW,* J & D Vol. 18, p. 420

Taylor, Thomas a Kempis, Cave's *Primitive Christianity*, etc. It is the evening meetings and publication of a hymnbook that make Georgia the "second rise" of Methodism. These formats would morph into the class meetings at Bristol, England, in 1739 and the consequent theology would be reflected in many of Charles Wesley hymns.

Charles Wesley's Georgia Ministry

Since Charles Wesley had been appointed personal secretary to Governor Oglethorpe, and Oglethorpe stationed himself and a garrison of soldiers on St. Simon's Island for fear of Spanish attacks from Florida, Charles Wesley had to be there, not in Savannah. He, Benjamin Ingham, Robert Hows, and others began a society at St. Simon's which looked much like later versions of Methodist societies.

Charles had a dreadful experience. His asthma was terrible and he and Oglethorpe did not work well together. After only five months, he returned to England. Benjamin Ingham returned after a year. The pastoral care of this Frederica group then fell to John, and prompted the several occasions when he was at Frederica for protracted periods. The abortive attempt to establish a disciplined group at Frederica might well have been Wesley's first design of a society meeting on Sunday mornings followed by "class meetings" on Sunday afternoons and after evening prayers. He notes this development in his *Journal* (written four years later) as the date of June 10, 1736, citing "singing, reading, and conversation with the most serious of the communicants."[158] Six months later, on January 26, 1737, he recorded, "After having 'beaten the air' in this unhappy place for twenty days ... I took my final leave of Frederica."[159]

John labored on in Savannah and with the Indians. In addition to the meetings at Frederica, John made sojourns into Indian Territory, trips to Charleston where he attempted to explain God to the slaves, and repetitive visits with the Moravians. All the while he was parish priest at Christ Anglican Church in Savannah. Even then, "holy conversation" was perhaps developing in Wesley's mind as a means of grace. He met late every Sunday

---

[158] Op. cit., Heitzenrater, *People Called Methodists*, 64

[159] Op. cit., Ward & Heitzenrater, *JWW*, J & D, Vol. 18, 175

evening with a group of what we would today call "seekers." Among the young adults in this small Sunday evening session was Sophia Christiana Hopkey.

Ministry with a few African Americans

Oglethorpe did not allow the slave trade in "his" Georgia colony as long as he lived. Slavery came in 1751, after his death. Wesley was horrified by slavery and moved with compassion for the Africans with whom he came in contact, particularly in Charleston and Purrysburg, SC, an upriver settlement by the French near Savannah. His heart went out to God's children who were being treated as chattels and told nothing of their spiritual nature. He tried hard to communicate with them the nature of the soul, and was bitterly disappointed that no Christian planter had bothered to offer them Christ. He began to convince the slaves that they had a soul. He sought for language to explain our "soul" and used the wind as a metaphor. All his ministry with slaves and masters was in South Carolina.

Wesley even devised a plan for missionaries to go onto the plantations, teaching reading and writing, and explaining the concept of the image of God shared by all humanity, without regard to race. His plan involved using some slaves who had learned to read and write. He reports that "I met with three or four gentlemen between Charleston and Purrysburg who would be exceeding glad for such an assistant."[160] However, his brief time in America and his deep involvement in parish and personal issues prevented his ever launching this endeavor.

Ministry with the Native Americans

Communicating the Christian concept of God to the Native Americans was a challenge. However, Wesley was impressed by "natural revelation" (in creation) that he discovered among the Indians. In one of his first encounters, he "asked an old grey headed man what he was made for." He said, 'He that is above knows what he made us for. We know nothing. We are in the dark. But white men know much. And yet white men build great houses as if they are to live forever. But white men can't live forever. In a little time, white men will be dust as well as I.' I told him, 'If red

---

[160] Ibid., 504

men will learn the Good Book, they may know as much as white men.' He answered, 'I believe that. Our men do what they know is not good; they kill their own children. And our women do what they know is not good; they kill the child before it is born."[161]

He made several attempts to evangelize the Native Americans near Savannah, but to little avail. Most of his descriptions of various tribes were stereotyped reports he copied from biased sources. However, he did try. He and Benjamin Ingham, a veteran of the Oxford "Holy Club," established a school for Indian children. An Indian woman gave them a jar of milk and a jar of honey. She said, "The milk is so you will remember that we are babies in the Great Word; the honey is so you will be sweet to us."[162] What a profound statement from the Native American.

To one girl Wesley resorted to nature, especially the starlit night sky to convey the concept of God. Then, he explained that after we die, we go "above the sky where no one will beat you or hurt you." He was impressed that the next day (April 24, 1737) "she remembered all I had said, readily answered the questions I proposed, and said that she would ask Him who is above the sky to show her how to be good."[163]

Sadly, the longer Wesley stayed in Georgia, the more his time was taken by trivial pursuits.

Thomas Causton, Sophia Hopkey, William Williamson

Much innuendo has arisen, and loads of curiosity persists, around John Wesley's falling in love with Sophia Hopkey. People who know nearly nothing about Wesley's ministry in Georgia will repeat something they have heard about his having to leave Georgia during the night, and that his departure is related to his love affair with a young woman. We choose to go into this relationship in more depth than is customary for four reasons:

- First of all, we wish to set the record straight, not from secondary sources, but from Mr. Wesley's daily diary and the *Journal* that he published immediately after he returned

---

[161] Ibid. , 164

[162] Op. cit., McTyeire, 93

[163] Op. cit.,Ward & Heitzenrater, eds. *JWW*, J & D, Vol., 18, . 502

to England. Much of his time with Sophia Hopkey was spent reading the Christian classics to her. He also ended every French lesson with reading a Psalm.

- Secondly, Methodists have too little knowledge of John Wesley's struggle with his natural attraction for women that repeatedly conflicted with his monk-like understanding of God's will for his ministry. From his days at Oxford to his old age, he demonstrated his failure to understand his own feelings as being naturally romantic and his conflicted conviction that he must "not ever enjoy the company of women more than the company of God." He repeatedly failed in verbalizing to women his human love and his divine call.

- Thirdly, he sought the counsel of too many mentors, mentors who added to his confusion.

- Fourthly, one does wonder why he wrote down such tantalizing details, but his record does help us to see the spiritual giant as a dedicated Christian man who had a consistent but troubling romantic dimension to his nature with regard to human sexuality. His dysfunctional family could have been a contributing factor. He did not grow up in a home with a happy marriage.

Who were the Caustons and Sophia Hopkey?

Years earlier, back in England, an insolvent Brit named Thomas Causton had married Martha Clarkson whose father owned a profitable calico business when calico was a new material in high demand. When Clarkson died, the beneficiaries of his considerable estate were Martha Clarkson Causton, and her niece, Sophia Hopkey. Thomas Causton became executor of the estate and guardian of the teenage Sophia. He decided to invest his wife's and niece's small fortune in the new Georgia colony. Sophia had no choice but to leave her comfortable life in London.

Upon arrival in Oglethorpe's colony, Causton was one of the few men of means. The land that Causton occupied overlooked Saint Augustine Creek, five miles east of downtown Savannah. It is still known as "Causton's Bluff." During Wesley's ministry, there was little there but a house and enclosed yard where Wesley and Sophia met to talk. Being English, Wesley referred to the Causton's back yard as "the garden." Orchards were developed later, eventually claiming "4000 mulberry trees" (for a silk industry that never materialized) and pastures for "200 head of cattle."

The Trustees of the Georgia Colony set up company stores that held a monopoly on food, clothing, piece goods, and supplies. They also instituted a program of "public works" for building rock walls, laying out the parks and squares which still mark Savannah. Thomas Causton was named by Oglethorpe as the proprietor over all the company stores. They used the company stores both for credit and as a "bank" for paying the workers. Many of the skilled craftsmen were Germans who did not speak or read English.

Causton was also named the chief of three magistrates who would hear cases of litigation. The upshot was that this Thomas Causton was second only to General Oglethorpe in authority and power. The plot thickens. John Wesley detected that the store clerks were cheating the Germans who charged merchandise and had their purchases deducted from their pay checks. Wesley called their hand and was immediately considered "meddling." The other complicating issue was that one of the clerks whom Causton hired for the Trustee Stores was William Williamson who, in the spring of 1737, would marry Sophia Hopkey.

The Trustees and Oglethorpe insisted on a ban on both slaves and rum, but Causton used some slaves in building Savannah and allowed rum to be bootlegged. As chief magistrate, he was breaking the law.

John Wesley and Sophia Hopkey

In Richard Heitzenrater's edition of Wesley's "Manuscript Georgia Journal–March 7, 1735–December 16, 1737," we can follow the Sophia Hopkey relationship in Wesley's own words, not those of subsequent authors. In this section of his *Journal*, "Wesley must justify himself against charges of misconduct in Georgia ...."[164] Much of the *Journal* was copied from his daily diary, but some of it was from memory. Granted, it was written virtually as a brief to be used in his defense before the Georgia trustees upon his premature return to London. This is how Wesley begins!

---

[164] Op. cit., Ward & Heitzenrater, *JWW*, J&D, Vol., 18, 37

"At my first coming to Savannah in the beginning of March, 1736, I was determined to have no intimacy with any woman in America. Notwithstanding which ... on March the 13th, I spoke to Miss Sophy Hopkey ... and endeavored to explain to her the nature and necessity of inward holiness. On the same subject, I continued to speak to her once a week, but generally in open air and never alone."[165]

(Later, as a parenthesis, he inserted) "Soon after being at Mrs. Causton's house, Mrs. Causton, when I was out of the room, said to others present, 'There goes a husband for my Pilky' (her common title for Miss Hopkey). And in June the following she told me, 'Then take Phiky; she is serious enough.' I said, 'You are not in earnest, madam!' She said, 'Indeed, sir, I am; take her, and do what you will with her.'"[166]

After counseling her regarding a former boyfriend (Mr. Mellichamp) who was now in a Charleston prison, and consulting with friends, he broke his intended policy, and began counseling with her alone.

"In all those conversations I was careful to speak only on things pertaining to God. But on July 23, after I had talked with her for some time, I took her by the hand, and kissed her (hand). And from this time, I fear there was a mixture in my intention, though I was not soon sensible of it."[167]

Some mornings, she came to his and Charles Delamotte's home for breakfast and devotions. Then, she remained alone to have French lessons. All summer and fall, Wesley continued to be tormented with feelings about which he felt guilty and a vocation to which he was determined to be faithful. In October, 1736, he wrote, "But the next morning, I was obliged to (return) to Savannah, and there again I groaned under the weight of an unholy desire. My heart was with Miss Sophey all the time. I longed to see her but at a distance and for a moment. On the fourteenth, I blurted out, to her, 'I am resolved if I marry at all, not to do so until I have been among the Indians.' That did it! Her response was,

---

[165] Ibid., 365)

[166] Ibid., 366

[167] Ibid., 367

'People wonder what I can do so long at your house. I am resolved not to breakfast with you anymore. And I won't come to you any more alone.'"[168] The next day she canceled her French lessons.

He knew now that he could not continue forever in the valley of indecision. Again he consulted his friends, and decided to write out three options and draw lots. The first option was "Marry." The second was "Think not of it this year." The third was "Think of it no more." Charles Delamotte drew. He drew the third. Wesley recorded his response to the lot that was drawn:

> "I saw and adored the goodness of God, though what he required of me was a costly sacrifice. It was indeed giving up at once what this world affords of what is agreeable (or desirable), not only honour, fortune, power, and the truly desirable conveniences of life: a pleasant house and a delightful garden on the brow of a hill at a small distance from the town; another house and garden in the town; a third a few miles off with a large tract of fruitland adjoining to it. And above all, what to me made all things else vile and utterly beneath a thought, such a companion as I never expected to find again, should I live a thousand years twice told. And so we prayed the prayer of a prophet denied the life of a common man: 'O Lord God ... I give thee not thousands of rams or ten thousand rivers of oil, but the desire of my eyes, the joy of my heart, the one thing on earth I long for.'"[169]

Her uncle, apparently convinced that Wesley would never marry his niece, had begun to arrange a marriage with William Williamson, one of the clerks whom Causton hired for the Trustee stores. Wesley did not describe Williamson very charitably. He wrote, "He was not a man remarkable for handsomeness, neither for genteelness, neither for wit or knowledge or sense, and least of all for religion."

So, on March 7 when Sophia denied any lingering feelings for her former fiancé, Mellichamp, Wesley asked about her relationship with Williamson. She responded that she could trust no one

---

[168] Ibid., 472

[169] Ibid., 480

but a Christian. Then Wesley remembers, "I looked upon her and should have said too much had we a moment longer. But in that instant Mrs. Causton called us in. So I was once more 'snatched as a brand from the fire.'"[170]

Wesley had no idea that his world was about to collapse. Earlier that very day, Sophia had buckled to her uncle's and aunt's insistence and agreed to marry William Williamson. In his *Journal*, written later, he enlarges on the visit to Mrs. Causton's:

> "She said, 'Sir, Mr. Causton and I are exceedingly obliged to you for all the pains you took with Sophy. And so is Sophy too; and she desires you would publish the Banns of Marriage between her and Mr. Williamson on Sunday.' I answered, 'Madam, I don't seem to be awake. Surely I am in a dream.' She said, 'They agreed on it between themselves last night, after you was gone. And afterward Mr. Williamson asked Mr. Causton's and my consent, which we gave him .... Speak to her; she is at the lot. Go to her. She will be very glad to hear anything Mr. Wesley has to say; pray go to her and talk with her yourself.' 'I said, 'No madam, if Miss Sophy is engaged, I have nothing to say."

> "From Mrs. Causton I went home full of perplexity. Later he did indeed go to the lot and found Sophia and her fiancé there. He recorded the conversation.

> "Williamson: 'I suppose, sir, that you know what was agreed on last night between Miss Sophy and me.'

> "I answered, 'I have heard something but I could not believe it unless I should hear it from Miss Sophy herself.'

> "She replied, 'Sir, I have given Mr. Williamson my consent— unless you have anything to object.' It started into my mind, 'What if she meant,"Unless you marry me."'

> "But I checked the thought ... and replied, 'If you have given your consent, the time is past. I have nothing to object.'

> "She replied, 'I hope I shall always have your friendship.'

> "I answered, 'I can be still your friend, though I should not stay in America.'

---

[170] Ibid., 482

"... I kissed them both and took my leave of her, as one I was to see no more.'"[171]

Wesley went home and walked in his garden, writing later, "And I did seek after God, but found him not. I forsook him before; now he forsook me. I could not pray. Indeed the snares of death were about me; the pains of hell overtook me .... About four o'clock (*in the morning*) he so far took the cup from me that I drank so deeply of it no more."

On Saturday, March 12, his diary shows a full day of pastoral duties and private readings, including Job and prayers. He also wrote his will. At the close of the daily entries, he wrote, "Today Miss Bovey and Miss Sophy were married at Purrysburg."

Actually, and foolishly, Wesley met with Sophy six more times, either privately or in the company of an angry husband. In one of these meetings he said to her, "In things of an indifferent nature, you cannot be too obedient to your husband. But if his will should be contrary to the will of God, you are to obey God rather than man." "It may be observed that this day, of her own free will, she fasted until evening."[172]

Contrary to most popular recollections of the events subsequent to Sophia's marriage, Wesley continued to serve her communion through the spring and early summer when she came to church. Indeed, he kept precise records of her attendance, and lack thereof. After noting the dates of her absence in May and June, he "determined to speak to her again." It was their sixth conversation since her wedding. "Accordingly, as we returned from church, Sunday, July 3, immediately after Holy Communion, I reproved Mrs. Williamson for her insincerity and other faults." He insisted she tell him if he had ever acted hypocritically toward her. "She answered, 'Indeed, I don't believe you have, but you seem to think I have dissembled with you.'" "I told her, I did so, and began to explain with her upon it. But the more I spoke, the more angry she appeared, till after a few minutes, she turned about and went abruptly away, thus putting an end to our sixth and last time together."[173]

---

[171] Ibid., 482-485)

[172] Ibid., 496

[173] Ibid., 487f

Then, he wrote it all down in a letter, itemizing her times of 'insincerity' and mailed it to her. At that time his mind moved to question her spiritual qualifications to receive Holy Communion.

On July 11, Sophia had a miscarriage, and Mrs. Causton began to tell throughout the community that it was Wesley's conversation with her eight days earlier and his subsequent letter that caused Sophia to lose her baby. The long friendship with the Caustons was ending. Storm clouds were gathering. Wesley took no heed, but insisted that without confession of her deceit and repentance of her absence from church, she would not be served communion when the sacrament was served with her present. That occurred on August 7, 1737.

The Infamous Refusal to Administer Communion to Mrs. Williamson

Wesley's Diary read,

> "From [6 July] till 7 August (part of which she was ill), neither Mrs. Williamson spoke to me nor I to her; though she had several opportunities of doing it. So that I was surprised as well as much grieved to be then reduced to the necessity of telling her in the church (indeed so softly that none heard it but herself, and in the mildest manner I was master of), 'I can't administer the Holy Communion to you before I have spoken with you.'"[174]

Sophia spoke that Sunday afternoon to a Mrs. Burnside about being repelled at communion. Apparently, she told Wesley what Mrs. Burnside said because his *Journal* records her having said, "… you may easily put an end to this by going to Mr. Wesley now, and clearing yourself of what you are charged with." The diary records that Sophia replied, "No, I will not show such a meanness of spirit as to speak to him about it myself, but somebody else shall."

A Warrant Is Served on Rev. John Wesley

The next day, August 8, the following warrant was issued. This shockingly illustrates what happens when civil government has control over ecclesiastical polity and practice:

---

[174] Ibid., 535

"Georgia; Savannah: To all Constables, Tithingmen, and others, whom these may concern:

You and each of you, are hereby required to take the body of John Wesley, Clerk:

And bring him before one of the bailiffs of the said town, to answer the complaint of William Williamson and Sophia his wife, for defaming the said Sophia and refusing to administer to her the sacrament of the Lord's Supper in a public congregation without cause; by which the said William Williamson is damaged one thousand pounds sterling. And for so doing this is your warrant, certifying what you are to do in the premises. Given by my hand and seal the 8th day of August, Anno Dom. 1737."

Thomas Cristie [175]

The warrant was served on Wesley, Tuesday, August 9, and he was "carried before the bailiff." Williamson showed up, and Wesley wrote in his diary, "after much reviling, he inserted on the edge of the warrant that I had endeavoured to alienate her affections from him. This I denied. As to the other [charges], being purely ecclesiastical, I could not acknowledge their power to interrogate me. Mr. Parker endorsed the warrant, whereby I was ordered to appear before the next Court."[176]

Causton Threatens Wesley with Defamation of Character

Then, Thomas Causton played his hand as a major perpetrator. After two angered verbal attacks on Wesley because so many people were calling Causton "Judas," Causton said on August 11, "I have drawn the sword and I will never sheath it till I have satisfaction." After Wesley tried to reason with him, he said to Causton, "Sir, if you thus wrest and pervert my words, even before my face, I must never speak to you again without witnesses. But if you come in at one door, I will go out at the other."[177] Wesley found in the evening lesson of the Lectionary these comforting words,

---

[175] 171bid., 537

[176] Ibid., 538

[177] Ibid., 542

"I will never leave thee nor forsake thee. So we may boldly say, The Lord is my helper. I will not fear what man shall do unto me" (Hebrews 13:5-6).

Causton began to seek witnesses, the first being James Burnside, an accountant in the Trustees' supply store. When Burnside refused to sign a statement sustaining the accusations in the warrant, Causton "discharged him from his employment." Wesley heard that the same effort was made to other communicants, "all to no avail." Then a long, accusative narrative appeared from Sophia which was sworn before a court recorder on August 16. Next came an affidavit from Burnside's wife, Margaret, and Wesley's friend, Charles Delamotte, exonerating Wesley.

By August 18, Causton, chief magistrate of the colony, had named a Grand Jury of twenty-six, with eighteen alternates. By August 31, they had indicted Wesley with ten True Bills. His response was to read to the congregation the instructions he read on his first Sunday back in March, 1736, at which time he announced that if for a time absent from church, to be served communion on Sunday, one must "register" beforehand. This Sophia had not done, and he insisted he was therefore justified, which, technically, he was. He was advised by his friends to go to England, but he resisted. Four times he went to court, only to have Causton postpone his case. By October 7, he consulted his friends and they advised, "You should go, but not yet."

He continued his multiple ministries to and beyond his own parish. He initiated two ministries with French Huguenots, one in an outlying settlement and one in Savannah proper. He continued reading prayers to the Germans from Salzburg who had no clergyman. He moved James and Margaret Burnside into the rectory, rescuing them from the small hut they had built in the country after Causton fired James from the company store.

His diary lists several burials. In late November, he baptized several children and adults and posted public notice of his intent to leave the colony. On December 2, the magistrate sent for him and forbade him to go. Wesley replied that he had appeared four times before the court, desiring a trial, and had been refused. Causton, the chief magistrate, published an order requiring all officers to prevent Wesley's departure. Wesley concluded, "I saw clearly I had nothing to do but to fly *('escape')* for my life."[178]

Wesley, foolishly, had written another note to Sophia, closing with the words, "And when you have openly declared yourself to have repented, I will administer to you the mysteries of God."[179] The note was hand delivered and Causton intercepted it, responding, "I have made his character public to all the world. I have sent it to England already; and I will publish it in every newspaper in England and America. I am the person who is injured, and I will espouse the cause of my niece .... And I will never leave him until my life's end.'"[180] Wesley's friend Delamotte, the courier, brought this message back to the rectory.

Wesley Leaves Georgia

With this threat from Causton and Causton's control of the colony which would make a fair hearing by the Grand Jury unlikely, Wesley was finally convinced to leave, which he did after posting notice on the town square. His final departure was secret and at night, just before Christmas, 1737.

The diary records, "And the tide serving as soon as Evening Prayers were over, I shook off the dust of my feet, and left Savannah, after having preached the gospel there (with much weakness indeed, and many infirmities) one year and nine months."[181] It was Friday, December 2, 1737. His trip to Port Royal near Charleston was secretive, circuitous, miserable, frustrating, and dangerous. The guides he hired either did not know the way or deliberately took wrong routes. They suffered nearly every deprivation imaginable. After eleven horrible days of walking in the swamps and sleeping in freezing clothes under the stars, they reached Charleston and civilization. By December 16, he felt his "soul renewed."

{Here his diary breaks off and we learn of the voyage from his Journal which he sent to press in Bristol on June 2, 1740}

On December 22, he bade his friend, Charles Delamotte

---

[178] Ibid., 569

[179] Ibid., 543

[180] Ibid., 543

[181] Ibid., 569)

("from whom I had been separate few days since October 14, 1735") farewell and wrote, "I took my leave of America (though if it please God, not forever) and boarded the *Samuel.* On Christmas Eve, "we sailed over Charleston bar, and about noon lost sight of land."

On board ship, he wrote that he immediately, "began instructing a Negro lad in the principles of Christianity."

Wesley's Return to England

His diary during the return voyage recorded these words: "By the most infallible of proofs, inward feeling, I am convinced ... of unbelief, having no such faith in Christ as will prevent my heart from being troubled" and prayed, "Lord save, or I perish. Save me by such a faith as implies peace in life and in death." This clearly showed the influence of Moravian theology. He also wrote the oft quoted passage, "I went to America to convert the Indians, but Oh. Who shall convert me? I have a fair summer religion. I can talk well and believe myself, but, nay, ... my spirit is troubled."[182]

On Sunday, January 29, 1738, "we saw English land once more and on January 30, a strong wind brought us safely into the Downs." It was finally "four in the morning" on February 1 when they climbed into the small boat that in "half an hour landed us in Deal."

Thomas Causton carried out his threat to defame Wesley in England. Less than six months after Wesley left Savannah, Causton had prompted a returning sea captain named Robert Williams to publish in London a sworn affidavit outlining Wesley's relationship with Sophia Hopkey and Causton's appointment of a Grand Jury with "ten true bills" for his arrest. It continued that Wesley had left Savannah "under the cover of darkness." Wesley is most fortunate that, then or later, this threat came to nothing.

Wesley Back in London

When back in London, Wesley had a legal issue to settle with the Georgia Trustees. There were three concerns:

• He had not stayed out his contract

---

[182] Ward & Heitzenrater, *JWW,* J & D, Vol. 18, 211

- The reports forwarded to England from Thomas Causton

- An uncertain future at the hands of the Anglican Bishop because he had left an episcopal appointment in Savannah without permission from the bishop.

In preparation for his meeting with the Trustees, Wesley published the first edition of his *Journal*, itemizing in great detail his ministry and personal life in Georgia. The *Journal*, dated January 29, 1738, contained pertinent excerpts from his daily diary, letters, memoranda, and his own recollection of every issue addressed in the affidavit. He bracketed the narrative and gave his editorial reflections, especially with regard to his relationship with Miss Hopkey.

This document was printed as a book and read in all the society and band meetings as well as being available to the public.[183] Dr. Richard Heitzenrater tells about that development in his well-documented book, *The People Called Methodists,* but he does not indicate that the matter became a problem for Methodism in England, or later, in America.

As has been true of many of us in life, our successes have sometimes had the seeds of failure, yet our failures have been learning experiences that ultimately bore good harvests. Wesley learned a lot through his missionary experience as a pastor in Savannah. Just as he was a "brand plucked from the burning" when he was five years old and the rectory in Epworth burned, so he was rescued by the grace of God from the efforts of Thomas Causton to destroy his character and deny him of a future. Even Sophia Hopkey's "jilting him" was perhaps the hand of God in human affairs. The Trustees of the Georgia colony did not press any charges. John Wesley's Georgia chapter was closed forever, but God, quite obviously, was not finished with him._

George Whitefield's Evaluation of Wesley's Georgia Ministry

Wesley considered his mission a failure and put himself down immeasurably indeed, to the point of depression and despair. But George Whitefield sailed for Georgia a few hours before Wesley left Savannah for London. As Wesley's successor, Whitefield wrote this:

---

[183] Op. cit., Heitzenrater, *People Called Methodists,* 117

"The good Mr. John Wesley has done in American is inexpressible. His name is very precious among the people, and he has laid a foundation that I hope neither men nor devils will ever be able to shake. O that I might follow him as he followed Christ."[184]

For the unscrupulous Thomas Causton, the future was grim. After the havoc that he caused in Wesley's personal life and ministry, his shenanigans caught up with him. By May of 1738, Causton was removed from his control of the Trustee stores because £13,382 was unaccounted for. He was recalled to England in 1744 and asked to defend himself. Attempting a return voyage in 1745, he contracted a fever and died at sea.

Conclusion of the Sophia Hopkey Relationship

Whatever happened to Sophia Hopkey Williamson? Following Causton's death, the trustees ran the Ockstead Plantatin from 1745 - 1750, but in that year they paid Mr. Williamson £110 for his services as administrator in the selling of the plantation. There is no historical data to follow Sophia after Wesley's departure from Georgia. One can only conjecture whether she followed the later life of the revered John Wesley and his founding of Methodism.

Casual readers of Wesley often imply that Wesley was guilty of sexual impropriety. While by today's standards, he was guilty of sexual harassment by virtue of his position of power as Sophia's pastor. Most credible scholars are agreed that Wesley avoided any moral turpitude. The Moravian mentors made decisions for his love life, not by counsel, but by casting lots. Also, we learn from his diary, that after her duplicitous marriage to Mr. Williamson, Wesley learned from others that she was "two-timing" Wesley. To say it colloquially in the words of the Appalachian folk song, "he lost his true love for a'courting too slow." His other mistake was that once she was married, he should have stayed out of her life with conversations and letters. No party in the confusion did what he or she should have done, and it cost him his job. The good news is that had he married her and settled as a long-term rector of Christ Anglican Church, the world would probably have never heard of John Wesley.

---

[184] Op. cit., McTyeire, 97

Wesley's Resumption of Ministry in England

Once Wesley had bared his soul regarding Georgia, he was invited to preach in some Anglican churches around London, but was not well received. He was at a very low ebb and had no clarity about his future. John Wesley's spiritual journey was coming to a climax. His long effort to be disciplined enough, to sacrifice enough, and to work hard enough to find the peace for which every human longs, was at a frustrating end. Going to Georgia had been his last best effort to find holiness through purity of heart and works of righteousness, which now seemed as filthy rags.

His major obsession in the spring of 1738 was with the condition of his soul. To fill that void, he turned to the people whom he had met on the way to Georgia, the Moravians. It was the Germans who would be the midwives of his new birth. Little did he know that in four agonizing months, he would reach a new plateau in his long search for the "peace that passeth understanding" and "strangely" receive God's unmerited grace at Aldersgate.

In his *Journal* he rehearsed what he had done in suffering, in poor judgment, and in hard work. Indeed, he asked in his diary, "Does all this give me a claim to the holy, heavenly, divine charter of a Christian? By no means."[185] I have "fallen short of the glory of God."[186] "I have no hope except that if I seek, I shall find Christ and be 'found in him,' not having my own righteousness, but the righteousness which is of God by faith."[187] "The faith that I want is a sure trust and confidence in God."[188] To be freed from sin is to be freed from doubt. He then quotes scripture, "Having the love of God shed abroad in his heart through the Holy Ghost which is given unto him'; which 'Spirit itself beareth witness with his spirit that he is a child of God."[189]

The winter of 1738 was a most miserable time in the life of a most incredible man.

---

[185] Op. cit., *Journal* & Diaries, V. 18, 214

[186] Romans 3:23

[187] Philippians 3:9

[188] Edwardian Homilies, "Of Salvation," Pt. III *(The definition of faith which Wesley quotes most frequently)*

[189] Romans 8:16

CHAPTER SIX

Aldersgate: The Third Rise of Methodism

Much of the scholarship interpreting what happened at Aldersgate reflects only the famous passage from his diary on May 24, 1738, upon his return to his rooms in London. Strangely, he makes no further reference to being "strangely warmed" that evening. Even at the laying of the cornerstone of Wesley's Chapel, he uses the 1729 date of Oxford Methodism as the place of origin and does not mention Aldersgate. Therefore, most scholars today consider Aldersgate as a seismic shift in Wesley's at last sensing the witness of the Spirit that he was a "joint heir with Christ." He "strangely" experienced the inner peace for which he had longed. Preachers, laity, and anyone studying the way in which Methodists have focused on Aldersgate need to appreciate more deeply the scholars who have spent much of their academic inquiry with the journals, letters, sermons, tracts, and diaries to bring a more accurate understanding of the mind, mission, and psychological disposition of John Wesley.

In this chapter we reflect the writings of scholars like Albert Outler, Richard Heitzenrater, Frank Baker, Randy Maddox, Rupert Davies, Ted Runyon, Rex Matthews, Ted Campbell, Charles Yrigoyen, Kenneth Collins, Jason Vickers, Chuck Hunter, Tom Langford, Robert Cushman, William Abraham, Karen Westerfield Tucker, Scott Jones, Roberta Bondi, Colin Williams, Sarah Lancaster, David Hempton, Steven Tompkins, Ben Witherspoon, Jean Schmidt, and many others.

Spiritual Journey from Oxford to Aldersgate

Before we leap immediately into John Wesley's experience on Aldersgate Street, May 24, 1738, let us reflect on the previous thirteen years of his spiritual journey. Since his decision in 1725 to "seek holy orders" while an undergraduate student at Oxford, he had devoted enormous emotional, spiritual, and physical energy to his faith journey. More than once, after continuous reading, self-discipline, personal and social holiness, and an unrelenting examination of his soul, Wesley had concluded that he was a "good Christian." However:

- 1720-1735 - He was for fifteen years, either as a student or faculty member, on the campus of Oxford University with access to thirty-seven college libraries and sought inner peace by sincerity, self-discipline, and rigid holy living. He led the so called "Holy Club." He was ordained Priest in 1728 and elected Fellow at Lincoln College, Oxford. Deeply influenced by reading devotional classics, he identified sincere "holy living" as the confirmation of one's being obedient to God.

- 1735-1737 - He spent two years of parish ministry as rector of Christ Episcopal Church in Savannah, during which time the Moravians were his mentors and confidants.

- In a "dark night of the soul" on January 8, 1738, still aboard ship en route to London, he prayed, "Lord, save me or I perish. Save me by such a faith as implies peace in life and in death ... by such humility as may fill my heart ... by sobriety of spirit."[190] While still on the boat in Deal Harbor, Wesley demonstrated that his spiritual longings were a prelude to Aldersgate: "The faith I want is the faith of a son, a sure trust and confidence in God, that through the merits of Christ my sins are forgiven and I reconciled to the favor of God." A footnote traces this definition of faith to the *Edwardian Homilies, 'Of Salvation,' Pt. III.*[191]

Back in London: The Miserable Mr. Wesley

John Wesley's boat docked at Deal, England, on January 29, 1738, "two years and almost four months since I left my native country." Typical of him, despondent as he was, he went imme-

---

[190] Op. cit., Ward and Heitzenrater, *JWW/J&D*, Vol, 18, 209

[191] Ibid., 215,216

diately to Oglethorpe and the colony trustees to explain why he came home prematurely. He received a tongue lashing from them and edited his *Journal* as a document of defense.

According to Rupert Davies, "John had followed the path of 'inward and outward holiness' for fourteen years and he had arrived nowhere."[192] Wesley wrote in his *Journal,* "... I who went to America to convert others was never myself converted to God."[193] This was of course exaggerated as Wesley himself admitted when, <u>years later</u>, he wrote in the margin of this 1738 *Journal* entry, "I'm not sure of this." But, his emotions were not all masochistic. The reality was that he was not at peace with himself or God. Interestingly, this is the last page of *Journal I.* His troubled life and times in Georgia and the cold reception he received from his fellow Anglicans upon his return to London brought Wesley almost to despair.

The Wesleys and Peter Bohler

On February 7, 1738, John went with his brother, Charles, to meet Peter Bohler, a Moravian who had just arrived from Germany en route to America. Wesley's request of him was, "Give us of the oil of your lamp, for ours is gone out."

From February 7 until early May when Peter Bohler left London, the Wesleys saw him many times. They conversed either in German or in Latin, for Bohler knew little English. Bohler kept repeating, "My brother, my brother, that philosophy of yours must be purged away."[194] The philosophy was probably Wesley's having adopted John Locke's theory of reason: a process of utilizing one or more of the five physical sensations (sight, hearing, touching, smelling, and tasting) followed by reflection. As time revealed, Wesley would never cease to be Lockean in this regard, however he would add a "sixth sense" that he called "spiritual sense."

Bohler insisted that Wesley should have, immediately, a "feeling, a sense of his sins being forgiven." Wesley did not have that. Bohler wrote in a letter to Germany that Wesley wept bitterly and asked if he should stop preaching. Then came that famous (*but*

---

[192] Op. cit., Davies, 49

[193] Ibid. 49

[194] Ibid., 50

often misquoted) Bohler line, "Preach faith till you have it; and then, <u>because you have it</u>, you will preach it"[195] We see Wesley's response through a letter that Bohler wrote back to Germany in which he referred to Wesley's repeated plaintive question, "How can I obtain such faith?"

During that spring, Bohler and Wesley walked the forty-three miles to Oxford. When they arrived, the Fellow of Lincoln College was mocked as he walked down the street because he was with a Moravian. Charles' illness made them hasten back to London. Charles, on May 1, was "strongly averse to the 'new faith.'" But on May 3, Wesley makes this *Journal* entry, "And it now pleased God to open his [Charles'] eyes, so that he also saw clearly what was the nature of that one true, living faith, whereby alone through grace we are saved."

The next day, Bohler urged John and Charles to meet with the Fetter Lane Moravian group on a regular basis. That was basically modeled after the Church of England Evangelical Society that Samuel and Susanna Wesley organized in Epworth, but the understanding of faith was Lutheran-Moravian and new to the Wesleys. Scholar Kenneth Collins wrote that it was so significant in Wesley's journey that he called it "the third rise of Methodism," but Collins cites no source.[196]

Bohler sailed the Channel for America, leaving John Wesley hungering and thirsting for the righteousness of faith. Wesley now made long daily entries in his diary. He was still a mourner, heavy in heart. On May 21, the day of Pentecost, Charles, mentored by a "lowly mechanic" named John Bray, recorded, "I now found myself at peace with God." He shared his news with John on May 22. Now John's soul became even more tortured; he stood alone.

As we focus on the evening of May 24, 1738, we too often forget what Wesley was thinking during the morning. In his London rooms, on May 24, 1738, John Wesley arose at 5:00 a.m., opened his Greek Testament, and his eyes fell on the passage, "Unto us are given exceeding great and precious promises: that by these ye might be partakers of the divine nature" (II Peter 1:4). Later in the morning, he wrote a letter to a friend. "I know that every thought,

---

[195] Ibid., 50

[196] Op. cit., Collins 83

every movement of my heart should bear God's image, but how deep I have fallen. How far I am from God's glory. God is holy; I am sinful."

Bohler had been insisting for months that living by faith, we are "freed from sin, freed from fear, and freed from doubt." In his *Journal* that went to press June 2, 1740, Wesley recalled that early in the day on May 24, 1738, he was struggling with Bohler's insistence that "true faith in Christ has two fruits: complete dominion over sin (i.e. immediate sanctification) and constant peace from sense of forgiveness." Wesley wrote, "If this was so, it was clear I had not faith. But I was not willing to be convinced of this."

He left his rented room, and walked the streets near St. Paul's, hearing the bells peal on the hour. Perhaps in a little tea room, he opens his Bible again. This time the text he sees first are the words of Jesus, "Thou art not far from the kingdom of God." At the time of Evensong, he went into St. Paul's Cathedral. The anthem was "Out of the depths have I cried unto thee, O Lord ..." (Psalm 130). He listened for an undetermined amount of time and left, walking out the north door facing Cheapside. (*This author has retraced those steps seven times, observing, thinking, praying, taking notes.*) As the shadows lengthened over the landmarks of London, he walked the streets experiencing the human heart as a lonely hunter.

Probably without supper, he walked down "Aldersgate," a street little more than an alley, quite near the old London Wall, built by the Romans to define the city as one square mile. He seemed both attracted and repelled. He wrote later that he went "very unwillingly" into the Moravian meeting. His Catholic writers and Anglican tutors understood salvation as holy living. Peter Bohler had convinced him that God's grace could be emotionally experienced. Indeed, Bohler promised "a peace that will come with the forgiveness of your sins."

Presumably, he sat down near the back of the small room. They probably sang hymns for a while. Martin Schmidt, in his *A Theological Biography,* notes that Wesley's triumphant moment came when the layman read from Luther,

> "Unbelief is the root, the sap, and the chief power of all sin. Faith however, is a divine work in us which changes us and makes us to be born anew of God. It kills the old Adam and makes us altogether different men, in heart and spirit and

mind and powers; and it brings with it the Holy Spirit."[197] Luther's preface continued, "This confidence in God's grace and knowledge of it makes men glad and bold and happy in dealing with God and with all his creatures." [198]

Let us listen to Wesley's words after Aldersgate that he wrote in his diary back in his room:

"About 8:45, as a layman was reading from Martin Luther's preface to St. Paul's Letter to Romans as he was describing the change that God works in the heart through faith in Christ, I felt my heart strangely warmed. I felt I did trust in Christ, Christ alone, for salvation and an assurance was given me that he had taken away my sins, even mine, and saved me from the law of sin and death."[199]

In the many recollections of what happened at Aldersgate, it is Ted Runyon who, to me, gives the most accurate analysis:

- "Being a student of John Locke's empiricism, Wesley typically begins his account like an entry in a laboratory book: 'about a quarter before nine.'"

- Then follows the layman's reference to Luther: "while he was describing the change which God works in the heart through faith in Christ ..." (Romans).

- Next comes the registering of empirical evidence: "I felt my heart strangely warmed." Note his use of the word "strangely" because his normal disposition was not to experience a wave of emotion, per se.

- Wesley's interpretation was, "An assurance was given me, that he had taken away my sins, even mine, and saved me from the law of sin and death."[200]

- But this is not yet the content of the experience. That

---

[197] Op. cit., Collins, 90

[198] Schmidt, Martin, *A Theological Biography*, Abingdon, Vol. 1, 1973, 221ff

[199] Op. cit., Ward and Heitzenrater, *JWW*, J&D, Vol. 18, 249-250

[200] Runyon, Ted, "Importance of Experience for Faith," IN Maddox, Randy, *Aldersgate Reconsidered*, Kingswood, 1990, 99

follows. As Christ's love was received, it created a responsive trust in Wesley's heart: "I felt I did trust in Christ alone for salvation." A relationship was established of which <u>Christ, not Wesley's feelings, was the guarantor. Trust is different from feeling.</u>

- Wesley concluded with, "I then testified openly to all who were there what I now felt first in my heart." [201]

Rupert Davies wrote his interpretation, "'Saving faith' had been given to him, and the assurance of forgiveness." Then, Davies explained that Wesley wrote the word "strangely" because "the conscious emotion which accompanied the great deliverance was strange to him; he was not an emotional man."[202] The Moravian's emphasis on feelings was attractive to Wesley. It seemed the answer to his long nights' journey in a spiritual wilderness where he lacked an experiential confirmation of God's love for him. He later called it "heart religion" but did not preach feelings as the experiential norm dimension of salvation. By autumn, Wesley was writing that he did not have the feeling of "joy and peace," but still trusted in the grace of God which we see in Christ. He adopted the words "trust and confidence" to describe his assurance in being changed from a "servant to a son."

Many Methodist preachers have referred to Aldersgate as Wesley's conversion, a *fait accompli* that minimized his ten years of "holy living." Others have called Aldersgate Wesley's sanctification. Certainly, it was a powerful and transforming experience in the spiritual journey and the public ministry of John Wesley. The Methodist movement in Britain and in America point to Aldersgate as the evangelical essence, the "experimental divinity" of Methodism's founder.[203]

Parkes Cadman, an American Congregationalist, wrote in 1916 about Aldersgate, "The conviction that then flashed upon one of the most powerful and most active intellects in England is the true source of English Methodism. That conviction set free the religious genius whose light flashed on England when the moral

---

[201] Op. cit., Ward and Heitzenrater, *JWW*, J &D, Vol 18, 250

[202] Op. cit., Davies, 51

[203] Sangster, William, *Methodism: Her Unfinished Task*, London: Epworth, 1947, p. 27

condition of her inhabitants was aptly summarized in the somber phrase of the Hebrew prophet, 'They sat in darkness and the shadow of death.'" Cadman continued: "Wesley's words have gone out unto the ends of the earth."[204]

On May 25, he wrote, "The moment I awaked, 'Jesus Master' was in my heart and in my mouth; and I found all my strength lay in keeping my eye fixed upon him, and my soul waiting on him continually. Being at St. Paul's again in the afternoon, I could taste the good word of God in the anthem from Psalm 89. The enemy injected a fear, 'If thou doest believe, why is there not a more sensible change?' I answered (yet not I), 'That I know not, but this I know. I have now peace with God and I sin not today, and Jesus my Master has forbid me to take thought for the morrow.'"[205]

On May 26, he went again to St. Paul's for evensong. "My soul continued in peace, but yet in heaviness .... Mr. Tltschig had taught me, 'You must not fight with them (*fears and doubts*), but flee from them the moment they appear and take shelter in the wounds of Jesus.' The same I learned from the afternoon anthem, 'My soul truly waiteth still upon God; for of Him cometh my salvation' (Psalm 62:1-2) ... for God is our hope."

In early June, he received a letter from a Moravian in Oxford who wrote that no doubting can accompany true faith, that whoever at any time felt any doubt or fear was not weak in faith, but had no faith at all."[206] The Moravian theology was German pietism, a deeply evangelical mutation of Lutheranism, but Wesley was steeped in high-Anglican holiness. To him what St. Paul called a "babe in Christ," can have "degrees of faith." Yet, only days after Aldersgate, he was still bothered by waking "in peace, but not in joy."

Wesley Goes to Germany for Support, Nurture

On June 7, he wrote in his *Journal,* "I determined, if God should permit, to retire for a short time into Germany."[207] His intent was to involve the German Moravians in his reflection

---

[204] Op. cit., Cadman,. 240

[205] Op. cit., Ward & Heitzenrater, *JWW,* J&D, Vol. 18, 250-251

[206] Op. cit., Ward and Heitzenrater, Vol. 18, 254

[207] Ibid., 254

and not trust his own. He and his old Oxford Methodist friend, Benjamin Ingham, joined six others, and "five English and three Germans" boarded a ship to cross the channel and travel on to Herrnhut, Germany. His sisters, especially Emily, really resented his going to Germany when they had personal needs.

So, it was that just as Saul of Tarsus had once left Damascus for Arabia, John Wesley left London for Germany. Since the English Moravians still looked to Herrnhut, Germany, for their spiritual roots, Wesley felt the need to seek out the source of Moravian inner peace.

Traveling by boat in Holland and on the Rhine River, walking many miles, and occasionally riding by coach, they arrived at a Moravian castle and heard Count Zinzendorf preach on July 9, thirty-two days after they left England. To the consternation of his sisters, John Wesley was in Germany, seeking the counsel of these people who had been his spiritual mentors since December, 1735. He attended their love feasts, conferences, prayer meetings, and Bible expositions. The Moravians became Wesley's faith community. He discovered that the teachings of the German Moravians were somewhat different from what Peter Bohler had taught and what was taught in the English Moravian societies.

At Herrnhut, Wesley was virtually lectured that at Aldersgate the previous May, he was made "completely righteous with a total victory over sin."[208] Zinzendorf, the Moravian leader in Herrnhut, insisted, "from the moment one is justified (saved), he is entirely sanctified." Zinzendorf further insisted that both happen in the same instance and thereafter, neither increases nor decreases.[209] This was foreign to the previous thirteen years of Wesley's growth in what he called "grace upon grace." God used the Moravians to confirm God's love, mercy, and grace, but Wesley did not become a Moravian. The "holy living" of Anglican pietism was too strong to be abandoned for *sola fide* or "only faith."

He stayed three months, returning to London on September 16, 1738. He wrote in his *Journal* in Herrnhut his conviction of God's mission for him upon his return to England. "I trust we shall allow God to carry on his own work within us in a way that

---

[208] Op. cit., Runyon, Ted, *"The Importance of Experience for Faith."* 101

[209] Ibid., 102

pleases God."[210] A lot of what he learned from the Moravians would forever be a part of Methodism. But, Anglican that he was, he did not like all he saw and heard. They made spiritual victory in Jesus instantaneous and absolute whereas for Wesley, the transforming work of God is primary and our feelings are secondary."[211] He never accepted the Moravian theory. Rather, he referred to St. Paul's terminology: "babes in Christ who need milk before they can take meat."[212] Two years later, on July 20, 1740, Wesley left the Moravians because he believed in "degrees of faith."

Wesley learned from the unlettered German Moravian carpenter Christian David that "for many years people can have forgiveness of sins and a measure of peace with God because they have a witness of the spirit which shuts out all doubt and fear."[213] He also learned from the elder member of the church, Michael Linner, that "the leading of the Spirit is different with different souls." *(Bohler had not admitted this.)* Linner taught Wesley that for many, forgiveness of sins and full assurance come at the same time, <u>but not for all</u>. The German Moravians taught that full assurance can come weeks, months, even years after forgiveness, as it had for Wesley himself. The Moravians in London did not teach this "degrees of faith."

Wesley back in London, September, 1738

Wesley's euphoria on May 24 did not last long. The Lockean/Wesley philosophy of "sensation/reflection" was ingrained in Wesley. The philosophy that Bohler told Wesley he must give up now "kicked in." That is, at Aldersgate, he had a sensation, which now required reflection, critical reflection. Therefore, he began to analyze by reflection the feeling at Aldersgate that he called "strangely warmed." The result was misgivings, soon after he returned from Herrnhut in September. He had been guaranteed that his deep feelings of peace and joy would abide without intermission, but at times he did not continually feel God's forgiving love. Therefore, according to Moravianism, he did not have true

---

[210] Op. cit., McTyeire, 143

[211] Op. cit., Runyon, 105

[212] I Corinthians 3:1-2

[213] Op. cit, McTyeire,. 143

faith. This troubled him deeply, but he gradually escaped from the Moravians' judgment of his Anglican paradigm of salvation.

Granted, at Aldersgate in London and with the Moravians in Herrnhut, Wesley had an unprecedented religious experience that changed his life. Without the Moravian influence, Methodism might never have been born. However, his *Journal* reveals that he learned by painful introspection that the Moravian emphasis upon feeling as the *summon bonum* of scriptural salvation tended to collapse the reality of God into the feeling itself. Many Methodists might well be surprised to learn that in his writings or sermons across the next fifty-six years, Wesley almost never referred to Aldersgate.

Wesley wrote in October, 1738, that he sometimes lacked "settled, lasting joy" or "such a peace as excludes the possibility either of fear or doubt."[214] The most he could affirm was "I nevertheless trust that I have a measure of faith and am 'accepted in the Beloved'" (Eph.1:5-6). His theology was transformed by and into missiology in field preaching.

We should be most grateful for the honest "confession that is good for the soul" which John Wesley shared with his movement. This is as current for 2018 as it was for 1738. Most Christians can identify with John Wesley when he wrote confessionally on January 9, 1739, seven and a half months after Aldersgate:

"My desire, though not gross and lustful, has been almost continually running toward this or that person. For many years I have been, yea, and still am, hankering after a happiness in loving and in being loved by one or another. And in these persons, I have from time to time taken more pleasure than in God. ...I have now and then some starts of joy in God; but it is not that joy; I have peace in my heart but it is not always that peace. I have health, strength, friends, a competent fortune, and a composed, cheerful temperament. Who would not have peace in such circumstances? But I have not a "peace that passeth all understanding."[215]

His self-examination found him short on "joy in the Holy Ghost, full assurance or witness of the Spirit with my spirit that

---

[214] Op. cit., Ward & Heitzenrater, *JWW*, J&D, , Vol. 19, 18

[215] Ibid., 30

I am a child of God, much less 'in Christ a new creature.'" Then, after reflection and study of scriptures, he added, "Nevertheless I trust that I am reconciled to God through His Son." In reaching that conclusion, he footnoted St. Paul's words in Colossians 2:14, "God made you alive with him when he forgave us all our trespasses, erasing the record that stood against us with its legal demands. These he set aside by nailing them to the cross."[216] In other words, our assurance is the assurance of God's grace, not the assurance confirmed by one's feeling.

He did not share publicly what he confessed privately. On January 25, he wrote, "I baptized John Smith and four other adults at Islington. Of the adults I have baptized lately, only one was at that time born again in the higher sense of the word; that is, had found a thorough, inward change by the love of God in her heart. Most of them were only born again in the lower sense, i.e. received the remission of their sins. And some (as it since too plainly appeared) not even in the lower sense."[217]

Ted Runyon analyzed Wesley's reflection on Moravianism. "As the source of the event, God remains the Holy Other, the external referent, the same transcendent Source we see in Scripture, tradition, 'Holy Conferencing,' and mature reflection (reason)."[218] This seems to be a dimension of what Wesley called, "prevenient grace." That is, being saved is divinely initiated. God whispers to the heart. In the vernacular of Leonard Sweet, God "nudges." Long ago, Methodists called this "being under conviction." These preceded Aldersgate.

After Aldersgate, Wesley became increasingly suspicious of the Moravian understanding of the role of feelings. Rather, Christian experience means participating in the reconciliation of God and humankind, a salvation event that was initiated by God, not the seeker. This qualification did not mean that Wesley's newly found experience of God's grace was not real. Indeed, it was like fire in his bones. The affirmation that we are justified by grace remained a central part of both Wesleys, but they were careful to affirm that salvation is a manifestation of God's love, not an expression of human enthusiasm or emotionalism.

---

[216] Ibid., 19

[217] Ibid., 32

[218] Op. cit., Runyon, 95-96

Also contrary to the Moravians, he was very Arminian, insisting that Jesus died for all humankind. God used the Moravians to tutor John Wesley, but their education was very provincial in their Germany pietism. John Wesley, on the other hand, was an ordained Anglican priest and Fellow of Lincoln College. He "brought to the table" the light from many lamps and the spiritual insight from Eastern Christianity, Roman Catholic saints, Enlightenment philosophers, Puritan dissenters, and Anglican orthodoxy, as well as his own journey. The Moravians were much more parochial in their knowledge of what God had done in other faith communities.

Aldersgate Reconsidered and Reaffirmed

Many years later, Wesley was still of that conviction as he wrote to a friend, "It is undoubtedly our privilege to 'rejoice evermore' with a calm, and heartfelt joy. Nevertheless, this is seldom long at one stay. Many circumstances cause it to ebb and flow. This is not the essence of religion. The essence is no other than humble, gentle, patient love."[219] In short, our spiritually exuberant feelings are not the dependable source of inner peace. Feelings, as Wesley said, "ebb and flow." The solid rock of our faith is our confidence in the Scriptures that God's love is steadfast and immovable. God is still standing when our faith enters a twilight zone. Wesley came to prefer the words "trust" and "confidence." Therefore, as we seek a recovery of Aldersgate, we must find it through reassessment.

Parkes Cadman, a British-born American Congregationalist, wrote of Methodism,

"Many streams fed the mighty river of gracious influence which issues from Wesley's personality, a river still flowing, and bearing the life of men toward a happier heaven beyond."220

Dr. Cadman was right. Wesley had the benefit of philosophical and theological reflection. He was deeply steeped in the Church's

---

[219] Wesley's letter to Ann Loxdale in 1782. Copied from Theodore Runyon's "
The Importance of Experience for Faith," IN Maddox's *Aldersgate Reconsidered,*
   Kingswood, 1990, 105

[220] Op. cit., Cadman, 239

tradition, and he was a master student of the Scriptures. What he lacked was the confirmation of God's grace, that is, the experience of knowing God's forgiving love, not just for "the world," but for himself. That is the hallmark of Methodism.

Rupert Davies of British Methodism sees Wesley's internalization of Aldersgate in these ways:

- **"Psychologically**, he had spent much of his energy brooding upon the state of his soul and trying to improve it. Now those energies were released, and immediately directed outward to those of his fellow men who stood in need of the same liberation as he had received. Personal salvation for himself was no longer his all-absorbing aim. In fact, he virtually found it in his enterprise to bring salvation to others. Sure enough, tired and weary with his used tools in his hands, he found what he had been seeking."

- **"Theologically**, after at least thirteen years of intensely seeking personal holiness, he saw that he had missed the personal witness of the Holy Spirit that Jesus Christ was not only Savior of the world, but his personal Savior. He realized that without that personal relationship with Jesus Christ, it is useless to try to be holy."

British Methodist preacher, William Sangster, wrote, "Wesley blended the Protestant ethic of grace with the Catholic ethic of holiness."[221] The more Wesley searched the Scriptures, read the lives of the saints, and dialogued in what he called "holy conversation," the more Wesley discovered that the Moravian emphasis on feeling tended to make faith totally subjective. Wesley's position was that the final authority of faith is what he called "trust and confidence" in God. "He could not ignore the fact that there were fundamental differences between his understanding of experience and that of the Moravians."[222]

Let us go to Dr. Richard Heitzenrater who has an encyclopedic memory of "all that is Wesley." On the last page of his essay, *Great Expectations: Aldersgate and the Evidences of Genuine*

---

[221] Op. cit., Sangster, 27

[222] Op. cit., Runyon, 103

Christianity,[223] the wise old Wesleyan scholar tells us, "Aldersgate is the point in his spiritual pilgrimage at which he experienced the power of the Holy Spirit and at which his theology is dominated by pneumatology (work of the Holy Spirit)." Here is my own summary of Heitzenrater's synopsis of Wesley's main challenges to the Moravians:

- **There are degrees of faith.** We grow from a weak faith to a mature faith, or as St. Paul put it from being "a babe in Christ, nurtured by milk, to nurture by meat."

- **The means of grace should be encouraged.** They must never be "ends" but are means to the ends of spiritual nourishment and growth in "grace upon grace."

- **Justification (or forgiveness) does not necessarily result in assurance.** It is an awakening of the soul. It is the threshold of grace. We are forgiven by the love of God, and being saved cannot be measured by our feelings. We might feel the assurance in the instance of a "God Moment" and frustratingly lack that emotional assurance sometime later. Salvation depends on the unfailing grace of God. (John 3:16)

  There are "seasons" of assurance. Feelings are an attribute of humanity that can be fickle, that ebb and flow with changes in life circumstances and life seasons. Assurance must be based on our trust and confidence in God, not in our feelings.

- **Doubt and fear** can return with circumstances and life seasons, and depend on our psychological disposition. Christians are like snowflakes; no two are identical.

- **Sanctification or *"perfecting grace"* is the call of the Spirit to grow with "grace upon grace."** As we grow, God heals, restores, and brings the "balm of Gilead" to the sinsick soul that is forever buffeted by temptations and human weakness, enabling us to be free from sin, *one day at a time.*

---

[223] Op. cit., Heitzenrater, Richard, *"Great Expectations,"* 88-89

- **Full love, peace, and joy** *come to some occasionally, some consistently, and to some, never.*

In what Wesley occasionally called "experimental divinity" and more often is called "practical divinity," we see a mingling of what he owed to the Anglicanism of his Epworth and Oxford years and the pietism of the Moravians that brought him to Aldersgate, and what we Methodists call "grace theology." Wesley also loved the term "scriptural way of salvation." It is salvation by God's grace through our faith: the spiritual discipline enhanced by the practice of means of grace which were a discipline to prevent backsliding and "working out your own salvation" through acts of mercy and deeds of kindness.

At the Conference of 1744, Wesley used his customary "Q & A" to adopt a standardized doctrine to preach, the method of teaching and evangelizing, and the practice of holy living. To do this he presented, and answered questions with answers that the lay preachers would hold in common.[224]

- **What to teach?**
  To the first question, regarding doctrines, four were defined: "Repentance, Justification by Faith, Assurance or "witness of the Spirit" but with the understanding that Christians had differing degrees of faith, and Sanctification is spiritual growth or "grace upon grace."

- **How to teach the doctrines and the means of grace?**
  To the second question, the response was "invite, convince, offer Christ; then build up the fellowship." To guide this process, the General Rules were adopted at the first annual conference. The oversimplification, but helpful summary, of the General Rules are (a) Do no harm, (b) Do all the good you can, and (c) Attend public worship regularly. The "means of grace" were emphasized: prayer, searching the scriptures, frequent communion, "holy conversation," and public worship.

- **What to do?**
  The third question, "What to do?" in Wesley's day meant the affirmation of loyalty to the Church of England.[225] Later

---

[224] Op. Cit,, Heitzenrater, *People Called Methodists, 144-145*

[225] Ibid., 145

"what to do" meant "acts of mercy and deeds of kindness" which differentiated Methodism from Moravianism's "stillness and sitting quietly before God." While Wesley did not believe that we are saved by good works, he did believe that the saved will do good works. He questioned Luther's insistence on *sola fide* ("only faith") because faith results in good works.

For two years after Aldersgate, Wesley launched the Methodist Revival with his preaching, his class meetings and societies, his tracts, and his ingenious organization skills. He also incorporated much of what he learned from the Moravians, but he used the term "witness of the Spirit," a doctrine for which he drew heavily from Paul's eighth chapter of Romans.

Feelings are tricky, depending on our psyche. Many years ago, Dr. Carlyle Marney helped me in my own concern that I did not have a dramatic "born again" experience. He said to a group of us young ministers, "Don't let a strike of lightning weaken your faith. Pack up your tools and go to work. Work hard for God every day. Soldier on as a servant. Then, walking home one day, tired and weary with your toolbox in your hand, you will meet Him. That day you will know you are a son." [226] Those words kept me in the ministry. *(The same is true for daughters.)*

Both Richard Heitzenrater and Randy Maddox use the term "orthopathy" to describe Wesley's theology. That is, God's saving grace has an inherent essence of healing. Maddox tracked Wesley's spiritual odyssey to Eastern Christianity's emphasis on inner healing. Wesley adopted the language of the clinic over the language of the court. He called being saved, "taking the cure." He considered personal scriptural salvation as "restoration of the image of God" that we see in Genesis 1:27.

Randy Maddox, always helpful in interpreting Wesley, has concluded that one's interpretation of what God did with Wesley at Aldersgate is influenced by the interpreter's own theology as much as by Wesley's experience! The preachers have often been the interpreters. Maddox sees the prevailing interpretation of Aldersgate through the lens of historical eras, using an American Methodist calendar.

---

[226] Marney, Carlyle, This writer's notes from a lecture at Lake Junaluska, North Carolina, 1969.

- **From 1760-1850,** Aldersgate was ordinarily interpreted as Wesley's conversion. The narrative was used in preaching as a means of inviting seekers to an "Aldersgate experience" of one's heart being "strangely warmed." This meant "a thorough change of heart and life from sin to holiness." He uses an American Methodist calendar.

- **From 1850-1870,** some widespread homework into Wesley's late journaling convinced many scholars that "It is not at all clear that this event was such a dramatic and thorough change in Wesley's life, as he admitted later himself.[227] Research into Wesley's own diaries began to affirm that before 1738, Wesley was already a Christian. The difference was that prior to Aldersgate, the emphasis was on obedience to God and holy living, whereas after Aldersgate, the emphasis was on God's love in which we have trust and confidence, but not always euphoric assurance.

- **From 1870-1890,** Methodist seminaries were being built, and the British "Oxford Movement" rediscovered Wesley's Anglicanism. Except in churches still "holding revivals," conversion was giving way to "gradualism" as the journey to discipleship was defined in the Sunday School literature.

- **By the 1880's,** the "holiness movement" called Aldersgate a "second work of grace," "second blessing" or "baptism of the Holy Spirit" that nullifies our "carnal nature." The doctrine, using Wesley's terminology was called either "sanctification" or "Christian Perfection." After the 1920's the major academic center for holiness teaching was Asbury Theological Seminary. Nazarenes, Free Methodists, Salvation Army, and Wesleyan Methodists adopted this as their standard interpretation of Aldersgate. Too little credence has been given to the reality that Wesley himself wrote and preached the "witness of the Spirit" and "grace upon grace" or "perfect love." It is now usually called "perfecting grace." By this time, and until the 1960's most "professions of faith" came through the Sunday School, not the mourner's bench.

- **From 1900-1963,** Methodist scholars showed the influence of German theologian, Friedrich Schleiermacher. During

---

[227] Maddox, *"A Tradition History,"* IN *Aldersgate Reconsidered,* 136

this era, American Methodism was embracing "19th century liberalism." We can see it in Gilbert Rowe's *Meaning of Methodism*, published in 1926. The essence of this era was Rowe's answer to the question, "What is the object of the Gospel?" His answer: "It is to free us from the bondage of sin and fear and put us in peaceful communion with God and in love and fellowship with one another." There are many theories about religion, and disagreement over speculative questions, but there can be no doubt that essential Christian religion is having the spirit of Jesus Christ."[228] Rowe was very non-sacramental as was Methodism in his generation.

- **In 1934,** Edwin Lewis, with his *A Christian Manifesto*, brought neo-orthodoxy to Methodism. The emerging neo-orthodox movement, fathered by Karl Barth, taught a recovery of the doctrine of original sin. Lewis brought Barthism to Methodism. This brought Wesley more in line with the Protestant Reformers like Luther and Calvin. Some called it "neo-Wesleyanism." It was preached and taught as Wesley's Aldersgate rejection of "works righteousness" and dependence on the Reformation doctrine of justification by faith. Its weakness of accuracy was that it negated Wesley's high-Anglican heritage of "holy living."

- **In 1938,** World Methodism celebrated the bicentennial of Aldersgate with a flurry of books and celebrations, once again giving Wesley's experience a "conversionist" interpretation. From that time, in Methodism, Aldersgate became the defining interpretation of evangelism. Wesley's spiritual journey up until Aldersgate was defined as "his search for a satisfying religious experience."[229] The interpretation was that Wesley's experience on May 24, 1738, is emblematic of what every Christian's should be. Harry Denman, Executive Secretary of the Board of Evangelism of The Methodist Church, dedicated his long lay ministry to the recovery of a Wesley-like experience as the definitive conversion of every Methodist. However, the prevailing emphasis of post-World War II Methodism was Christian education, camping, youth retreats, and conventional Christian morality.

---

[228] Rowe, Gilbert, *The Meaning of Methodism*, Cokesbury Press, 1926, 18-19

[229] Ibid., 141

- None of the above were the overarching emphasis of Methodism by the 1950's. By that time, the seminaries and denominational leaders were committed more to merger with the Evangelical United Brethren and other merger conversations. The era of Christian Education as "queen" was giving way to ecumenism, not to evangelism.

- Few were the prophets who foresaw the decline of the Sunday School, the effects of the 1960's cultural revolution, the end of the Baby Boom, the sheer formality of confirmation, and the rise of social justice issues that would almost mute any and all emphasis of Wesley.

Whatever Wesley's "spiritual temperature" at the several seasons of his life and ministry, he did two things that we all must do. First, he kept "examining his heart." Secondly, he kept preaching, remembering Peter Bohler's words, "Preach faith until you have it; then, because you have it, you will preach faith."

If we read Wesley closely, and if we are as honest in examining our own souls as Wesley was, we know that we also have the need to re-process, reinterpret, and reflect deeply, asking, "Is it well with my soul?" There are times in life when the Holy Spirit gives us a deep sense of peace and joy. However, we know that there have been times when, as Wesley put it to Bohler, "the oil in my lamp burns low." Let us take heart that the founder of Methodism kept working, kept preaching, kept praying, kept searching the Scriptures during these times of what he called "doubt and fear." The witness of the Spirit is a dynamic relationship, not a static one.

Maddox helps again in saying that Aldersgate represents a paradigm that "changes our motivation from seeking *to insure* God's acceptance to our *living out* of that acceptance."[230] Aldersgate is not a rigid model of every Christian's being "born again" at an identifiable moment in one's spiritual journey. We must incorporate the "witness of the Spirit," which leads us toward an emotional or mystical experience, with the work of God in Christ. Wesley reaches for St. Paul's support that "removes all imagination of merit from man, and gives God the whole glory of his own work."[231] The wellspring of saving grace is not our feeling, "for it

---

[230] Op. cit., Maddox, *"A Traditional History,"* IN *Aldersgate Reconsidered,* 143

[231] Wesley, John, Sermon #85, *"On Working Out Our Own Salvation,"* JWW, Vol. 1, 202-203

is God that worketh in you both to will and to work for his good pleasure."[232] God provides in us the energy for doing good works: the motivation and the power. God infuses every good desire, accompanies it, and follows it. God's infusion of grace is a dimension of *Imago Dei* (Genesis 1:27).

Even the author of Ecclesiastes realized that "God hath planted eternity in the human heart" (Ecclesiastes 3:11). This implanted grace whispers to our souls, nudges us, and makes an "inward impression on the soul" which places us under conviction of our estrangement from our heavenly Father. This "nudging" calls us home as we, like the prodigal son, "come to our self." Repentance is proactive and calls us to "rise and follow Jesus." We then "walk through the threshold of grace" into a long-life journey of divine-human encounters. All of these are "syncretistic." Each of us can grow in grace, or, if we quench the Spirit and reject God's "nudges," we can slowly grow further from God's whispers. We grow in grace if we follow the advice of Psalm 46:10, "Be still and know that I am God."

Some experiences of "witness of the Spirit" are intermittent "God moments" or "baptisms" of the Spirit like Elijah's hearing "the still, small voice" at Horeb. These can be interpreted as instantaneous conversion, but seen from a macro view of our spiritual journey, they are gradual experiences of "grace upon grace." Thus, Wesley loves to use the term "growing" in grace just as growth occurs in the plant world or learning occurs in the mind or training occurs in the domesticated animal world.

So, it is most of us have our "Aldersgate." Some are more "game changers" than others in our lifestyle, relationships, or disposition. Our lives have many dimensions, many relationships, many trials. We live not by sight but "by faith in God's grace" until we breathe our last. For Wesley, at age eighty-eight, that was expressed at his last with a soft but firm affirmation, "Best of all; God is with us."

As two of his sisters were dying, they were asked if they were ready to die. Their answer, with a nod and a gentle nod was, "Methodists die well." That, in final analysis, is the litmus paper test for Aldersgate.

The prayer of Methodism, and of every Methodist today, is to

---

[232] Philippians 2:12-13

study Aldersgate and pray, "Do it again, Lord, do it again." Let us make it personal: "Do it to me, Lord, do it to me."

CHAPTER SEVEN

Methodism Is Born, Takes Unique Shape

Hallmarks of Methodist Missiology

While Wesley was characteristically still reflecting on his experience of salvation at Aldersgate, God provided a ringing call to mission. In the spring of 1739, George Whitefield issued a "Macedonian call" to come to Bristol and preach in open fields, mine shafts, and factory gates without notes and to pray extemporaneously. Wesley saw in Whitefield's "SOS" letters that God was now calling him to move out of a time of deep reflection and invest himself in the needs of the world around him.

The context for Wesley's ministry is important. A real case can be made that Methodist polity emerged out of missiology more than tradition, doctrine, or preliminary planning. In Bristol in 1739, form followed function. In so many ways, he demonstrated that he was a pragmatist. With a different paradigm, he was still "finding a need and meeting it."

Our tendency in regaling the unparalleled puzzle of Methodism is to describe Aldersgate as a norm for everyone and growth as the phenomenal consequence that can be birthed anew in our time. The first fact is that Britain does not have another Wesley and American Methodism does not have another Francis Asbury. Secondly, twenty-first century culture with its most recent phenomenon of social media is radically different from previous generations. The paradigm is radically different. We cannot plant the cultural or spiritual dynamics of early Methodism in the vastly different context of the twenty-first century.

However, we can look carefully and listen intently to the mission and message of the first hundred years of Methodism in

England and America, and from that reverential inquiry, we can be led by the Holy Spirit to new wineskins for the taste of new wine. As William Sangster wrote in pre-World War II England, "Methodism can be born again."

Socio-economic Context of the Methodist Revival

Once again, let us look at "The Church" of Wesley's England. Of the 11,000 Anglican parishes or "livings" in 1750, 6,000 were occupied by men who lived in London or on the continent and farmed their parishes out to curates, whose training and pay were both paltry. Puritanism, which had brought revival to English religion in the seventeenth century, had dwindled in numbers and had been splintered by doctrinal hair-splitting. Also, the Industrial Revolution brought the rise of factory life and break-up of strong village ethos, eroded morals, and fractured family structures.

In Wesley's England, there was no middle class. Peasants were condemned to peasantry from one generation to the next. The lower classes were economically helpless, emotionally demoralized, and for the most part, morally irresponsible.[233] To these of God's children who did not know the meaning of the word "dignity," and certainly not a word like "child of God," Wesley talked about salvation:

- as "taking the cure"

- or "being restored to your original identity as a human being who was made in the image of God"

- or the self-discipline, by God's grace, to overcome addictions like alcohol abuse, gambling obsession, and physical abuse of wives and children.

Sociologically, Methodism was a child of the Industrial Revolution. Peasants escaped the farm and went to the slum where those who worked the mines, the textile mills, and the new factories lived. The Established Church did not adjust, and hardly any new churches were built. Clergy preferred "livings" where farmland provided extra income but urban parishes had no means for providing parish income. Bristol's population had skyrocketed

---

[233] Sherwin, Oscar, *John Wesley, Friend of the People,* Twayne Publishers: New York, 1961, 39 (paraphrase)

from 29,000 to 100,000 and Liverpool's from 4,000 to 300,000 since the time of Wesley's birth. The poor had to sit at the back of the parish church on backless wood benches and listen to sermons on "referencing your 'betters.'" Class-lines were rigidly drawn. Typical Anglican religion in that day argued that the masses should obey their "uppers."

Hugh Price Hughes, a leading Methodist voice, said, "The Methodists were the first preachers since the days of the Franciscan friars who reached the working classes. The Reformation on the continent was essentially a middle-class movement." For the crushed and despised to be told over and over again that God loves them, that they could be saved from their sins and given "grace-strength" to resist habitual temptations, sounded strange to their ears, and astonished them with a new sense of dignity and hope.

For hundreds and then thousands, the sermons, singing, revivalistic "group-think," and outpouring of the Holy Spirit resulted in awakened souls. Attendees, of whom there were about 70,000 by Wesley's death, learned "earnestness, sobriety, industry, and regularity of conduct."[234] By the grace of God, many of these converts became "exhorters, class meeting leaders, lay preachers, or stewards." By the time of his death, in England alone, Wesley had "set aside" over eight thousand persons in one of the leadership roles. Parkes Cadman wrote, "Mob leaders became class leaders."[235] It is quite amazing that a person of John Wesley's disposition, education, and cultural sophistication could entrust the Methodist movement to unlettered laity.

For the most part, Anglican worship was highly liturgical, was regimented by the *Book of Common Prayer*, and sermons were defined as "a dull discourse on a boring subject." The bands, classes, and societies were adopted and adapted by Wesley because of their missional value for reaching people and enhancing their lives. He knew well that most of those attending his services were uneducated and there he wanted to "unite those two so long disjoined – knowledge and vital piety." To that end,

- "He kept and dramatically changed Whitefield's "Kingswood School" outside Bristol.

---

[234] Ibid., 35-37

[235] Op. cit., Cadman, 310

- He also wrote numerous books and pamphlets sold at two pence each and written in the most basic vocabulary.

- He campaigned for the improvement of prisons.

- He opened dispensaries for the sick poor.

- He worked with authorities to counteract smugglers at the ports of Cornwall.

- He worked to abolish "that execrable villainy, the scandal of religion: slavery."[236]

Wesley had a choice. Would he try to reform England from the top down, with his being an Oxford don and an intellectual with lots of well-placed contacts? The answer was, "No." Wesley referred to Paul's description of the Corinthian Church in the description of the Methodists: "Not many of you were wise by human standards, not many were powerful, not many were of noble birth" (I Corinthians 1:26b). His evangelical promise was, "He (God) is the source of your life in Christ Jesus, "who became for us wisdom from God, and righteousness and holiness and redemption" (I Corinthians 1:30).

Wesley's work in London was experiencing phenomenal response. Societies were springing up among all social classes. The last Sunday in February, 1739, John preached three times: near the Tower of London, rural Islington in the afternoon, and back near the Tower at 5:00 where three hundred were gathered to hear him. However, his ministry was about to change.

"That Vile Thing" – Open Air Preaching

Rupert Davies, an English Methodist scholar, has written, "The originator of the Methodist revival was neither John nor Charles Wesley, but George Whitefield (1714-1770)."[237] Shut out of London churches, George Whitefield left for Bristol soon after the 1739 New Year's Eve meeting on Fetter Lane where the group sensed that God was going to do something in him and through them. In Bristol, he found a spectacular response to his preaching

---

[236] Op. cit., Davies, (selected and adapted from his book, *Methodism*, 78-80

[237] Op. cit., Davis,56

in open air to the miners as they emerged from the bowels of the earth, covered in coal dust, carrying the lanterns that lit the black holes, and one of them carrying the canary cage. If the canary quit singing, the miners knew oxygen in the mine was getting low and they must quickly evacuate. That was their daily danger and to them George Whitefield preached the "good tidings of great joy." Many were converted, but Whitefield had a commitment to take John Wesley's place as pastor of Christ Anglican Church in Savannah, Georgia. So, his ministry was to be short-lived.

Wesley in the West Country - Bristol

In March, 1739, a letter came from Whitefield in Bristol England's "West Country," asking Wesley to come and take his place. The "Macedonian call" was for him to come to Bristol and preach in open fields and mine shafts and factory gates without notes, and to pray extemporaneously. Shocked by Whitefield's letter, Charles Wesley wrote, "We strove to dissuade my brother from going to Bristol from an unaccountable fear that it would prove fatal to him."[238]

A second "Macedonian call" letter came from Whitefield. John put Whitefield's proposal before the faith community at Fetter Lane. He considered open air preaching "a vile thing" and hesitated. "Wesley was reluctant to leave London, and his brother Charles vehemently opposed his doing this." In their complexity they reverted to the customary practice of letting the Bible fall open and reading as God's message for them the first words that their eyes fell on. Charles opened his Bible at the words of Ezekiel 24:16ff, "Mortal, behold I take away in one stroke the desires of thine eyes; yet neither shall you mourn or weep...." Upon this he (Charles) withdrew his opposition and John decided to go to Bristol.[239] John saw in Whitefield's "SOS" letters that God was now calling him to move out of a time of deep reflection and extreme "self-examination," and to invest himself in the needs of the world around him. John went west, reaching Bristol and meeting with Whitefield on March 31, 1739.

Whitefield was returning to America. He preached his farewell sermons the very next day to "all ranks of society, including

---

[238] Ibid., 152

[239] Op. Citl, Cadman, 293

the rich in their coaches, others on horseback, and most on foot." Wesley was shocked. "I could scarce reconcile myself to this strange way of preaching in the fields ... having been all my life so tenacious of every point relating to decency and order, that I should have thought the saving of souls almost a sin, if it had not been done in a church."[240] His own first sermon was from Jesus' "Sermon on the Mount," which Wesley realized was "a pretty remarkable precedent of field preaching." More amazingly for an Anglican priest, Wesley had preached without his "canonicals." His robe and vestments were still on the road from London. He wrote, "I want my cassock and gown every day."

On Monday, April 2, he wrote, "I submitted to be more vile, and proclaimed in the highways the glad tidings of salvation, speaking from a little eminence of ground to the city (Hanham Mount), to about 3000 people." His text was the same Isaiah text (61:1-2) that Jesus used in his first sermon at the synagogue. "The Spirit of the Lord is upon me because he has anointed me to preach the gospel to the poor. He has sent me to heal the broken-hearted" (Luke 4:18-19). It occurred to Wesley that Jesus' sermon was in "open air." That was the motivation for his mission to continue "that vile thing" of field preaching and form a grass roots movement. To do the latter would mean that his ministry would be with the teeming masses: the tired, the weak, the addicted, the abusive, the abused, and the poor. *That choice faces every generation and every preacher in which the flame of religious reform is ignited anew.*

The path Wesley chose was to minister to the masses. This eventually cast the die which molded Methodism as a separate denomination. The old wineskins of 18th century Anglicanism could not contain this new wine. When he again visited Oxford, he was to be rebuked by the deans of both Lincoln and Christ Colleges. In the next nine months, John Wesley worked in Bristol, preaching over five hundred times, only eight of them in a church.

George Whitefield was a more powerful preacher than John Wesley, and, within the same time frame, more people were converted under his preaching. He brought that gift to the fields, factory gates, mine shafts, and town squares. As Wesley's successor in Savannah, Whitefield became known as the most flamboyant and effective orator in the colonies. However, Whitefield lacked

---

[240] Op. cit., Ward & Heitzenrater, *JWW*, J & D, Vol. 19, 46

organizational skills.

Wesley on the other hand was a genius in organization. In Bristol, as the miners came to Kingswood, Hanham Mount, and the several Anglican Society meetings, Wesley did not leave their resistance to temptation to their individual will power. The life of sin was too entrenched in habit, language, attitude, and behavior for an instantaneous conversion to complete the process of discipling. He saw the need for small support groups. He also had a passion for "growth in grace" and saw the small groups as the most effective way of encouraging means of grace like searching the Scriptures, prayer, holy conversation in the small groups, and beginning something most had never practiced: worship at the parish churches. But to Wesley, "The main thing was to keep the main thing the main thing." His stated priority was "to save souls" and to organize new groups for fellowship and Christian nurture.

The die was cast. His new method of preaching his faith was bearing incredible fruit in attendance. His mission was "to spread scriptural holiness throughout the land." The people's response was to experience a life change in themselves. To the objection of the Bishop of Bristol, he responded, "I look upon the world as my parish; thus far I mean, that, in whatever part of it I am, I judge it meet, right, and my bounden duty to declare unto all that are willing to hear the glad tidings of salvation."[241]

John Wesley was a patrician in every sense of the word, and had friends in the upper classes who enjoyed his learned conversations, but he followed his calling to the point of greatest need. In one of his letters, he wrote, "My part is to improve the present moment." The Methodist chapel provided an equalitarian fellowship, a civilizing influence including literacy, and religion accented by singing and affirmation. To have always been told in church that you were a "worm" and then to be told in Methodist meeting that you were "created in the image of God" was exhilarating and redemptive. No longer were wages squandered in pubs, cockpits, and whorehouses. Wesley wrote to a critic, "The habitual drunkard is now temperate, the whoremongers flee fornication; he that stole steals no more, but works with his hands; he that cursed or swore perhaps at every sentence has now learned to

---

[241] Op. cit., Davies 67

rejoice with reverence."[242]

So it was that, thanks to the closed-mindedness of the Church, field preaching was like throwing "Br'er Rabbit in the briar patch." "It was by field preaching and in no other possible way that England could be roused from its spiritual slumber, or Methodism be born," wrote an objective critic of Wesley's.

A "Mrs. Hutton," with whom John lodged, wrote, "In the year 1739, open-air preaching commenced in England; for the clergy had closed all their churches against the Methodists. In open air, thieves, prostitutes, fools, people of every class, several men of distinction, a few of the learned, merchants, and hordes of the poor who had never entered a house of worship, assembled and became godly."[243] The Bible says of Jesus, "The common people heard him gladly because he spoke as one with authority, not as the scribes." So it was with John Wesley. As for Wesley, though some question his estimates, he recorded a grand total of 47,500 to have heard him in his first month of preaching out-of-doors in and around Bristol and just into Wales.

Methodism spread quickly to Welsh mine shafts, English factory gates, and town centers as a mission to the last, the least, and the lost. God's children could not get home alone and the Church of England had little interest in shepherding them to the fold.

Kingswood

The story of Kingswood epitomizes the Pentecostal power of the Methodist revival and the genius of John Wesley in converting the ethics of social holiness into a place of learning for those who had never had the opportunity of becoming literate in "ABC's" or functional in arithmetic. Wesley described Kingswood as "the middle of the wood between the London and Bath roads, about three measured miles from Bristol."[244] Mining had created a morass of open mine shafts, coal piles, and hovels where the coal miners lived in abject poverty. There were no schools. George Whitefield not only preached to the colliers (miners), he also had

---

[242] Op. cit., Sherwin, 44

[243] Op. cit., McTyeire, 154 (quoting a letter from a "Mrs. Hutton, widow o James Hutton of Bristol."

[244] Op. cit., Ward and Heitzenrater, *JWW J &D*, Vol. 19, 125

the vision for a school at Kingswood. The "colliers" subscribed money from their pitiable pay, enabling Wesley and Whitefield to build a "charity school!" Wesley followed through with a plan for a two-room building staffed by two schoolmasters. By mid-July, 1739, Charles and John were preaching inside the school in the rain because the roof was not yet in place! It was here, in the dedicatory hymn by Charles Wesley, that the phrase was first coined, "Unite the pair so long disjoined - knowledge and vital piety." [245]

Giving Whitefield the credit for beginning a ministry of evangelism there, Wesley enunciated the results: "Kingswood does not now, as a year ago, resound with cursing and blasphemy. It is no more filled with drunkenness and uncleanness, and the idle diversions that naturally lead thereto. It is no longer full of wars and fighting, of clamor and bitterness, of wrath and envying. Peace and love are there. Great numbers of the people are mild, gentle, and easy to be entreated. The students could be any age, and many gray-heads came to 'learn their letters.' "The curriculum was reading, writing, and 'casting accounts.'"

Dr. Heitzenrater reflected with his knowledge and wisdom, "Wesley's parish was not only without boundaries and his congregation without pedigree, but his concept of ministry was without limits so long as the activities fit into his vision of scriptural Christianity by helping a person receive the wholeness that God's salvation could bring to humanity."[246] For the crushed and despised to be told over and over again that God loves them, that they could be saved from their sins and given "grace-strength" to resist habitual temptations sounded strange to their ears and filled them with a hope they had never known. Years later, in 1753, Wesley wrote of Kingswood, "I have spent more money and time and care on this than almost any design I ever had, and still it exercises all the patience I have. But it is worth all the labour."[247] "This proved to be true for in the course of time it became one of the great schools of England, with a noble succession of masters and scholars, many of whom were distinguished in every branch of learning and in every walk of life. Its fame has

---

[245] Op. cit., Heitzenrater, *Wesley and the People Called Methodists*, 219

[246] Op. cit., 106

[247] *The Historical Tablets of the New Room*, Andreas Haaf & Sons, 1930, 13

spread to the ends of the earth."[248]

When Wesley first visited the Newgate prison in Bristol in 1739, he wrote that the filth, stench, misery, and wickedness shocked him. In 1760, the Methodist influence had altered the situation miraculously. Wesley wrote, "The place is as sweet and clean as a gentleman's house." During the last year of his life, on Sunday morning, 14 March, 1790, he wrote, "I met the Stranger's Society, instituted wholly for the relief, not of our Society, but for the poor, sick, friendless strangers. I do not know that I ever heard of or read of such an institution till within a few years ago. So this also is one of the fruits of Methodism."[249]

Culturally, it was in the West Country that Methodism had perhaps its greatest impact. A lot of the lay preachers from Wales and Ireland are the "fathers of Methodism" in America. In the generation prior to John and Charles Wesley, Anglicans like their own father had sponsored "societies." Even in Georgia under the auspices of S.P.C.K (Society for Promoting Christian Knowledge), there were Anglican societies. In Bristol, he referred in his diary to attending a society at "Nicholas Street," "Baldwin Street," "Back Lane," "Castle Street," and others that were already meeting regularly.

Anglican society meetings, which had been in existence before the outdoor preaching of Whitefield and Wesley, quickly mushroomed and changed. As Anglican societies, they were devoted primarily to "knowledge" whereas under Wesley, the curriculum became both "knowledge and vital piety." The society meeting was the follow up of the large gatherings in the fields. They were the logical new faith community for people whose souls were awakened, who repented of their sins, and intended to "lead a new life following the commandments of God and walking from henceforth in his holy ways."[250]

The New Room is Built in Bristol

For this much of a following, John Wesley needed an indoor

---

[248] Ibid. 13

[249] Ibid., 12

[250] Young, Carlton, ed., *The United Methodist Hymnal, 1989, 26 (from "Invitation" of Service of Word and Table of the former Methodist and Evangelical Brethren Churches)*

preaching place, a training center, a reading room for the unlettered laity to be taught, and a "stay place with beds." Wesley wrote in his *Journal* for May 9, 1739, "We took possession of a piece of ground in the Horsefair (*near the livery stables where people came to rent or buy horses, carriages, carts, etc.*).[251] Wesley associated the word "church" only with Anglican churches. Therefore, he called his building simply "The New Room." "Though he quickly accumulated a debt of a hundred and fifty pounds, he had no money except his stipend from Lincoln College. But as the Bible says of Nehemiah's building the Temple in about 445 B.C.E., "The people had a mind to work" (Nehemiah 4:6). Even though poor, they also had "a mind to give all they could."

"The New Room" construction began soon after the property was acquired in 1739. Still standing, it has a large room where the lay preachers preached under the watchful eye of the Wesleys. Upstairs is a library/reading room, a band room, and bedrooms, including what Wesley described as "a garret in which is placed a bed for me."[252] There were stables for the horses. "In 1741 the New Room in the Horsefair was completed. "[253]

Charles Wesley and his family later moved to Bristol and lived in a brick home nearby. Charles did not itinerate. Later generations of Methodists, many from the United States, built two statues. At one entrance is a life-sized statue of John on a horse. At the other entrance of the New Room, is a life size statue of Charles with his hands open to the street. At the base is engraved a verse he had written. It is the epitome of the Methodist message:

"O let me commend my Saviour to you."[254]

Though the Foundery was called "the cathedral of Methodism," and Wesley's Chapel is called the "mother church of Methodism; it is the New Room in Bristol that lays claim to the title, the "cradle building of Methodism." In the 1930's, the history of the New Room and lots of Wesley's quotes were displayed on the New Room walls as "tablets." They were edited and improved in décor

---

[251] Op. cit., Ward and Heitzenrater, *JWW*, J&D, Vol. 19, 56

[252] Op. cit., Ward and Heitzenrather, *JWW* J & D, Vol. 19, 56

[253] Op. cit., Davies, 62

[254] Ibid. No. 9

in the 1980's, and their contents were published as a booklet, *The Historical Tablets of the New Room.*

The class meetings originated in Bristol although the concept of that paradigm came from Monsieur de Renty, a French Catholic to whose writings Wesley had been attracted, and from Samuel Wesley who organized a "society" in Epworth when Wesley was a teenager. For the Bristol class meetings, immediate credit was given to a "Captain Foy" whose suggestion about the debt on the Room led to "a division of the Society into classes under the care of a leader." [255] Wesley reported that "in two or three days, two hundred and thirty pounds were subscribed."[256] However, that was not enough to amortize the rising indebtedness. Almost immediately, the class meeting became a meeting for encouraging the "babes in Christ" to give, using both testimony and teaching to sustain their spiritual growth, practicing "grace upon grace," and his conviction that though good works do not save a seeker, a saved person will do good works!

Methodism reached all classes, but just the fact that it grew most rapidly in the English "West Country" and in Wales reveals that Wesley gave them religious freedom from their plight long before the government gave them a vote. He had gone to prisons with food and listened to the prisoners' stories since his own student days. He developed what we know as "food pantries." In his second "Sermon on the Mount" sermon, his proposition was "to show that Christianity is essentially a social religion, and that to turn it into a solitary one is to destroy it. "The Gospel of Christ knows of no religion but social, no holiness but social holiness."[257]

Eighteen annual conferences were held in the New Room from 1745 until 1790. At the first, Wesley gave an imperative to lay preachers, "You have nothing to do but to save souls. Therefore spend and be spent in this work. And go always not only to those who need you most, but to all who need you."[258] From the beginning there was a library set up in the New Room, just as there was at the Foundery in London and a meetinghouse in Newcastle.

---

[255] Ibid. No. 4

[256] Ibid. No. 7

[257] Warner, Wellman, *The Wesleyan Movement in the Industrial Revolution,* London, 1930, 266

[258] Op. cit., *The Historical Tablets,* No. 10

Meanwhile, back in London, Charles had been threatened with excommunication from the bishop. John returned to London to encourage his distraught brother. John preached "on the Moor-fields" just east of St. Paul's Cathedral in London to a thousand lost souls. The paradigm of preaching outside an Anglican Church now became "the Methodist way," even in London.

CHAPTER EIGHT

Movement Meets Opposition: Spreads, Grows

Wesley's Syncretistic Theology

From age seventeen until age thirty-two, John Wesley was either a student or a teaching fellow at Oxford University. Oxford had thirty-seven college libraries and it was a time of expansion of the British Empire in Asia, the Middle East, Africa, and Australia. Explorers had brought home troves of observations and some writing from the minds and pens of Muslims, Buddhists, Hindus, Confucians, and Zoroastrians. It was the heyday of what historians call "The Enlightenment" and Wesley was well read in Enlightenment philosophy but did not accept their theology which was Deism. This philosophy is often called "the watchmaker theory" that God created the world and lets it run on its own just as a watchmaker makes a precision watch, but never keeps in touch with its new owner. The eighteenth century was also the climax of the Industrial Revolution.

In Christian theology, John Wesley was shaped by strong mentors. He read and ingested the work of rigidly strong Anglicans who insisted on a life of moral rectitude as the will of God for every Christian. As we noted elsewhere, he was deeply influenced by the writing of Thomas à Kempis, Jeremy Taylor, and William Law. From them, he adopted a lifestyle and a theology of "holy living." He mastered a knowledge of Catholic theology from Augustine in the fifth century forward. He also was drawn to the pre-Augustinian theology developed by the Cappadocians of Eastern Christianity. With "light from these many lamps," he developed a theology of salvation through holy living and self-discipline.

Then in Georgia, he met the Moravians of German pietism who seemed to have in their spiritual life specifically what he

lacked in his own - the witness of the Holy Spirit that gives a
"blessed assurance that Jesus is mine as a personal savior."
However, try as he did, he could not become a Moravian. He could
not accept the Moravian concept of "stillness." He was deeply
couched into his own tradition that includes good works and
degrees of growing in grace through one's faith.

Though Calvinism was the prevailing theology of Anglicanism in the early eighteenth century, Wesley could not escape the
conclusion that Calvinism makes "God the author of evil." He
adopted the theology of Jacob Arminius of The Netherlands and
gave that theological stamp to Methodism in perpetuity. The
bottom line of Arminianism is that Jesus died for everyone and
"whosoever comes to Him he will in no way reject."

England was Anglican. Even generations later, Methodists
would still be called "chapel people," noting not only the humble
meetinghouse they built, but the stratum of society from which
most of the converts and lay preachers came. Indeed, Methodism's
limited influence in England was at least a component of the motivation of lay preachers to migrate to the English colonies in America from the 1760's onward.

He also was a pragmatist who adopted and adapted what he
saw as being effective. In this he was deeply influenced by the
writings of several Enlightenment philosophers like John Locke,
David Hume, Adam Smith, and Montesquieu.

John Wesley was very cosmopolitan in his knowledge when he
taught at Oxford's Lincoln College, but he remained a seeker and
a pragmatist. From "all of the above" and his own spiritual journey, the theology and polity of Methodism were shaped. Now let us
look at the doctrine itself, a doctrine that Dr. Robert Cushman of
Duke Divinity School called "experimental divinity." Most call it
"grace theology." Methodist doctrine was the confluence of many
doctrinal streams and drew light from many lamps. It was shaped
by each and it is different from each: Catholic, Lutheran, Calvinist, Anglican and Moravian theology.

Anglican Church Opposition

Many pulpits were closed to John and Charles Wesley, but
their situation was under more threat than is usually realized.
John and Charles Wesley were ordained Anglican clergy, not independent, roving evangelists or registered Dissenters under the

Toleration Act of 1689. Anglican clergy could not preach anywhere without written permission from their bishop. In the few parishes where the priest had invited Charles or John to preach, they had to present to the Vestry the permit signed by the bishop. This rule was not enforced rigidly, but it was enforceable canon law. Bishop Edmund Gibson of London called in the Wesley brothers in 1739 and "urged them to moderate their actions and undertake more traditional ministerial roles."[259] When John followed George Whitefield in open air preaching in Bristol, word filtered back to London and Charles was suddenly denied pulpits. The Anglican Church at Islington, London, even hired men to prevent his entering the pulpit.[260]

Suffice it to say that for a number of years, John and Charles Wesley were both criticized and ostracized by the Anglican Church to which they assiduously remained loyal by not performing the sacraments in their field preaching, society meetings, or other Methodist venues. They walked a constant tight rope between their loyalty to the Church they loved and their practice of the "new light mission" to which they had been called.

The Wesleys' unorthodox evangelism was well known across Anglican England. The prestigious "St. Martin-in-the-Fields" Church had an attack on the Wesleys published:

"What is this but an outrage upon common decency and common sense? It is folly that approaches very near to madness. They are schismatical; they make religion ridiculous and contemptible. Go not after these imposters and seducers; but shun them as you would the plague."

Contrary to Methodist memory, Charles was considered a more effective preacher than was his brother. Their first official biographer regarded "Charles' sermons as more 'awakening and useful" and John's more "dry and systematic." It was the Archbishop of Canterbury who "summoned Charles and threatened to excommunicate him."[261] Charles was invited to Oxford to preach at St. Mary's but "felt that his words fell on stony ground."

An Anglican minister wrote a book entitled *A Caution Against*

---

[259] Op. cit., Best, 111

[260] Ibid., 114

[261] Ibid. 115

Religious Delusion. In it he accused the Methodists of overturning respect for authority and creating "tumultuous assemblies" which disturbed the public peace by permitting "wild fancies." Biographer Tyerman quoted an Anglican writer,

> "Young quacks in divinity are running around the city, and taking great pains to distract the common people, and to break the peace and unity of the Church. They look upon themselves as exquisite pictures of holiness and patterns of piety; they represent us (the clergy) as dumb dogs, profane, and carnally minded. They talk much of their pangs of new birth, inward feelings, experience, and spiritual miracles, but their faith is an ill grounded assurance and their hope an unwarrantable assumption."[262]

Whatever the criticism, field preaching increasingly attracted hordes of people, the Methodist movement grew, and by the 1740's, one can see the establishment of Methodist ministries in two large buildings, the New Room and the Foundery, and societies in the geographic triangle of London, Bristol, and Newcastle upon Tyne in the north. Within that triangle Wesley preached in hundreds of villages and city settings. Beyond that triangle, he established a strong Methodism in Wales and in Ireland. (He crossed the Irish Sea fifty-four times.)

It is not historically accurate to paint a "rosy picture" of the ministry of John Wesley or the growth of the Methodists in England. The opposition was constant and from many sources. In so many ways, John Wesley was not the revolutionary which would arouse such opposition from the establishment. His manner was conservative, as was his politics. He loved the British Empire and obeyed every law he knew. He loved the Church of England and never left it. He tried mightily to place his converts under the care of Anglican pastors, desperately wanting his "babes in Christ" to have access to the sacraments. Yet, he was consistently branded "an Enthusiast." The Anglican bishops did not place new churches in the growing cities. Most priests still were provided "livings," which meant rural farm and pasture land!

The Bishop of Bristol, in England's West Country bordering Wales and Cornwall, said to Wesley, "Sir, since you ask my advice, I will give it freely – you have no business here. You are not

---

[262] Ibid. 119

commissioned to preach in this diocese; therefore I advise you to go hence." Wesley explained that he had been ordained at Lincoln College, not by a diocesan bishop. He concluded, "I have no parish, nor probably ever shall.... I look upon all the world as my parish. I am ordained to preach in any parish of the Church of England; I must preach the gospel anywhere in the habitable world; indeed the world is my parish. Therefore here I stay for now."[263] The bishop did not contest the well-taken point of ecclesiastical law and closed the interview. (Bristol and Wales became the largest centers of Methodism.) Though his brother Samuel constantly warned John of possible excommunication, and Charles objected to field preaching, John Wesley knew that the Bishop of Bristol had shared with his peers this "loophole" in canon law which limited their control over John Wesley who was ordained at Oxford University, not a diocesan center.

The Bishop of London had complaints from everywhere: vicars, deans, curates, rectors, chaplains, and other bishops. He called the Wesleys to his chambers to see if they really were preaching the full assurance of personal salvation. Almost uniformly, the sole means of grace accentuated in the 18th century Anglican Church were the sacraments; to the bishop, baptism and the Eucharist were sufficient means of grace. Would anyone dare subject the sanctity of Christianity to the whims and fancies of feelings and emotions? He seemingly ignored Wesley's faithful practice of "holy living" which he learned from the divines of his Anglican theology. As time bore out, Wesley's insistence of experimental grace and other means of grace like prayer, searching the Scriptures, holy conversation, and attending church were great additions and, to a degree, the genius of Methodist grace theology. The old wineskins simply could not yield enough to accommodate the Wesleyan revival in England, and Anglicans were not about to sanction the ordination of uneducated lay preachers in America. Anglicanism missed the opportunity to benefit from a paradigm shift.

Ignoring Wesley's journey of holy living and means of grace, Anglican bishops called the Methodists "antinomians" for preaching justification by faith only. To this Wesley replied, "Can anyone preach otherwise who agrees with our Church and the Scriptures?" The Bishop responded with a fifty-five page "Pastoral

---

[263] Op. cit., Cadman, 303

Letter to the people of London on Caution against Lukewarmness on the one hand and Enthusiasm on the other." Two-thirds of it was invective against the Methodists before one Methodist society was formed. Were the Wesley brothers heretics? When, in 1755, the Bishop of London excommunicated one of the Methodist lay preachers, John said to Charles, "If we must *dissent* or be *silent,* it is all over. Adieu."[264]

- The Anglicans because of the Wesleys' outdoor preaching and evangelical enthusiasm

- The Moravians because Wesley kept his belief that we are saved to do good deeds, not to retreat into a cocoon and "be still." They also did not believe that faith can be "in degrees" but the converted person was instantaneously free of doubt or fear. Wesley refuted them with St. Paul's use of the term "babes in Christ."

- Lastly, Calvinism was a theological opponent. Methodism's co-leaders were the Wesley brothers and George Whitefield. As their spiritual journey's advanced, Whitefield became a Calvinist and Wesley deepened his conviction to be an Arminian. Calvinists believed that God's grace is granted to only the elect and that God preordains everything. Arminians believe that God's grace is granted to every human, and that we are given the free will to accept it.

Methodism had several Christian opponents:

- As Methodism grew, so did opposition, not only from the unchurched, but from other Christian communions: the Anglicans, the Moravians, and the Calvinists.

From 1732 through Wesley's death, 606 officially published articles or books attacked either the Wesleys as persons or Methodism as a sect. Against them were the mob, the clergy, the aristocracy, and the press. But Wesley pressed on. He preached in the Yorkshire moors, the Cornish wastelands, the Welsh mountains, the cheap inns, the factory gates, the mine shafts, the pub yards, and the streets where mud and raw sewage made all gentlemen ride in carriages. John Wesley, clergyman, professor, evangelist,

---

[264] Op. cit., Tomkins, 151

walked ... and walked ... and walked. When he rode, it was a solitary rider on horseback, usually reading as the horse plodded the
paths.

His fear of excommunication gradually abated, but most
pulpits remained closed to Wesley. A number of Anglican *divines*
loved to preach on the texts, "Be not righteous overmuch," and
"Let your moderation be known to all." They also abhorred enthusiasm in any form, and were still paranoid about the Puritanism
of the Cromwell era.

Until the 1760's Wesley would beg the Bishop of London
annually to ordain Methodist preachers for America, but was
always denied. Yet the fields, as Jesus said, "were white unto
harvest." There were vast areas of the colonies where no Anglican clergy was available to baptize the children or administer the
Holy Eucharist. Hundreds were being converted, but unlike the
Baptists, the Methodist preachers could not baptize or celebrate
The Lord's Supper.

Wesley and the Moravians

As an Anglican, Wesley led a devoutly disciplined holy life
that was confirmed by what he learned from his mother as
"sincerity." However, on board ship as a missionary pastor headed
to Georgia when he was thirty-two years old, he met a group of
German pietists called Moravians. They had something he lacked
- assurance of their salvation. As we have rehearsed, the Moravians had a deep influence on him for the next five years. We have
traced that influence leading to and following Aldersgate, but the
relationship with the Moravians was always strained. We dare not
romanticize the Methodist-Moravian relationship.

The trouble which arose with the Moravians was the fault line
between German pietism rooted in the Reformation and English
pietism rooted in Anglicanism.

- Anglican theology called for a life disciplined in the "image
  of Christ" that resulted in "holy living." That included
  acts of mercy and deeds of kindness, but lacked assurance. The contrast between his Anglican understanding of
  "holy living" and the Moravian insistence on *"sola fide"* or
  "faith alone" was so sharp that he used the term "strangely
  warmed" to interpret his Aldersgate experience.

- The Moravian position that Wesley could never accept was their insistence that justification and sanctification were a simultaneous and instantaneous *fait accompli* followed by meditative "stillness." They believed that following that emotional experience, you had no doubt or fear; just peace and joy. Wesley's post Aldersgate experience, even after a summer with the Moravians in Germany, had not been that serene!

- He believed in "degrees of faith." He cited St. Paul in his insistence that a Christian can be a "babe in Christ" and have only degrees of faith, and that all Christians are subject to having "a spiritual funk." The Church of England and, before it, the Catholic Church, had believed in a journey of growing in grace by such "means" as praying, searching the Scriptures, taking communion, having mentoring relationships, and going to church!

Less than a year after Aldersgate, John Wesley had spent three months in Germany, had begun open air preaching in Bristol and Bath, had purchased and begun construction on the New Room, developed "The United Societies" in the West Country, and had begun open air preaching in London. The revival had begun, both in and around Bristol and in London. Obviously, he was not going back to Oxford to teach nor was he going into parish ministry.

He was building an organization, a "connexion" of lay preachers, exhorters, and stewards; an organizationally ingenious way to draw large crowds to hear him preach, to train laity to be leaders, and to publicize his writing ministry. He also still felt a commitment to the needs of the poor and wanted "social holiness" always to be a major commitment of Methodism. This was demonstrated in the multiple ministries of the New Room which provided a "West Country" base, but he needed a London base.

1739: Wesley Left Moravians; Leased old Foundery

The conflict with the Moravians worsened. Then, "On October 31, 1739, two businessmen approached him to create a preaching house in London similar to the one in Bristol. They suggested that he lease and renovate a large brick building on Windmill Street near Finsbury Square. They offered him the capital with which to remodel the cavernous building. It was called the Foundery because it had originally been built by the Royal Navy to re-cast bronze cannons captured by the Duke of Marlborough at Blenheim on the Upper Danube in Bavaria, but the building was abandoned in 1716. 'The grounds were laid out pleasantly with walks and promenades, shaded by trees, and in summertime decorated with flowers and shrubs."[265]

For Wesley's multiple needs, its cavernous interior was perfect. He raised the money to lease the building for £115 and to spend £800 to upgrade what he called "this vast uncouth heap of ruins" into what was euphemistically dubbed "the cathedral of Methodism." It stood just east of St. Paul's Cathedral. The Foundery "band room" or chapel held 1,500 people! At the end of the chapel were rooms for the preachers when they were in London. The north end was petitioned for a school, the south end became a "Book Room" for retailing Methodist literature. Above the band room were apartments in which Susanna, Emily, and Hetty lived. Susanna died there in 1742. There were also rooms for John, traveling preachers, and domestic staff.

By the following summer, Wesley tired of arguing with the Moravians at Fetter Lane in London about their doctrine of "stillness" and their objection to his emphasis on deeds of kindness and acts of mercy as part and parcel of being Christian. According to some good research by Gary Best, "Control of the Fetter Lane Society had been taken away from John and Charles by a Moravian, Philip Henry Molther."[266]

To Molther, being "still" was more important than charitable work. He insisted that complete sanctification was simultaneous with conversion, and that subsequently the Christian is to be "still." He even objected to Holy Communion. Charles called this "diabolical stillness." Both Wesleys insisted on the necessity of "frequent communion" as a means of grace and that every Christian should obey the commands of Christ such as we see in Jesus' ministry and in the Parable of the Last Judgment in Matthew 25. The Wesleys saw in "stillness" both laziness and pride, and saw Molther as a "wolf in sheep clothing."[267] Molther was not a man of compromise.

---

[265] Op. cit., Best, 125

[266] Ibid. 126-127

[267] Ibid., 127-128

Storm clouds had gathered for some time between Wesley and the Moravians before the final break came. The New Room in Bristol was a Methodist center while at Fetter Lane in London, the Moravians and Methodists met together. By June, 1740, Wesley verbalized in his *Journal* his feeling about the Moravians:

> "But eight or nine months ago certain men arose, speaking contrary to the doctrines we had received. They affirmed that faith admits of no degrees and consequently that weak faith is no faith; that when one is justified, he has a clean heart and is inescapable of doubt or fear. ...They affirmed also that there is no commandment in the New Testament but to believe; that no other duty lies upon us; and that when a man believes, he is not bound or obliged to do anything...; in particular he is not subject to ordinances. ...They affirmed that a believer cannot use any of the means of grace."[268]

Wesley, in his *Journal,* attempted to prove by quoting Scripture that the Gospels and Epistles do teach faith as beginning with limitation and growing on to have "the mind that was in Christ Jesus." Wesley called these "degrees of faith" and the Moravians insisted he was wrong. Indeed, Wesley quoted Jesus, "If you love me, keep my commandments." Did not Jesus say that "All ought to pray?" Did not our Lord give the sacrament in the Upper Room with the words, "Do this in remembrance of me?"

Finally, July 20, 1740, marked Wesley's final date of fraternal unity with the Moravians. "In the evening I went with Mr. Seward to the love-feast in Fetter Lane, at the conclusion of which, having said nothing till then, I read a paper, the substance whereof was as follows:

- That there is no such thing as 'weak faith'; that there is no justifying faith in one where there is still doubt or fear, or where there is not...a new, clean heart.

- That a man ought not to use those ordinances of God which our Church terms 'means of grace' before he has such a faith as excludes all doubt and fear....

- You have often affirmed that to 'search the scriptures' to pray, or to take communion before we have this faith is to

---

268 Op. cit., Ward & Heitzenrater, *JWW,* J & D, Vol. 19, 154

seek salvation by works and that until these works are laid aside no man can receive faith.'"

"I believe your assertions to be flatly contrary to the word of God. I have borne with you long, hoping you would turn. But as I find you more and more confirmed in the error of your ways, nothing now remains but that I should give you up to God. If you are of the same judgment, follow me."

Wesley then noted in his *Journal*, "I then, without saying anything more, withdrew, as did eighteen or nineteen of the society."[269]

More recently Michael Henderson has done an excellent piece in dissecting the theological and missiological differences between Wesley and the Moravians:[270]

Moravian Elements Liked	**Moravian Elements Disliked**
Hymn singing	Lack of openness, candor
Women's place of service	Exclusiveness
Love Feast, Watchnight services	Count Zinzendorf's domination
Ecclesiolae in ecclesia (small groups)	Antinomianism (rejection of works)
Intense fellowship	Doctrine of "stillness"
Emphasis on conduct	Rejecting means of grace,
Instantaneous conversion, assurance	Lack of social holiness
Simplicity of lifestyle	Casting lots for decisions
Distinction between instruction and edification	mysticism tendencies

So it was that the Moravians and Methodists went their separate ways, unable to reconcile one of Christianity's recurring debates: grace and works. An early Methodist historian writes, "July 20, 1740, is in strict propriety the real commencement of the Methodist Societies."

The old Foundery renovation was completed sufficiently for occupancy on July 23, 1740, only three days after Wesley's offi-

---

[269] Ibid., 162

[270] Henderson, Michael, *John Wesley's Class Meeting*, Francis Asbury Press, 1997, 64

cially leaving the Moravian Fetter Lane Society, taking some members with him. Wesley wrote in his *Journal*, on Wednesday,

> *"About twenty-five of our brethren God hath given us already, all of whom think and speak the same thing; seven or eight and forty likewise of the fifty women that were in band desired to cast their lot with us."*[271]

By August, Wesley wrote in his *Journal*, "A meeting at St. Luke's Parish Church was such a sight as, I believe, was never seen there before; several hundred communicants."

After a visit to Kingswood in Bristol, he returned to London on September 14. "As I returned home in the evening, I had no sooner stepped out of the coach than the mob, who were gathered in great numbers about my door, quite closed me in. I rejoiced and blessed God, knowing this was the time I had been looking for, and immediately spake to those who were next me of 'righteousness and the judgment to come.' At first not many heard, but the silence spread farther and farther, till I had a quiet, attentive congregation. And when I left them, they all showed much love and dismissed me with a blessing." With such unexpected growth, he remained in London until November 10, 1740, when "early in the morning I set out, and the next evening came to Bristol."[272]

The Foundery was a site for multiple missional and evangelistic ministries. By 1745, he appointed twelve stewards in charge of social welfare. Since his days at Oxford, John Wesley, Fellow of Lincoln College at Oxford, had devoted time, money, and imagination to relieve the multiple needs of England's "working class." They were not only poor, they were locked in a socio-economic underclass destined for perpetual poverty. Ten thousand persons each year, in England, were condemned to debtor's prison, which in turn, sentenced their families to begging. Oscar Sherwin wrote in 1961, "John Wesley taught liberty, equality, and fraternity long before the French Revolution."[273]

In the Foundery, Wesley opened the first free dispensary in London since King Henry VIII had destroyed all Catholic

---

[271] Op. cit., Ward & Heitzenrater, *JWW*, J&D, 163

[272] Ibid. 172

[273] Op. cit., Sherwin, 41

monasteries two hundred years earlier. He hired a pharmacist and a surgeon to provide medical needs to the poor. He founded a free school with sixty children and two teachers. He established a lending library in 1747. In 1748, he rented an adjoining house as a free almshouse for widows and poor children. These multiple ministries demonstrate that when Wesley spoke of "social holiness," he was serious! It was never considered to be a church. No services were held when the nearby parish churches had worship, but they were held after Anglican Evensong on Sundays and at 5:00 every morning. The Foundery continued until 1777.

"For thirty years, it was Wesley's London headquarters and "family residence.""[274]

Wesley's Breach with the Calvinists

Since college days and correspondence with his mother, Wesley had considered the teachings of John Calvin to "make God the author of evil." Now, to his shock and awe, George Whitefield, whom Wesley had mentored since youth, became a Calvinist! Whitefield's preaching was so powerful that much of Welsh Methodism followed him into the doctrine of predestination and Christ's atonement as being limited to only the Elect.

Wesley was forced to break with them because he believed that every person, not just the elect, can respond to God's grace. At his own Kingswood, Wesley had a lay preacher named John Cennick to promote predestination among the bands. That controversy ruptured the friendship of Whitefield and the Wesleys, splintered Welsh Methodism into a different denomination, and robbed the Wesleys of considerable financial support.

Whitefield, back in London from the colonies in 1741, pledged to preach election from the rooftops and did it! Wesley offered Whitefield a "right hand of fellowship," but Whitefield refused to shake on it. According to some biographers, "it was the lowest point in Wesley's career. He could face hostile crowds, but it broke his heart to be engaged in an evangelistic war with your closest friends."[275] Wesley soldiered on, staking out for Methodism as a "middle way."

---

[274] Op. cit., Urlin, 207

[275] Op. cit., Tomkins, 94

A Digest of "Wesleyan Grace Theology" Core Beliefs

Q: What was taught or exhorted from the Scriptures at the Methodist Society meetings?

A: Grace theology and holiness of heart!

Those who insist that Wesley was not a theologian ignore his concerted efforts to delineate several doctrinal themes which were a departure from the trends of the Church of England or the Calvinists. We are indebted to a number of distinguished scholars who have brought much new light to Wesley's works. We can now define Wesley's curriculum for his societies which we now know as "Wesleyan Grace Theology."

1. The Universality of God's Love or what Wesley called "Original Righteousness"

Wesley turned from the theology of Augustine and Calvin to the theology of Eastern Christianity in its use of the term "original righteousness...."[276] In his sermon, *The Image of God*, (#141) he said in exegeting Genesis 1:27, that the most overlooked verse in the Bible was, "And God made man in God's own image...."

- The first characteristic of *imago dei* was identified as "understanding." Later, philosophers began to call it "reason."

- The second endowment is love. At creation, love filled the whole expansion of his soul. It possessed him without a rival." "Man <u>was</u> what God <u>is:</u> Love." Wesley cited the only formal definition of God in the entire Bible, "God is love" (I John 4:7-21). God's love is not a passive ideal. It is a proactive, seeking, God-given initiative. However, it is not "monergistic," meaning that God forces love or that love is irresistible. Rather, God's love is "synergistic."

- The third endowment is two attributes of God himself: "political image" and "moral image."

  ○ The "political image" means our free will to make choices, good or bad, right or wrong. Free will is not a

---

[276] Op. cit., Outler, 290

human source, but a gift of God's grace. With our spiritual sense, we "hear" God's "whispers to the heart," but with our free will, we can say, "No."

- ◦ The "moral image" is our God given conscience or "spiritual sense" to know what is right.

2. The Universality of Human Sin

We must carefully avoid Pelagianism. Pelagius, a contemporary of Augustine, believed we are morally neutral, not "prone to wander." He did not believe in salvation by grace, but by good persons making good choices and doing good works. Pelagianism is a form of self-salvation, not grace salvation.

The third chapter of Genesis portrays picturesquely the origin of sin with Adam and Eve's disobedience. In Chapter 4, we see an immediate response to the parents' disobedience when Cain murdered his brother, Abel! That sinful act is called in theology, "the Fall."

Subsequent to the Fall, sin is universal. Paul wrote to the Romans, "All have sinned and fallen short of the glory of God." That narrative was God's inspired way of documenting a "stain" on God's perfect creation. Like Lady Macbeth who screamed, "Out damned spot," our "bent to sinning" is an indelible stain, an irresistible temptation. In Christian doctrine, we call it "original sin." To those who denied it in the "Enlightenment" philosophy of Wesley's day, he asked, "But what do we do with our Bibles?" He believed in original sin, and in total depravity, but, in Albert Outler's euphemism, not "tee-total depravity." That is, God endowed every person with what Wesley called "spiritual sense."

We were all created in that *Imago Dei*. Paul spoke to that truth in Romans 1 even as he insisted on the universality of sin: "For what can be known about God is plain to them *(all humankind)*. Ever since the creation of the world, his eternal power and divine nature, invisible though they are, have been understood and seen through the things he has made. So they are without excuse..." (Romans 1:19-20).

3. The Universality of God's Grace

Jesus said, "Whoever comes to me I will in no way reject." John recorded, "For God so loved the world ... that whoever believes in Him shall have eternal life." Jesus said, "Come to me you who are weak and heavily burdened, and I will give you rest. My yoke is easy and my burden is light." These are the bedrock biblical affirmations of Arminian theology. Charles Wesley's invitational hymn has the congregation singing,

> **"Come sinner to the gospel feast;**
> **let every soul be Jesus' guest.**
> **Ye need not one be left behind,**
> **for God had bid all humankind."**[277]

4. The Synergism of Grace—Freedom of choice.

Wesley's third point in his "Image of God" sermon led to his subsequent Arminian insistence on free will, the priority of choice over circumstance! He preaches to his Oxford peers,

> "What was made in his (God's) image yet plainer in his human offspring was the liberty he originally enjoyed; the perfect freedom implanted in his nature.... Man was made with an entire indifference, either to keep or change his first estate; it was left to himself what he would do; his own choice was to determine him in all things. The balance did not incline to one side or the other unless by his own deed. ...In this sense, he was the sole lord and sovereign judge of his own actions."[278]

Most Anglicans were Calvinists, but Wesley insisted that predestination frees us from responsibility. For Wesley, Adam's fall was predicated on Adam's possessing a freedom of choice, a will of his own, and the responsibility for choosing to obey or disobey. Adam disobeyed and all human progeny has born his choice's consequences. If humans are but robots or actors reading scripts, then God is responsible for our actions. However, if, as the Bible says, we were created in God's image, we make responsible choices with consequences. Wesley would have endorsed James Russell Lowell's late 19th century poem:

---

[277] Young Carlton, ed., United Methodist Book of Hymns, Methodist Publishing House, 1989, 339

[278] Op. cit., Outler, Sermon #141, 295

> "Once to every man and nation
>   comes the moment to decide,
> In the strife of truth with falsehood
>   for the good or evil side...."

Many misunderstand "free will" as Pelagian's "self-salvation." No. We are saved by grace. Free will is simply the human capacity for accepting or rejecting God's saving grace. The term "self-made man" is patently false. The maxim, "God helps those who help themselves" is at best a half-truth. Salvation is our choice to accept the most unimaginable gift: preparing, saving, and perfecting grace.

5. Witness of the Spirit.

We can know our sins forgiven. This is the doctrine of assurance. This was the focal point of Wesley's own spiritual journey at Aldersgate. This is a uniquely Methodist contribution to historical theology. What John preached, Charles had the society sing:

> "How can we sinners know our sins on earth forgiven?
>   How can my gracious Savior show my name inscribed in
>   heaven?
>   We who in Christ believe that he for us hath died,
>   We all his unknown peace receive and feel his blood
>   applied.
>   Our nature's turned, our mind transformed in all its
>   powers,
>   And both the witnesses are joined – the Spirit of God
>   with ours."[279]

Wesley called this "Witness of the Spirit" and two of his standard sermons are by that title. Then he asks, "what is 'the witness of the Spirit?'" Acknowledging that it is "hard to find words in the language of men to explain the deep things of God," he tries anyway! He explains that it is the testimony given by the Spirit of God to our spirit that we are "children of God" (Romans 8:14-17). He calls it "God's whispers to the heart." Scholar Leonard Sweet calls it "God's nudges." So, the experience of assurance flows into witness. The result of this testimony is the 'fruit of the Spirit' (Gal. 5:22). Without these fruits the testimony of witness cannot long endure."

---

[279] Op. cit., *UMC Hymnal,* Hymn #372

He calls the witness of the Spirit the "inward impression of the soul" whereby the Spirit of God immediately and directly witnesses to my spirit that I am a child of God, that Jesus Christ loved me and gave himself for me, that all my sins are blotted out, and I, even I, am reconciled to God. He called this experience moving from being a servant of God to a son.

Wesley continues that when the Spirit of God nudges our souls,

> **"the stormy winds and troubled waves {of the soul} subside, and there is a sweet calm; the heart resting as in the arms of Jesus, and the sinner being clearly satisfied that God is reconciled, that all his sins are forgiven." [280]**

The Quaker, John Greenleaf Whittier has us sing about "the silence of eternity, interpreted by love." In the hymn, we move from affirmation to a prayer:

> **"Drop thy still dews of quietness, till all our strivings cease; Take from our souls the strains and stress,**
> **And let our ordered lives confess the beauty of thy peace."**

We cannot love God until we know that God loves us. And we cannot know his love until his Spirit witnesses it to our spirit. Wesley wrote two discourses entitled "Witness of the Spirit," one in 1746 and one in 1767. He was carefully delineating a "middle way" between what he called "the danger lest our religion degenerate into mere formality" and the temptation "to run into all the wildness of enthusiasm." Concerning "witness of the Spirit," Wesley continued, "It is by his peculiar blessing upon them (the Methodists) in searching the Scriptures, confirmed by the experience of his children, that this great evangelical truth has been recovered, which had been for many years well-nigh lost...."

6. The Gospel of Christ knows of no religion but social, no holiness but social holiness.

Dr. Heitzenrater corrects any who speak of Wesley's adopting a paradigm of social justice as is known today. He simply believed that the road to right living leads through relationships, reform, and systemic repentance, not solitary religion. Wesley wrote,

---

[280] Op. cit., Outler, *JWW, Sermons,* Vol. 1, "Witness of the Spirit II," 287

"'Holy solitaries' is a phrase no more consistent with the Gospel than 'holy adulterers.' The Gospel of Christ knows of no religion but social, no holiness but social holiness."

7. Wesley then proceeds to outline the way we avoid what he calls "enthusiasm."

It is to see that in our lives there is evidence of the "fruits of the Spirit" immediately following the inward experience or testimony of the Spirit. In short, he agrees with James. "Faith without works is dead." (To Wesley, "experience without good works is froth and fizz!")

Faith working by love is the length and breadth and height of Christian perfection. Jesus said, 'My Father has worked until now, and I too work."

8. Perfecting Grace or "Grace upon Grace."

Charles' great hymn on this subject ends, "Finish then thy new creation, pure and spotless let us be." "Sanctification" is a word that took on so much negative baggage that Wesley's term "grace upon grace" is preferable. Current preferred phraseology is "perfecting grace." Being saved brings forgiveness. The "second rest" of which Charles Wesley has us sing is our Spirit filled "peace that passes understanding."

We may allow the Holy Spirit to perfect us in love gradually, or we might grow in grace "two steps forward and one step back." We grow spiritually, or atrophy and die. Christians whose salvation theology believes only in being saved can testify only to the forgiveness of their sins. Wesleyans believe that we grow in grace as God constantly nudges us toward "being completed as a new creation in Christ Jesus."

Wesley insisted, and could document, that nothing in his doctrine was outside the Protestant dimension of Anglican theology. However, his accent on "holy living" offended the Moravians who saw that as "works righteousness" or "popery." Conversely, his insistence on "witness of the Spirit" sounded like "enthusiasm" or "antinomianism" to the Anglicans. The upshot was that Methodist emphases were offensive to many: the Anglicans, Moravians, and Dissenters!

The Revival Paradigm: Preaching, Worship, Organization

Many streams fed the mighty river that flowed through John Wesley's mind and soul. He saw the light of God's truth from many lamps. Though he preached in fields and pubs without notes, he was still an Oxford don, and he required that his lay preachers have some substance in their sermons. In a letter to Mary Bishop in 1778 he rejected the term "Gospel sermon:"

> "The term has become a mere cant word. I wish none of our Society would use it. It has no determinate meaning. Let but a pert, self-sufficient animal, that has neither sense nor grace, bawl out some something about Christ and his blood or justification by faith, and his hearers cry out, 'What a fine Gospel sermon." I find more profit in sermons on either good tempers or good works than in some that are vulgarly called 'Gospel.'" [281]

John Pollock in his biography notes that when asked to define this new movement, Wesley would reply by emphasizing "in very plain words the difference between the true, old Christianity, now commonly called by the new name, Methodism, and Christianity now generally taught.[282] In his last letter to his brother, Samuel, before Samuel's death, Wesley wrote, "How is it that you can't praise God for saving so many souls from death, and covering such a multitude of sins? Why should his work be contained within consecrated walls; why should He not fill heaven and earth? I love the rites and ceremonies of The Church, but I see that our great Lord can work without them."

To an Anglican bishop who queried, "Sir, what do you mean by faith?" Wesley answered, "My lord, by justifying faith I mean a conviction wrought in a man by the Holy Ghost that Christ hath loved him, and given himself for him, and that through Christ his sins are forgiven." After about an hour, the bishop finally said, "You have no business here. You are not commissioned to preach in this diocese. Therefore, I advise you to go hence." Wesley refused, saying, "My lord, my business on earth is to do all the good I can. At present I think I can do most good here. Therefore I here stay." It was then that he used the term so often repeated,

---

[281] Vickers, Jason; Maddox, Randy, eds., *The Cambridge Companion to John Wesley,* Cambridge Press, 2010, 107

[282] Op. cit., Pollock, 130

"The world is my parish." The bishop did not contest that and closed the interview. Wesley's course was clear in his mind. His face was set like a flint to "preach the gospel wheresoever I am in the habitable world." Bristol became, and is until this day, a stronghold of Methodism.

- After this point in time, the term "rise" is no longer used. Bishop McTyeire insists that following Aldersgate, we should use the term "epoch!"

- Heitzenrater's next table is entitled, "Early Period of the Revival, 1740-1755"[283]

- Jason Vickers uses "early, middle, and late" without assigning specific transition dates. This is probably a more accurate terminology.

"The North" - Newcastle upon Tyne

For three years, from 1739-1742, Wesley had preached, established societies and class meetings, and built two "preaching houses," one in Bristol of the West Country where his ministry spilled over into Wales, and one in London. It was Lady Huntingdon, Whitefield's dear friend, who urged Wesley to take his ministry north to Newcastle upon Tyne on the North Sea. A young stone mason named John Nelson had heard Wesley preach in London and "found his preaching to be effective and personal."[284] Now, without permission, Nelson was preaching in the North like "an owl in the desert," and found that people gladly received "the doctrine of *conscious pardon.*"[285]

So it was that Wesley went north to Newcastle upon Tyne in 1742. On May 30, he began in "the poorest and most contemptible part of town," which was Sandgate. He began by standing at the end of the street and singing the *Doxology.* Before he ended his sermon, there were four or five hundred folks listening. His text and topic were something they probably had never heard from the Bible before: "He was wounded for our transgressions and bruised

---

[283] Op. cit., Heitzenrater, *People Called Methodists,* 156

[284] Op. cit., Heitzenrater, Mirror and Memory, 164

[285] Op. cit., Heitzenrater, *People Called Methodists,* 137

for our iniquities, and by his stripes we are healed" (Isaiah 53:5). It is best if you read of this occasion in John Wesley's own words:

> "Observing the people when I had done to stand gaping and staring upon me, with the most profound astonishment, I told them 'If you desire to know who I am, my name is John Wesley. At five in the evening, with God's help, I design to preach here again.' At five, the hill on which I designed to preach was covered from the top to the bottom. I never saw so large a number of people together.... I knew it was not possible for the one half to hear, although my voice was then strong and clear, and I stood so as to have them all in view." The Word of God which I set before them was, 'I will heal their backsliding, I will love them freely.'" (Hosea 14:4)

> After preaching, the poor people were ready to tread me underfoot, out of pure love and kindness. It was some time before I could possibly get out of the press. I went back another way than I came, but several were got to our inn before me, by whom I was vehemently opportune to stay, at least a few days."[286]

That was the beginning of a Methodist presence in Newcastle which remains strong until this very day. In the late 1990's Dr. Peter Graves was pastor of a large and influential church there. From May 31 until June 5, John rode horseback from Newcastle to his home town of Epworth. At every village, his reputation had preceded him and he preached to large crowds. At Birstall, "a multitude of people gathered from all parts."[287]

On June 5, he arrived in Epworth in Lincolnshire. He went to the Red Lion Inn at the junction of the road that to the left leads to St. Andrews Anglican Church where his father served over thirty-eight years and where John and his siblings were baptized, and, to the right where the road leads up hill to the rectory where John and most of his siblings had been born. He did not know if any would remember him, but "an old servant of my father's, with two or three poor women, presently found me out." The next day was Sunday and he went to St. Andrews where John Romley, who knew John Wesley quite well, was the curate. Wesley offered to either preach or lead prayers, but "he

---

[286] Ward & Heitzenrater, *JWW*, J&D, 269

[287] Ibid., 270

did not care to accept my assistance."

> "After sermon, John Taylor stood in the churchyard and gave notice as the people were coming out, 'Mr. Wesley, not being permitted to preach in the church, designs to preach here at six o'clock.' Accordingly at six I came, and found such a congregation as I believe Epworth never saw before. I stood near the east end of the church upon my father's tombstone, and cried, 'The kingdom of heaven is not meats and drink, but righteousness, and peace, and joy in the Holy Ghost.'"[288]

Spending the night with one Edward Smith, Wesley found people from a number of surrounding villages had sent word for him to come and preach to them. He spent several days doing so, then he returned to Epworth and again preached on his father's tomb, "as I did every day that week. "Again he preached in a circle of villages around Epworth, visiting in "the home of my brother and sister."[289]

Wesley's account of his establishing Methodism in the North is most fascinating. For instance:

> "I rode over to a neighboring town to wait upon a Justice of Peace whose angry neighbors had carried a whole wagon-load of what they considered new heretics." (Converts in response to his preaching!) As the "J.P." asked if there were other reasons to arrest them, an old man said, 'Yes Sir! … He convarted (sic) my wife. Till she went among them, she had such a tongue! And now she is as quiet as a lamb.' The Justice of Peace replied, 'Carry them back to your town and let them convert all the scolds in the town.'"[290]

Wesley kept staying in the area. He was invited to preach at Wroote, where he had been the curate for nearly two years as assistant to his father (1727-1729). The curate at Wroote was John Whitelamb, another man who had been Samuel Wesley's assistant. Whitelamb had married John's sister Mary, and she had died in childbirth the next year. On Sunday, June 14,

---

[288] Op. cit., Telford, 163

[289] *Likely his sister Anne and brother-in-law, John Lambert.*

[290] Op. cit., Telford, 163-164

"I preached for the last time at Epworth to a vast multitude gathered from all parts. Near forty years did my father labour there, but he saw little fruit of all his labour. I took some pains among this people too, and my strength also seemed spent in vain. But now the fruit appeared...The seed sown so long ago now sprung up, bringing forth repentance and remission of sins."

Of the Epworth experience, he wrote, "I am well assured that I did far more good to my Lincolnshire parishioners by preaching three days on my father's tomb than I did by preaching three years in his pulpit."[291] He preached his way through village after village southwest to Coventry and finally to Bristol. So it was that in the summer of 1742, he established a beachhead of Methodism from the new societies in Newcastle to the established societies back in Bristol.

Following his mother's death in 1742, Wesley rode back and forth from London to Bristol five times. Then on November 8, he again made the long journey north to Newcastle upon Tyne. The culture was different than in the south. The response was steadily increasing, so he preached in the city and surrounding villages for seven weeks, but he had no "preaching place."

Then a merchant named Stephenson sold Wesley for £40 a plot of ground, forty-eight by ninety feet. Winter came early. Wesley's desk at his rental quarters was only a yard from the fire, but he could write only for fifteen minutes before his fingers began to grow numb. However, the cornerstone was laid for the new building on December 20. The estimated cost was £700 and he had only twenty-six shillings! [292] Then came a letter from a Quaker that began, "I had a dream concerning thee." His dream was about a flock of sheep and a shepherd but no shelter from the storms. He enclosed a note for one hundred pounds! On March 25, 1743, John preached in the shell that still had no roof. He named it the "Orphan House" because in addition to a preaching place, it would be the home for forty poor children, a master and a mistress.

According to biographer John Telford, the Orphan House became the site of the first Sunday School in the north with a

---

[291] Ibid., 277

[292] Op. cit., Telford, 168

thousand scholars. "The colliers and keelmen of the district were so eager to hear the Wesleys that they would lie down on the benches at the end of evening service and sleep there till the early morning preaching began!"[293] By 1744 Wesley was back north in Newcastle.

Welsh Methodism

The English looked condescendingly on the Welsh. Geographically they were "west of the west country." Culturally, they were quite different. Economically, they were poorer. Linguistically, they spoke a different language.

Yet the Anglican Church had established Welsh parish churches, baptized babies there, and taught the Catechism as a means of religious instruction. They created a market or a "demand" that exceeded their supply of parish priests. Psychologically, the Welsh were more open to religious enthusiasm and the features of societies and class meetings than they were to the high church sacramentalism of the Anglican Church. They loved open air preaching and the new paradigm of hymn singing introduced by Charles Wesley, Isaac Watts, Edward Perronet, and others. Culturally, Methodism came to have more influence in Wales than in England.

In October, 1739, at the "pressing insistence" of a lay preacher named Howell Harris, Wesley went to Wales. He remained five days and preached three times each day. In his *Journal* he wrote that he "simply described the plain old religion of the Church of England as is now almost everywhere spoken against." He wrote further that he found the people to be "ripe for the gospel ... and as utterly ignorant of it as the Creek Indians in America. He was convinced that these poor creatures should not perish but have the opportunity to "believe in Jesus Christ and have eternal life." Wesley's success in Wales is evidenced by the numerous Welsh lay preachers who came to the American colonies without Wesley's permission or knowledge.

The sad element of Methodism in Wales is that this same Howell Harris who invited Wesley to come later followed Whitefield into leading many Welsh Methodists to become Calvinists. Indeed, most joined a group who called themselves "Primitive Methodists."

---

[293] Ibid., 170

Wesley's Writings and Publications

As the movement spread, several media were used. In addition to "conferencing," a second way of building uniformity in doctrine and discipline was to write and publish. Charles did indeed write over 6,600 hymns which were very "singable" for people having no worship experience. John wrote tracts and, beginning in 1746, published his *Sermons on Several Occasions.*

In the preface to the three-volume set, he wrote, "Every serious man who peruses these will see in the clearest manner what those doctrines are which I embrace and teach as the essentials of true religion."[294] They were reprinted at least four times between then and 1787, each edition larger than the earlier one. These brought to unlettered laity the great doctrines of the Reformation, some unique contributions of little-known mystics, and such writings as Robert Gell's book on the potential of "loving God and neighbor in such degree as to displace all desire to sin." Soon thereafter Wesley began to preach on the perennially misunderstood experience of Christian perfection or sanctification. However, Wesley insisted that this is no permanent state, but that any who were living a life of perfect love might fall away, yielding to temptations, usually those of the spirit.

The same year that he first published his three-volume set of *Sermons on Several Occasions,* he preached his sermon, "The Way to the Kingdom," based on Mark 1:15. In it, he denounced orthodoxy or "right doctrine" as the true Christian faith:

"Neither does religion consist in orthodoxy or right opinions.... A man may be orthodox at every point—the incarnation of our Lord, the ever-blessed Trinity, and every other doctrine in the [Bible]. He may assent to all three creeds—the Apostles, the Nicene, and the Athanasian—yet 'tis possible he may have no religion at all, no more than a Jew, Turk, or pagan. He may be almost as orthodox as the devil...and all the while be as great a stranger as he to the religion of the heart."[295]

Then he identified "right opinion" with Jesus' definition of "the law and the prophets." That is, "Love the Lord thy

---

[294] Op. Cit, Outler, ed., *JWW*, Vol. 1, 103

[295] Ibid., 221

God with all thy heart, and with all thy mind, and with all thy soul, and with all thy strength." And the second is like unto it: "Thou shalt love thy neighbor as thyself." He then explained that "neighbor" means "not only thy friend, thy kinsman, or thy acquaintance; not only him who loves you or returns every kindness, but every child of man, every human creature, every soul which God hath made – screeing him from whatever might grieve or hurt his soul or body."[296]

Oxford Faculty Closes Chapel Pulpits to Wesley

On August 24, 1744, he was scheduled to preach again at Oxford, this time in St. Mary's College chapel. He was deliberately scheduled during the student's Long Vacation. Most of the congregation were intended to be faculty, but according to an undergraduate named Benjamin Kennicott, Wesley had been in town two days "preaching among the poor and in inns and private houses." So, a multitude of Oxford citizens "with general faces and plain attire" turned out to fill the chapel.

The sermon was entitled "Scriptural Christianity" and is #4 in the *Sermons on Several Occasions* which he arranged. Wesley began with a history of Christianity but could not refrain from "zeal and satire." When he came to the point of saying, "it remains only that I should close ... with a practical application," he went into an "in your face" diatribe that might have been accurate, but could not be well received by several Oxford college faculties:

- "Is this city a Christian city?

- "Is scriptural Christianity found here?

- "Are all the heads and governors of colleges and halls and their respective societies 'of one heart and of one soul?' ... I pray those who are in authority over us, whom I reverence for your office's sake, to consider, 'Are you filled with the Holy Ghost?'

- "Ye venerable men who are more especially called to form the tender minds of youth ... Are your thoughts and tempers in keeping with your calling?

---

[296] Ibid., 222

- "Do you abound in the fruits of the Spirit?

- "Is this the general character of the fellows of the colleges? I fear it is not. Are we 'taught of God' that we may be able to teach others also?

- "Do we know God? Do we know Jesus Christ? Where are our seals of 'apostleship?'

- "Are you humble, teachable, advisable, or stubborn, self-willed, heady, and high-minded?

- "Do you behave as seeing him who is invisible?

- "Or, are not drunkenness and uncleanness found among you?

- "Or, are you a generation of *triflers?*

- "How few of you spend from one week to another a single hour in private prayer?

- "Indeed, what religion are you of? Even the talk of Christianity you cannot, will not, bear! O my brethren!

- "What a Christian city is this?

- "Where is that scriptural Christianity that should be the religion of this place? Lord save us or we perish! Take us out of the mire, that we might sink not!"[297]

The congregation, mostly faculty, was understandably hostile! As he, Charles, and two Methodist friends left the church, they were shunned. The Vice Chancellor sent a beadle to ask for a written copy of the sermon which Wesley gave him. William Blackstone, the brilliant jurist, was in the congregation. He noted that "they thought it proper to punish him with mortifying neglect." Though he lived fifty-six more years, Wesley was never allowed in a university pulpit again.

(In the 20th century, Wesley's portrait was hung in the refectory of Christ Church College as one of their alumni "greats," a bust is mounted at Lincoln College on the wall outside his room, a room is kept as a museum, a statue of him is in the garden of St.

---

[297] Op. Cit., Outler, Albert, ed. *JWW, Sermons,* Vol. I, 172-180; (selections)

Paul's Cathedral, and a stained-glass window in Lincoln Cathedral portrays John and Charles.)

Wesley's Ministry of "Social Holiness"

From a twenty-first century vantage point, it is tempting to say that Wesley was an advocate, even an activist, for social justice issues. This writer was duly corrected several years ago by Methodism's pre-eminent historian, Richard Heitzenrater. Dr. Heitzenrater calls Wesley's a "Methodist scheme of social action." *(In Britain, "Scheme" has no negative connotation as being nefarious. It is much like the American English word, "strategy.")*

Wesley's conviction about and commitment to what he called "social holiness" began in his student days at Oxford, and especially during his teaching years at Oxford's Lincoln College. Acquiring the title "Holy Club" did not arise from pietism as much as from daily visits with warm bread to the Castle Prison and to the city jail, food and clothing for the poor children on the streets, and other acts of mercy and deeds of kindness. By 1731, Wesley's diary listed the following as daily commitments: "Monday, Bocardo city jail; Tuesday, Castle Prison; Wednesday, the children; Thursday, Castle Prison; Friday, Bocardo (prison); Saturday, Sunday, poor and elderly."[298] One of Wesley's favorite Scriptures was, "By their fruits ye shall know them." He saw the mission of Methodism as ministering relief to every form of human sorrow and distress, "doing good, as far as in our power, to the bodies and souls of men."[299]

The need for social holiness was immense. The *Lloyd's Evening Post* editorialized in 1765, "The distresses of the poor are melancholy beyond description." The *London Chronicle* wrote, "The poor are reduced to the greatest extremities of want and distress, to the point they are obliged to rob, steal, or perish." Wesley wrote, "People have been assured in every part of the kingdom that 'trade was as plentiful and flourishing as ever and the people as well employed and as well satisfied.' A more notorious falsehood could not have been palmed off upon them."

The *Lloyd's Evening Post* agreed in a 1765 editorial, "Many

---

[298] Op. cit., Heitzenrater, *People Called Methodists*, 42

[299] Hyde, A. B., *The Story of Methodism from the Beginning to the Present Time*, Willey & Co., 1889, 261-262

thousands of people at Manchester, Birmingham, Leicester, and Nottingham will probably starve this year for want of work and money to buy food." Long letters on the starved condition of the country were published in newspapers and magazines. When the king opened Parliament, he referred to the dearness of corn and recommended, "My lords and gentlemen, we must develop a scheme for alleviating the distresses of the poor."

Miners in Wales worked for a penny an hour for sixteen hours a day. Children of five and six years of age worked in mills and factories twelve hours a day, six days a week. Girls dug coal in the bowels of the earth in an atmosphere of coal dust and little oxygen, and dragged it on little wagons pulled by harnesses over their little shoulders. For the slightest of crimes, men were executed. "The gallows were busy and the prisoners were like hungry sheep awaiting slaughter. The sharp distinction between sordid squalor and starvation on the one hand and plenty and abundance on the other did not disturb the minds of those in power."[300] Wesley preached against this situation and worked for its alleviation.

That was "Wesley's England." Wales and Scotland were even more deplorable. Wesley knew the poor better than any man of his age. He wrote in his *Journal,* "Suppose a great man ... oppresses the needy; suppose the rich grind the face of the poor; what remedy against such oppression can he find in this Christian country?" This was the backdrop for John Wesley's emphasis on what he called "social holiness." He did not organize protests in the streets, which he could have. Wesley was a loyal political Tory, a lifelong Anglican who opposed Methodism's becoming a Church, a constant supporter of the Crown, and never the perpetrator of anti-government protests.

What he did do was to develop a Methodism that "wept o'er the erring one" and "lifted up the fallen." He insisted that Christianity cannot be a solitary religion. It must be one that loves one's neighbor and expresses that love with acts of mercy and deeds of kindness. "He was a restless advocate of self-improvement and the improvement of society; in his view, 'the ideal Christian life was one of ceaseless, cheerful activism.'"[301]

---

[300] Op. cit., Sherwin, 123-124

[301] Op. cit., Hempton, 42

This writer, in 1977, had the privilege of sitting where Wesley sat in Lincoln College. The Oxford Methodist Institute was entitled, *"Liberation Theologies in Light of the Wesleyan Tradition."* Eleven Methodist theologians from five continents compared and contrasted "sanctification and liberation." Ted Runyon set the stage in the first lecture with this statement:

> "When Wesley calls Christianity a social religion, he is of course not using the term in the full-blown, twentieth century sense of the social gospel—that is the application of the Christian message to social, political, and economic institutions and structures of corporate life. Rather, he is arguing from his own eighteenth century context. He is opposing William Law and the German pietists and the Christian mystics."

Then Runyon quotes Wesley:

> "'If thou will be perfect,' say they, 'trouble not thyself about outward works.... He hath attained true resignation (to God) who hath estranged himself from all outward works that God may work inwardly in him, without any turning to outward things.'"

> "Directly opposite is the Gospel of Christ! Solitary religion is not to be found there.'Holy solitaries' is a phrase no more consistent with the Gospel than 'holy adulterers.' The Gospel of Christ knows no holiness but social holiness."[302]

For Wesley, sanctification is the transformation of the individual in that s/he loves God and loves fellow humankind. Wesley called it moving from a servant relationship with God to a son relationship: "I can do all things through him who strengthens me." He abhors a religion that "abstracts itself from all sensible things." "Sensible things" are the constitutional dimensions of human society: poverty and wealth, oppressiveness and being oppressed, the unlettered and the educated elite, powerlessness and being empowered, disenfranchised and franchised. Randy Maddox and others define Wesley's theology as "orthopraxis" (practical divinity) or orthopathy" (therapeutic grace) rather than orthodoxy ("doctrine that does not reach to the marrow of Chris-

---

[302] Runyon, Theodore, ed., *Sanctification and Liberation*, Abingdon, 1981, 42

tian truth"). Runyon defines Wesley's theology as "God's pouring himself into the world to renew the creature after his image (sanctification) and creation after his will."[303]

Wesley was not a societal revolutionary, he was a social reformer. His last letter was dictated to William Wilberforce, urging the young Parliamentarian not to give up or give in with his fight to get slavery abolished in the British Empire. At the 1977 Oxford seminar, scholars from holiness Wesleyan denominations pointed out that in 1843 in America, the Wesleyan Methodists were created because they insisted on the evil of slavery and wanted instant abolition. The Salvation Army, created by William Booth, was motivated to help the lot of ragamuffins on the streets, and, later, to ordain women. Historically, the holiness people need to be given more credit for creating social change. Some of them had as their mottos: "We salvage wrecked lives" and "Down, but never out."

Social holiness was led often by women. Nancy Hardesty, a feminist theologian, quoted historian Robert Wearmouth, who affirmed, "The emancipation of women began with Wesley."[304] John Fletcher and his wife, Mary Bosanquet, were virtually co-pastors to a Methodist Society in London. In 1787, Wesley gave a preaching license to Sarah Mallet, with the commentary, "we have no objection to her being a preacher in our connection so long as she preaches the Methodist doctrine, and attends to our discipline." It was General Booth's wife who led him out of the Methodist Conference when his proposal to help the poor was rejected.

Certainly, no human being had the influence on John Wesley that his mother did. When she led a study in the rectory kitchen while Samuel was away, pouting in London, her husband reprimanded her. Susanna's response was, "… in your absence I cannot but look upon every soul you leave under my care as a talent committed to me, under a trust, by the great Lord of all the families of heaven and earth."[305] Suffice it to say that though Wesley was not a feminist theologian by any stretch of the truth, he did, for his day and time, recognize and authorize a place of leadership

---

[303] Ibid. 45-46

[304] Wearmouth, Robert, *Methodism and the Common People of the Eighteenth Century,* Epworth, 1945, 223

[305] Clarke, Adam, *Memoirs of the Wesley Family,* New York:Lane and Tippett, 1848, 412

for women that we must consider most admirable. Again, he was
a reformer.

Wesley had a deep sense of commitment to physical health.
We have his letter to Alexander Knox on August 16, 1778, who
wondered if God were punishing him with bad health, "Mercy
rejoices over judgment. Therefore expect from Him not what you
deserve, but what you want—health of soul and health of body."
His book *Primitive Physick*, sold thousands of copies with royal-
ties that made Wesley a wealthy man, but he gave it all away or
invested it in places like the New Room, Foundery, and Newcastle
Orphan House.

After buying and refitting the Foundery in London, Wesley
was a pioneer in providing medical care to the poor. He had studied both anatomy and medicine. When he found many who were
sick and too poor to pay physicians, Wesley said, "I will prepare
and give them physic (*sic)* myself." His volunteer "staff" included
an apothecary and a surgeon. In one five-month period he treated
five hundred patients, of whom seventy-one were cured. The
Foundery also had rooms for up to fifteen "sick widows" with
whom he and the lay preachers ate "the same food at the same
table." His mother, Susanna, lived there the last three years of
her life.

He created Lending Stock for the industrious poor who needed
a mite of capital to get a new start toward fiscal independence.
Managed by two stewards, the fund loaned money in amounts of
from five to twenty-five pounds for three months. Records show
they helped two hundred and fifty persons to "get on their feet,"
financially.

He rode horseback over a quarter of a million miles, preached
no less than 52,400 times, wrote 233 books and pamphlets, thousands of long hand letters, kept a shorthand diary, edited at least
three editions of his *Journal*, and appeared in over fifty towns as
much as thirty times each! There are two hundred recorded visits
to London. He crossed the Irish Sea fifty-four times.

Wesley's Personal Life

Wesley lived a very regimented life. Normally, he rose at
four o'clock, read his books and the Bible or answered letters
until five, preached to miners or factory workers at daybreak,
breakfasted at seven, mounted his horse at eight and usually

read as the horse meandered down the well-trodden path. At noon he stopped to preach in a village, often in front of the pub. In the afternoon he rode rapidly and preached again at 5:00. After supper, he preached again before retiring for the evening by 10:00. He insisted that six hours is enough sleep. On Fridays, he did not eat until 2:00. Then, he had a cup of tea. He ate dinner each day but was basically a vegetarian. He advised, "Eat no flesh at supper but something light and easy for digestion."[306] He truly was a force for hygiene and preventive medicine in his day.

Many people think that the quotation, "Cleanliness is next to godliness" is in the Bible, but this was in one of John Wesley's sermons:

> "Be cleanly, in this let the Methodists take pattern of the Quakers. Avoid all nastiness, dirt, slovenliness, both in your person, clothes, house, and all about you. Let none ever see a ragged Methodist. Do not cut off your hair but clean it and keep it clean. Cure yourself and your family of the itch. … Cleanliness is next to godliness. [307]

We should not think of Wesley as dour and glum. He also distinguished himself with his cheerfulness and affability. He preached and wrote in letters, "sour godliness is the devil's religion." He was not a "monk." He wrote, "Every Christian ought to enjoy life."[308] A contemporary wrote of Wesley, "His was a beautiful contrast to the austere deportment of many of his preachers and people. …It was impossible to be long in his company without partaking of his hilarity."[309]

Actually, he was one of the most sought-after conversationalists in England because he was informed on so many subjects. Samuel Johnson loved his company, but complained, "The little man was always in a hurry." Wesley was a well-read classicist who admired Socratic virtue and reason as much as the apogee of human wisdom without Christ. Like Jesus, Wesley also periodically retreated from his public regimen and rested up to

---

[306] Op. cit., Sherwin, 78

[307] Op. cit., Wilder, 162

[308] Ibid. 163

[309] Op. cit., Tomkins, 143

six weeks, usually using the time for writing another book or sermons.

Wesley wrote voluminously in sermons, books, tracts, personal letters, his *Journal,* and his daily diary. He earned a lot of money, but constantly gave it away and died with almost no estate. It is almost accurate to say that his biographers have had more written documentation than any public figure in history. His contemporary critics and supporters had a trove of documentation. Yet in many ways, he was elusive.

Wesley's marriage was a disaster. Molly Vazeille was a wealthy widow, was extremely jealous of him, and resented his exchanging letters with women. Molly found being Mrs. Wesley hard to get used to. When he wrote, "I am discontented with nothing. To have persons at my ear fretting and murmuring at everything is like tearing the flesh off my bones."[310] She often felt neglected and was repeatedly upset by John's relationships with others, especially women."[311] Once she broke into his bureau and read letters. She found no evidence of impropriety, but was nevertheless infuriated. On January 20, 1758, after seven stormy years of marriage, she left him. "A short reconciliation was demolished in March 1760 with a row over her putting a dismantled bed in his study. Wesley exploded in a ridiculous letter,

> "If you was a wise, whether a good woman or not, you would long ago have said, 'Tell me what to do and I will do it; tell me what to avoid and I will avoid it.'"[312]

They had married in 1751. In 1774, the long, torturous relationship ended. She wrote him a final letter to which he responded with a typical epistle, ending, "Neither was guilty of any great crime beyond the folly of agreeing to marry in the first place."

> "As long as I can hold a pen, I will assert my right of conversation with whom I please. If the unbeliever will depart, let her depart. I am giving an account only to God

---

[310] Op. cit., Tomkins, 147

[311] Ibid. 142

[312] Ibid., 179

and my own conscience."[313]

After 1776, there is no record of their ever meeting. When she died, Charles had her funeral. From her £5000 estate, she left John a mourning ring. So it was that he remained in touch with a wide variety of people and enjoyed their company.

---

[313] Ibid., 155

CHAPTER NINE

Early Methodist Structures

For John Wesley the term "church" could be ascribed to only the Catholic and Anglican Churches. Therefore, he borrowed from historical and contemporary Anglican, Quaker, and Moravian paradigms the terminology and "psychology" that was appropriate to Methodism as a movement.

The Congregation

Anglicans literally objected to the worship of Almighty God outside the Church. So it was that the idea of the gospel being preached to an *ad hoc* group of village people was unthinkable. Yet, that was the paradigm developed by George Whitefield and the Wesley brothers. The word "congregation" was whoever gathered in fields, streets, pubs, or rented buildings to hear a sermon. The numbers they report are hard to believe: 3000, 5000, 10,000! The first were in early 1739 in Bristol and in Moorfields, London, outside the city wall. Then the phenomenon spread to Cornwall, Wales, the Midlands, Yorkshire, and down through East Anglia. No one was converted to Christ through Methodism in a church. Everyone's first contact was the outdoor or "preaching house" congregation. The intent was to have the Holy Spirit use the sermon to "awaken the soul" of the casual listeners. Some of the people who were previously converted were designated to study people's reaction and ask some to join a society, usually the next morning at 5:00.

Congregational Singing

A major life-changing element of the early Methodist services was the hymns of Charles Wesley. Hymns were at the emotional heart of evangelical Christianity. They were part of the "heart and soul" of Methodist worship from the days of Wesley through the gospel hymns of the nineteenth century. Almost every Methodist gathering began and ended with a hymn or a medley of hymns. As David Hempton said it so well, "They inspired the imagination, mediated biblical metaphors, and helped build a system of symbols; they defined for Methodists a religious content and style of a more vibrant and populist kind than was tapped by confessions of faith or chanted liturgies or tunes sung best by professionals."[314]

Charles Wesley was not a composer of a single tune. He did not write music. It is not accurate to say that Charles Wesley wrote lyrics to be sung by the tunes of pub songs, but it is accurate to say that he wrote lyrics that could be sung by existing tunes, most of which were very singable. Some were sung to classical music, soundtracks of plays, or even operettas. There were no hymnals with musical notes printed above each line of lyrics. Song leaders would "line out" hymns, sometimes improvising tunes. In *The United Methodist Hymnal* published in 1989, more of Charles Wesley's hymns, and more hymns normally called "gospel hymns" were included than for any hymnal since the nineteenth century. Andy Langford deserves a lot of singular credit for this. The Gospel hymn lyrics' usual emphasis is on the journey of faith from invitation, to repentance, to blessed assurance, to the expectation of heaven."[315] The medium of music and the message of the evangel were in perfect harmony. Even more recently, the hymns that quickly become "favorites" are those with the gospel message and singable tunes that resonate with every person's life journey: ethos, pathos, and telos.

From the poor and unlettered of England in Wesley's day to the American frontier at the height of the Second Great Awakening in America *(c.1800-1850's)*, hymnody reflected the interplay of sin and salvation in everyday life. The lyrics and tunes spoke to the angst, temptations, hopes, and fears of pre-Christian people. Music was a major motivator in coming to Christ. If a person had no self-esteem and was a victim of the "school of hard knocks," think what it would mean to hear a congregation singing:

---

[314] Op. cit., Hempton, 73

[315] Ibid., 73, (paraphrased)

"Come sinners to the gospel feast; let every soul be Jesus'
   guest.
   Ye need not one be left behind for God hath bid all
   humankind.
Sent by my Lord, on you I call; the invitation is to all.
   Come, all the world!
 Come sinner, thou! All things in Christ are ready now.
Come, all ye souls by sin oppressed, ye restless seekers
   after rest;
Ye poor, and maimed, and halt, and blind, in Christ a
   hearty welcome find.
My message, as from God, receive; ye all may come to
   Christ and live.
   O let his love your hearts constrain, nor can we let him
   die in vain.
   THIS IS THE TIME, NO MORE DELAY!
This is the Lord's accepted day.
Come thou, this moment, at his call and live for him who
   died for all."

Another hymn of invitation was,

"I have long withstood his grace, long provoked him to his
   face,
Would not hearken to his calls, grieved him by a thousand
   falls.
There for me the Saviour stands, bears his wounds and
   spreads his hands.
God is love! I know, I feel; Jesus weeps and loves me still."
Now incline me to repent, let me now my sins lament;
I my foul revolt deplore: I weep, believe, and will sin no
   more."

Think of the multiple millions in every generation for whom
that is their story. Coupled with the power of music, those words
awaken one's heart for the Holy Spirit to bring a person to conviction of sin, repentance, and the "still small voice of calm" whispering to our hearts that <u>we are more than we have become</u>. That has
pathos and comfort, reality and hope, inclusion and motivation.
The music and the message move us to "rise and go to Jesus."

The drumbeat of Arminian theology is in the hymns and the
sermon. Jesus died for everyone, not just the "elect." Some contemporary hymns in the 21st century are very Wesleyan. One by Chris
Tomlin is,

"Amazing love. How can it be
that thou, my God, shouldst die for me?"
Long my imprisoned spirit lay fast bound
in sin and nature's night;
Thine eye diffused a quickening ray;
I woke, the dungeon flamed with light;
My chains fell off, my heart was free.
I rose, went forth, and followed Thee."

After such words were sung by a soloist, a choir, or the congregation, then John Wesley or a lay preacher stood to proclaim the Gospel. The preacher announced a biblical text and began to speak extemporaneously. The language was plain, the vocabulary was simple, and the illustrations were often anonymous biographical references or personal testimonials of what God had done in the lives of people just like those listening. The sermon, like the hymns, hooked the sinners' own stories. Some illustrations brought tears and some brought laughter.

The sermon was "preaching for a verdict," a human response of the soul's being "awakened" to what Wesley called "God's whispering to the heart." They were not intentionally manipulative as a charlatan might be, but were "heart to heart."

Wesley called their message "plain truth for plain people." It was not "hell fire and damnation" or "sinners in the hands of an angry God." His emphasis was always on God's love.

The themes, according to David Hempton, were "grace, godliness, repentance, temporal and eternal joy, perseverance, vigilance, and assurance."[316] Listen.

"It was love that took my place on the cross of Calvary;
It was grace, redeeming grace,
That paid my ransom full and free
Over sin, without within. I have the victory
Thro' grace, marvelous grace, that lives in me."

That is powerful. Souls were awakened, people repented and found their "victory in Jesus." Their lives at home changed, they began going to church, their language cleaned up, and their ethics became cleaner. Indeed, according to the research of Nathan Hatch and John Wigger, Methodist converts in the first half of the

---

[316] Ibid., 75

nineteenth century formed the foundation of what sociologists later labeled "The Middle Class."

Extemporaneous Praying and Preaching

As was said of the prophet Ezekiel, so it must be said of early Methodist preachers, "They sat where their people sat." The location might be around the hitching post of the pub, or the water pump for the village, or the "green" where children played. Hanham Mount, just outside Bristol, is still a grassy knoll surrounded by a flat pasture. In Epworth where his father served for nearly forty years, John preached at the "Red Lion Pub" in the middle of the village, and on his own father's tombstone outside St. Andrews Parish Church. The crowd was the larger than the Sunday morning congregation in the church.

Both Wesley brothers preached extemporaneously with no notes. They held the Bible in their hands and stood close to their field audiences. This was in literal opposition to the position of the Anglican bishops. The parish priests urged their people not to go and hear such "tripe." However, people came, not only by the hundreds, but by the thousands. The Anglican pulpits were for the most part closed to the Wesleys who were ordained and Oxford graduates. They did not feel called to accept appointments to parish churches. Field preaching, undeniably, was the reason for the growth of the Methodist movement which upon John Wesley's death, numbered about 70,000 followers. To receive the sacraments, people still had to go to their parish Anglican Church.

For Wesley, the purpose of the sermon was to awaken, to reach the soul, to stir up the residue of the *Imago Dei* as "the deep reaches down to the deep" and moves one to conviction of sin and "desire to flee from the wrath to come." The sermon was not followed by emotional altar calls and invitational hymns as we saw in the later revival movement or in Billy Graham crusades.

George "Chuck" Hunter, when Dean of the E. Stanley Jones Institute for World Mission and Evangelism at Asbury Theological Seminary, has analyzed Wesley's method which his field preaching incorporated. "During open air services, his helpers scattered among the crowd observing responses, studying faces."[317] At the close of the service, Wesley invited any who sensed God's speak-

---

[317] Hunter, George, *To Spread the Power,* Abingdon, 1987, 57

ing to them to come at 5:00 a.m. the next morning to a local home for a Society meeting. If they came, they were nurtured from that point on by the stewards with a visit at least once a week.

If you read Wesley's sermons as printed today, you will wonder how they brought people to be converted! What we read is not what he preached! Albert Outler and Richard Heitzenrater have both documented that Wesley preached "on the stump" extemporaneously and without notes. The printed sermons available today were homiletical treatises that Wesley wrote to "teach preaching" to the lay preachers: doctrine, scriptural exegesis, and use of rhetorical questions.

There was a different theme in John's and Charles' preaching. John tended to arouse guilt, then preach forgiving grace. Charles' favorite text was "Come to me all you who are weak and heavily burdened and I will give you rest, for my yoke is easy and my burden is light."

Roots of Small Group Ministries

Religious societies were not an innovation of Wesley's. The Quakers and Moravians used this means of fellowship and spiritual accountability. The methodology of the Anglican Church's S.P.C.K. ("Society for the Propagation of Christian Knowledge") included small groups. Samuel Wesley organized a "society" in Epworth when Wesley was a boy. There were Anglican societies in Bristol before Whitefield and Wesley began preaching there.

Dr. Anthony Horneck, a German who was educated at Oxford and converted to Anglicanism, began small, parish-based societies in 1678 and wrote a manual for them, requiring "a talk, scripture including a psalm, and prayer." His fourteenth rule required that the minister approve each person who could attend. Samuel Wesley used this paradigm at Epworth. Both the Horneck and John Wesley models required "employment of the 25th chapter of Matthew in helping the poor and helpless."

Monsieur Marquis de Renty, a French Catholic, had developed societies in France, and Wesley read about de Renty while still at Oxford. Aboard the ship *Simmonds,* Wesley noted in his *Journal* for January 6, 1736, "I ended the abridgement of Mon. de Renty's life." de Renty was no stranger to Wesley. He had studied him and his small groups since Wesley's days at Oxford. Monsieur de

Renty was a French Catholic nobleman (1611-1649) who had been influenced by à Kempis' *Imitation of Christ*. After a transforming experience of Christ's presence, the Frenchman devoted his life to caring for the poor and living a regimented, holy life. Wesley admired his zeal, humility, and effectiveness.

According to Michael Henderson's research on Methodist class meetings, de Renty's societies served as the nearest prototype of Wesley's class meetings, described as "little gatherings of devout people meeting weekly for prayer, reading books, distributing food to the poor, and sharing personal religious experiences." A "high Frenchman" by birth and cultural refinement, de Renty often did manual labor alongside the peasants. His societies demanded acts of Christian kindness. de Renty also demanded of his Society members that they carry a sponge or cloth to wipe off offensive graffiti wherever they saw it. All of this deeply impressed Wesley before he sailed on the *Simmonds* for Georgia. Wesley wrote in his diary after reading de Renty again, "What cannot a man do that is zealous, disinterested, and full of God?" What he meant in his diary by "disinterested" was de Renty's ability to avoid the trap in which personal holiness can become self-centered narcissism.

Philipp Jakob Spener, August Hermann Francke, and Count Nikolaus Ludwig von Zinzendorf were Germans who had versions of small group ministry similar to de Renty's, except they did not require manual labor. On the ship *Simmonds*, the twenty-six Moravians met daily in just such a group. A frequent subject was the personal assurance of salvation, a question that haunted Wesley until Aldersgate. Wesley therefore studied the Moravian home study groups. It was in such a meeting on Aldersgate Street in 1738 that Wesley felt his heart "strangely warmed." Wesley's definition of a Wesleyan society was "a company of men having the form and seeking the power of godliness, united in order to pray together, to receive the word of exhortation, and to watch over one another in love, that they may help each other to work out their salvation."

However, in contrast to many German quietists, de Renty insisted that the road to holiness leads through the world of service. In one respect, the influence of this Catholic monk helped Wesley to see the error in the Moravian doctrine of "stillness" where people simply gathered and sat meditatively. Wesley later would go to great lengths to avoid the pitfalls of mysticism which encourages withdrawal from the world as one gets closer to God.

In an article for "London Magazine" in 1760, Wesley alluded to *The Country Parson's Advice to His Parishioners* as another source for his class meetings. He concluded that members of the small group "engaging each other in reflective conversation" will be "the most effectual means for restoring our decaying Christianity to its primitive life and vigor, and the supporting of our tottering and sinking Church."

George Whitefield was a more effective preacher in the field or pulpit than was John Wesley, but Whitefield had no organizational skills. Wesley's theology of experimental divinity was matched by his genius for organization: conferences, societies, class meetings, and bands. Whitefield lamented to a friend, "My brother Wesley acted wisely—the souls that were awakened under his ministry were joined into class and thus preserved as the fruit of his labours. This I neglected and my people are as a rope of sand."[318]

An historical analysis is also helpful. Let us now take a closer look at the three levels of groups that Wesley developed as the "spiritual culture" of Methodism:

Methodist Societies

The word "Society" was well known in English religious circles in Wesley's day. The society meetings were much like congregational worship services in churches. The Anglican S.P.C.K. (Society for Promoting Christian Knowledge) had actually sponsored Wesley when he went to Georgia in 1736. There were Anglican societies in Bristol before Whitefield or Wesley folded them into Methodist societies. Monsieur Marquis de Renty used the paradigm in French Catholicism. The Moravians also used the term "Society." For instance, it was to the "Fetter Lane Society," originally evangelically Anglican and now mostly Moravian, that Peter Bohler sent the Wesley brothers upon their return from Georgia, a time during which Bohler was their spiritual director. And, as we have recorded, Wesley revised the format and the curriculum. Let him tell us in his words:

"In November 1739, several persons came to me in London, and desired me to advise and pray with them. I said, 'If you will

---

[318] Op. cit., Telford 149

meet on Thursday night, I will help you as I can.' More and more desired to meet, till they were increased to many hundreds. The case was afterward the same at Bristol, Kingswood, Newcastle, and many other parts of England, Scotland, and Ireland." [319]

From London, he took the paradigm to Bristol. Wesley began by visiting every member "house to house." "Most of those who were sick had spotted fever, but Wesley went into their homes anyway. He also began an entrepreneurial venture, "We took twelve of the poorest and a teacher and trained them for four months in carding and spinning cotton."[320] He reported that they were soon employed and the cycle continued, but he had to delegate this to persons whom he called "stewards." Wesley introduced the requirement of tickets for admission. He wrote, "It can scarce be conceived what advantages have been reaped from this little prudential regulation."[321] Wesley was warned that his strictness might send the movement into extinction. Indeed, many were expelled, but he never wavered from his authoritarian examinations and judgments.

Actually, the first use of the term "Methodist United Society" dates from the opening of the Foundery in London in April, 1739. By June "that infant society" had increased from twelve to three hundred members."[322] "Form Societies in every place we preach," Wesley insisted to his preachers.

Society membership was at first probationary. When a person hearing the gospel presented and hearing exuberant congregational singing expressed her or his desire to join a Methodist society, only one question was asked as a prerequisite for admission, "Do you desire to flee from the wrath to come?" If admitted into "full connection," they were disciplined by practice of "means of grace," or they dropped away by what was called "backsliding." Organization of membership, disciplinary actions, congregational care, and finances were handled by "stewards."

Persons called and trained to exegete Scripture were called "exhorters." Gradually he licensed "lay preachers." He did not allow Methodist meetings during "church hours," did not allow the

---

[319] Ibid., 173

[320] Ibid., 173

[321] Ibid., 151

[322] Op. cit., Heitzenrater, ˆ 113

administration of the sacrament of baptism or the Lord's Supper, and did not allow the use of ecclesiastical titles such as "bishop."

Most met on early Sunday morning and adjourned before "church hour," or on Sunday evenings after Anglican Evensong. Once a quarter, the Chief Steward examined every member of the society "one-on-one." Disciplined living was a requirement. We have a record of that examination at the Newcastle Society when seventy-six were questioned about their self-discipline and sixty-four were expelled. Members in good standing had tickets for admission to society meetings. It was in Newcastle in 1743 that he wrote what we still have as "The General Rules." Indeed, in American Methodism, at the General Conference of 1808, they, along with the Articles of Religion, the episcopacy, and the itinerancy of pastors were called "Restrictive Rules."

Wesley wrote to Adam Clarke in 1787, "It is a true saying, 'The soul and body make a man; the Spirit and discipline make a Christian.'"[323] Wesley spelled this out in his sermon, "On God's Vineyard,"

> "It is certain that in this respect the Methodists are a highly favoured people. Nothing can be more simple, nothing more rational, than the Methodist discipline; it is entirely founded on common sense, particularly applying the general rules of Scripture. Any person determined to save his soul may be united (this is the only condition required) with them. But this desire must be evidenced by three marks: avoiding all known sin, doing good after his power, and attending all the ordinances of God. He is then placed in such a class as is convenient for him, where he spent about an hour in a week. And the next quarter, if nothing is objected to him, he was admitted into the Society. And therein he could continue as long as he met with his brethren and walked according to his profession."[324]

The Society was not the same as the open-air preaching service. Those who sensed an "awakening of their soul" were invited to attend a Society meeting. These met weekly, and were

---

[323] Richey, Russell, Campbell, Dennis, Lawrence, William, *Marks of Methodism*, Abingdon, 2005, 84

[324] Op. cit., Ward & Heitzenrater, *JWW, J &D*, Vol, 19, 511-512

not open to the public. After attending only three Society meetings, seekers indicated a desire to join. Each member was to be visited once a week. The decision to join brought with it a rather dramatically changed lifestyle.

The places of society meeting were plain and austere with no communion table, no kneeling bench, no paraments, no cross and candles. Unlike the band and class meeting which came later, the society meetings were not dialogical. The people sat in rows on backless benches, and listened to the leader. There were no pews reserved for higher classes as the seating was egalitarian. Fine ladies and landed gentry had to sit beside uncouth miners or unwashed factory workers.

This was highly irregular in the English class system of that day. Society meetings never were scheduled at the hour of established church services as every effort was made to avoid being in conflict with the Anglican parish church. It was the umbrella group, the identifying symbol of Methodism, even to outsiders.

Class Meetings

Henry Ward Beecher, a Calvinist, said, "The greatest thing John Wesley ever gave to the world is the Methodist class meeting." Dwight L. Moody said, "The Methodist class meetings are the best institution for training new Christians the world will ever see." The class meeting was the matrix for what historians call the "radical transformation of England's working classes" into persons of moral fiber, family responsibility, character integrity, and community betterment.

The origin of the Methodist class meeting is well known. They began in Bristol after the Societies in both London and Bristol were too large for pastoral care or spiritual mentoring. Wesley is characteristically specific: "While we were thinking of quite another thing, we struck upon a method for which we have cause to bless God ever since. I was talking with several of the Society in Bristol (Feb. 15th, 1742) concerning the means of paying the debts there, when Captain Foy stood up and said, 'Let every member of the Society give a penny a week, till all the debts are paid.' Another said, 'But many are poor, and cannot afford it.' 'Then,' said the first man, 'put eleven of the poorest with me, and if they can give nothing, I will give for them as well as for myself.' It was done. In a while some of these informed me they found such and such a one did not live as he ought. It struck me immediately, 'This is the thing, the very thing, we have wanted so long.' I called together the leaders of the classes and desired that each would make a particular inquiry into the behaviour of those whom he saw weekly. They did so. Many disorderly walkers were detected. Some turned from the evil of their ways, and some were put away from us." [325] "The class meeting was thus endowed with a pastoral, financial, and devotional function.

D. Michael Henderson calls the class meeting the "behavioral mode" of Wesley's method. In the eighteen months prior to December, 1743, in London, one Society grew from 455 members with 65 classes at 7 per class meeting to 1404 members with 117 classes at 12 per meeting. Unlike the revival ethos where the penitent was asked doctrinal questions, seekers in Wesley's time were nurtured into an experience of saving grace over a period of days, weeks, or months. There were catechumen instructions initially, and then encouragement, reproof, and accountability for seekers. There was a six months probationary period followed by a vote of the class as to whether the candidate was ready for full membership.

This has a striking similarity to the Celtic evangelism that George Hunter has described in his volume, *The Celtic Way of Evangelism*. It also syncs with the emotional needs of 21st century pre-Christians who are leery of leaping into a new construct of religious beliefs. Many "church refugees" have been disenchanted with what they call "organized religion." "Discipling" involves a process of trust, caring fellowship, and honest inquiry. The class meeting paradigm, in Wesley's day and now, meets needs that neither Sunday worship nor Sunday School can meet. The pastor appointed the leader, who was in charge in the pastor's absence.[326] He was called the "Steward."

It was soon resolved that each class meet in one place at a given time, beginning and closing with song and prayer. This practice became general, and gave efficiency and organization to the Wesleyan Societies. Class meeting participation continued indefinitely, with home visits by the stewards in between meetings

---

[325] Op. cit., McTyeire, 202 (quoting Wesley without citing the specific source)

[326] Ibid. p. 203

and society worship on Sunday mornings. They met at times not conflicting with the Established Church services of worship. And so it was that early Methodism was shaped ... and grew.

The first Methodist hymnal was organized entirely around Wesley's *Ordo Salutis* so that in class meeting, you sang your faith. After being virtually ignored over two hundred years, Albert Outler revived the term *"Ordo Salutis."* In the 1989 edition of *The United Methodist Hymnal,* Andy Langford arranged the hymns in the order of the work of God's grace in our lives preparing, saving, and perfecting. The hymns numbered 337-536 are arranged accordingly!

However, the exhorter or lay preacher at "society meeting" reminded everyone of Wesley's combination of faith and witness. Today we call this Methodist "orthopraxy"; it is "orthodoxy in practice."

Questions of faith:

- Do you believe in God's never-ending love for you and do you love God and love your neighbor?

- Do you believe that God's mercy and grace are for all humankind?

- Do you repent of your sins and respond with your heart to God's prevenient and forgiving grace?

- Do you intend to follow a spiritual journey that leads to perfect love?

As a member, you covenanted to three things:

1. prohibitions for things not to do (avoid strong drink, profanity, beating family members, etc.)
2. new behaviors to assume so habits are being re-formed
3. faithful practice of 'means of grace' meaning prayer, searching the scriptures, frequent communion, holy conversations with colleagues, public worship.

But for Wesley the society and class meeting did not replace the Church. To become a class leader, one studied and was examined on the studies for at least two years. The leader then knew the Methodist doctrine of grace theology, Arminianism, optional modes of baptism, and open communion.

The "means of grace" he divides them into two categories:

- "chief"– prayer, searching the scriptures, and taking the Lord's Supper

- "other" - the preached Word, holy conversations, public worship, and fasting. When the means of grace are done regularly and with perseverance, the practitioners "will be awakened in their souls and reach salvation." (Note that he does not list baptism or church membership.)

Philip Hardt has rendered all denominations of Wesleyan heritage a great service in his careful research of the class meeting in New York City.[327] In doing so, he sees the early use and subsequent decline of the class meeting as American Methodism's evolution from what Ernst Troeltsch's classic work, *The Social Teaching of Christian Churches,* calls a "sect" into a "church." He defines a sect as "lay Christianity, personal achievement in ethics and in religion, radical fellowship of love, religious equality and brotherly love, indifference toward the state, ideal of poverty, directness of personal religious relationship, criticism of official spiritual guides, appeal to the New Testament and the Primitive Church."[328] The Pilgrims, Quakers, and Moravians were sectarian. So were the English Methodists. Troeltsch sees the sects as historically corrective because they restored elements which the institutional church invariably either allow to lapse or become fearful of. In short, "churches" become acculturated, reflecting the ethos of their societal context. This illustrates exactly the development of Methodism from English sect to American denomination.

The Bands

The concept of bands came from the Moravians. All members of the societies or class meeting were not members of the bands. In contrast to the society which was cognitive and the class meeting which was behavioral in emphasis, Michael Henderson calls

---

[327] Hardt, Philip, *The Soul of Methodism,* University Press of America, 2000

[328] Troeltsch, *The Social Teaching of the Christian Churches,* Harper Torchbooks, 1960, 336

the bands "the affectional mode."[329] He observes that "the bands facilitated the cultivation of inner purity, the purging of hurtful additions to substances, attitudes, and spiritual sloth, and a more disciplined life."[330]

The "Twelve Step" programs of Alcoholics Anonymous and the several adaptations of the AA program have much of the psychological dynamics of these Methodist bands. Their method was what Wesley called "close conversation" which meant testimonial witness and soul-searching inquiry concerning motives, resistance and acquiescence to temptations, and feelings.

A band was a group of from four to six persons of the same gender and same marital status. Wesley used as the scriptural guide the words from the Book of James 5:16, "Confess your faults one to another and pray for one another, that ye may be healed." One must remember that most of these early converts to Christian discipleship lived a hard scrabble existence. Many had been abusers and abused, addicts and victims, exploited and oppressed, impoverished and disenfranchised, lonely and afraid. Now they had this intimate support group, this caring faith community, these soulmates.

Wesley wrote in defense of the bands, "They wanted to pour out their hearts without reserve, particularly with regard to the sin which did still easily beset them and the temptations which were most apt to prevail over them." No visitors were allowed and participants must be invited from persons already in class meetings.

The small band rules:

1. Meet once a week, at least.

2. Come punctually at the hour appointed.

3. Begin, exactly at the hour, with singing or prayer.

4. Speak, each of us ... the true state of our soul, with the faults we have committed in thought, word, and deed, and the temptations we have felt.

5. Appoint some person to speak first ... then ask the rest

---

[329] Henderson, Michael, *John Wesley's Class Meeting: A Model for Making Disciples,* Asbury Press, 1998, . 112

[330] Ibid. p. 115

searching questions ...

   a. "What sins have you committed since our last meeting?"

   b. "What temptations have you met?"

   c. "Were you delivered from their power?"

   d. "What have you done in thought, word, or deed that could be sin?"

   e. "Have you nothing you desire to keep secret?"

6. End with prayer.

In contrast to the class meeting where the leader was the major speaker, all band members were urged to share and bare their souls. One can easily see how the temptation to gossip about what was shared in band meeting became an issue for those present. Wesley did not require band membership, and perhaps, the insistence that all members of any given band were single men or single women or married men or married women proved to be more a liability than an asset. The bands were never used widely in America. One reason was the distance between homesteads, and the sheer geographic vastness of America compared to England. For whatever reasons, the bands simply faded away.

Penitential Bands

Another, and less utilized, Wesley model was the "Penitential Band." This was a "detox group" for persons who had resorted to drunkenness, theft, wife beating, etc. They were sought out and invited to join what we would call a recovery group so they could be re-claimed and set on the higher way again. They were used only in England where the times were tough, grog shops were everywhere, prostitutes abounded, gambling was practiced in a hundred ways, and few got home with their pay envelopes. The "victory song" of the penitential band is expressed in the old gospel hymn:

> **"Yield not to temptation, for yielding is sin.**
> **Each victory will help you some other to win;**
>   **Fight manfully onward, dark passions subdue,**
> **Look ever to Jesus, he'll carry you through.**
>   **Shun evil companions, bad language disdain,**
> **God's name hold in reverence, nor take it in vain;**

Be thoughtful and earnest, kindhearted and true,
Look ever to Jesus; he'll carry you through.
    To him that o'ercometh God giveth a crown,
Thro faith we will conquer though often cast down
He who is our Savior our strength will renew,
    Look ever to Jesus, he'll carry you through.
Refrain: Ask the Savior to help you, comfort, strengthen
    and keep you;
He is willing to aid you, he'll carry you through.

The "Penitential Bands" were congregational rehabilitation groups. The concept was wonderful but their use was never widespread.

CHAPTER TEN

Early Connectional Innovations

We must remember that Methodism in Britain was never a church in John Wesley's lifetime. Only the Church of England was the "Established Church." To be a "Dissenting Church" like the Quakers, Moravians, and others, the group had to be in existence in 1689 when the "Act of Toleration" was passed by Parliament. That allowed churches other than the Established Church to meet freely and openly. Of course, the Methodists were not in existence in 1689! Therefore, Wesley devised "innovations" that were legal because they were seen as practices of a reform movement in Anglicanism. Both Wesley brothers were careful to claim that they were ordained Anglican priests, that the sacraments were never a part of Methodism in their lifetimes, and that Methodist meetings were never held during "church hours."

The Message of Methodism

Methodism was and is much more than organization. Methodism was a new paradigm, different from anything in Britain's Established Church, Dissenters, or Puritans. The cumulative minutes of Wesley's annual conferences were collated to form what was called "The Large Minutes." Dr. Robert Cushman of Duke insisted in his book, *Experimental Divinity,* that these Large Minutes contained the message of Methodism.

Cushman, using a Latin term, called Methodism's "creed" *Consensus Fidelium ("consensus of faith")*. Albert Outler called Methodist doctrine "a marrow" of Christian Doctrine. By the twentieth century, the mainstream of United Methodism had allowed this consensus, this marrow, to suffer what Dr. William Abraham of Southern Methodist University called "doctrinal amnesia."

After a century of benign neglect, Wesley's theology was

resurrected by Albert Outler in the 1960's during his tenure at SMU. He, and, in his footsteps, many Methodist scholars, began a much-needed recovery of Wesley's sermons, tracts, letters, diaries, and journals. Sadly, few clergy and fewer laity have read deeply in Wesleyan grace theology. Rather we have resorted to maxims like "the quadrilateral" to summarize the *consensus fidelium,* the "experimental divinity."

To appreciate today the message of early Methodism, the setting in history is important. The roots of Methodism were in Oxford University. John Wesley lived on the campus of Oxford University from 1720 until 1735. The "new" and prevailing philosophy of the early 18th century was the Enlightenment. Wesley not only knew the emerging philosophy, he rather adroitly wove some of the "new" insights into Methodism. He set aside the traditional Descartes approach to philosophy and adapted John Locke's theories of knowledge into his "experimental divinity." Wesley was not a speculative theologian. He insisted that with one exception, Locke was right that all knowledge is received by one's five physical senses.

That one exception was Wesley's added sixth sense, a spiritual sense. It was this dimension of our knowledge that convinced him that a sensible, reasonable spiritual experience could result in the assurance that one's sins are forgiven. He called it "witness of the Spirit" based especially on Romans 8.

Wesley was an Arminian. That is, he was not a Calvinist. Jacob Arminius, a Dutch Calvinist prodigy, came to challenge predestination. Like Calvin, Arminius believed we are saved by God's grace, not by our free will, but he believed that God's is a universal grace and that Jesus died for all humankind, not the elect. He also believed that God's grace can be accepted or rejected. Randy Maddox called this "response-able" grace. Salvation is synchronistic, involving both God's will and our response, not monergistic which would leave humankind as a puppet on a string.

In addition to Enlightenment philosophy and Arminian theology, pietism arose in Wesley's time. Protestantism saw this in Germany among the Moravians, in Protestant France among the Palatinates and Huguenots, and in England among the Quakers. All were dissenters to their indigenous state churches and saw the Church as a voluntary association whose only authority was the consent of its members.[331] He knew them all. All also were allowing untrained laity to practice the functions previously reserved for clergy such as preaching, teaching, and administering the sacraments.

So it was that his mind was the "confluence of many streams." From it all he developed his "grace upon grace" theology. Dr. Robert Cushman ferreted out Wesley's term, "experimental divinity"[332] to define Methodism' essence.

Wesley's "Light from the Christian East"

Wesley's interest in, studies of, and attraction to, Eastern Christianity was long overlooked in Wesley biographies. It was Albert Outler in the 1960's who first cited Wesley's borrowing some theological insights from the first four centuries of the "primitive church" before Augustine. Outler pointed out that in Wesley's sermon, "Sermon on the Mount IV," he preached, "The providence of God has so mingled you together with other men that whatever grace you have received of God may through you be communicated to others."

Randy Maddox complemented Outler's pioneering work with Maddox's monumentally important textbook of grace theology—*Responsible Grace*. He points out, "Eastern theology based their anthropology more on Creation than on the Fall." Wesley repeatedly referred to conversion as "being restored," which was reflective of his emphasis on Genesis 1:27: the "original righteousness" that was inherent in humankind's being created in God's own image. "Wesley's understanding of human nature and the human predicament gives primacy of place to therapeutic concerns."[333] Maddox points out that Wesley called sin "dis-ease," used the term "plague of sin," and called being saved "taking the cure." Outler, Heitzenrater, and Maddox, all Wesley scholars, called Wesley's brand of theology, "orthopathy." In Charles Wesley's beloved Christmas carol, he has Methodists sing, "Light and life to all he brings, risen with healing in his wings."

Maddox adroitly points out that, prior to Aldersgate, Wesley

---

[331] Op. cit., Hempton, 51

[332] Cushman, Robert, *Experimental Divinity,* Kingswood, 1989

[333] Op. cit., Maddox, Randy, *Responsible Grace,* 67

"was making only a juridical claim that he was aware of God's pardon of the penalty of his sin. He actually came to Aldersgate expecting more than a juridical claim." He came seeking the assurance of which Peter Bohler had spoken and which Wesley's own brother, Charles, now had experienced. That morning John Wesley opened his Bible to 2 Peter 1:4 which he took as a direct promise that he could be a partaker of the divine nature. Finally, his *Journal* entry "placed as much stress on God's grace's giving us a new heart that would incessantly do good works as it did on forgiveness" (*per se*).[334] With great insight Maddox acknowledges that Wesley admitted "my wound was not fully healed," but that the idiom of this disappointment was still more the language of the clinic than of the court.

In Wesley's development of the doctrine of sanctification (perfecting grace), he focused on the therapeutic efficacy of the Holy Spirit to deliver us from the plague of sin:

> "By salvation, I mean, not barely... deliverance from hell or going to heaven, but a present deliverance from sin, a restoration of the soul to its primitive health, its original purity; a recovery of the divine nature; the renewal of our souls after the image of God in righteousness and true holiness, in justice, in mercy, and truth."[335]

Now we turn to the innovative ways in which Wesley communicated his message to a quite wide variety of people.

Societies

As has been documented, the "structures" of field gatherings, society meeting, class meetings, and bands were adopted, "tweaked" and woven into a new context, but each had predecessors that Wesley had known from somewhere. The paradigm of an evangelical society was not new, but Wesley began to use the term "United Societies," which obviously had a connectional implication.

Once the Foundery in London was occupied in April, 1739, Wesley was linking that society with Bristol societies and using the term "United Societies." By late summer, 1740, the Foundery

---

[334] Ibid., 144

[335] Wesley, John, *A Further Appeal to Men of Reason and Religion,* IN Maddox, Randy, *Responsible Grace,* 144f

society had grown from a dozen who had come from the Fetter Lane Society to three hundred. This meant that people who gathered for "field preaching" were being garnered into disciplined societies. "Those who were united together grew stronger in the faith."[336]

By 1742, Wesley was establishing societies in Wales and the Midlands when Lady Huntingdon suggested that he go north to Newcastle upon Tyne. He soon had a society there, and, thanks to the generosity of a Quaker, a meetinghouse which also served as a home for orphans. There in 1743, he drew up "General Rules of Our United Societies" and distributed them throughout the connection. By now, it was obvious that he needed "shepherds for the flocks."

To be admitted to a Methodist society, the only requirement was to affirm that you "desire to flee from the wrath to come." While that is the only requirement to be admitted, it was not true for remaining a member. To remain a member, one had to subscribe in lifestyle to what the various generations of the *Book of Discipline* know as "the General Rules." The General Rules have often been reduced to a brief philosophy and life style summarized in this way:

"Do no harm."

"Do all the good you can."

"Attend the ordinances of God" (meaning an Anglican Church).

However, Wesley's General Rules had much more specificity. For instance, under the section called "Doing no harm," the General Rules prohibit:

- "profaning the day of the Lord," either by doing ordinary work or by buying or selling";

- "uncharitable conversation..." particularly ministers

- "putting on of gold or costly apparel";

- "singing those songs or reading those books which do not tend to the knowledge or love of God";

---

[336] Op. cit., Heitzenrater, *People Called Methodists,* 113

- "laying up treasures on earth."

The threat of being "disfellowshipped" from the society
was explicit: "If there be any among us who observe them not,
who habitually break any of them, let it be known unto them
who watch over that soul...we will admonish him of the error
of his ways. We will bear with him for a season. But then, if he
repent not, he hath no more place among us." When the General
Rules were first employed in Newcastle, sixty-four persons were
expelled from the society. However, eight hundred remained.

In reality, a strict obedience to the General Rules did not
survive Wesley's own generation. In England, the Methodists
never shed the stigma of being called "chapel people," but they
did not require obedience to the General Rules. In America,
Methodists became gentrified and known as "The Middle Class."
In America, the General Rules are printed, but not long followed
legalistically.

Lay Preaching–Heresy and Necessity

As Anglicans, neither John nor Charles Wesley had ever
thought about preaching outside the Church, extemporaneously,
or without a manuscript. Then, less than a year after Wesley's
Aldersgate experience, George Whitefield, a colleague from
Oxford days, began preaching at the mine shafts, factory gates,
and open areas around Bristol, in England's "West Country."
Meanwhile, following their evangelical experiences of saving
grace, they were not being invited to preach in London's Anglican
pulpits. In March, 1739, John responded to Whitefield's second call
to help him in Bristol. Whitefield, in effect, said, "Come and See,"
Wesley was a pragmatist. He went, he saw, he adopted!

One year after Aldersgate, thousands were coming to hear
Whitefield. Most of those who came were baptized Anglicans who
had been sadly overlooked by the parish churches The Anglican
parishes were situated to serve an agrarian society and did not
create new parishes to serve the radical population shift associated with the Industrial Revolution in towns like Bristol, Liverpool, Birmingham, Manchester, and Newcastle.

Wesley was determined to take the good news of the Gospel
to the over-populated, under-paid, under-nourished, and abusive
industrial centers. The crowds were phenomenal. They had

never heard a preacher say that God loved them! Therefore, Wesley simply had to provide leadership for the growing number of converts who needed shepherding. As an Anglican, Wesley believed that only ordained clergy should practice either Word, Sacrament, or Order, but his exposure to the Moravians had softened that. Now Wesley faced a situation that would challenge his devout loyalty to Anglican tradition. Should he use laity to preach as the Moravians did? As the saying goes, "Necessity is the mother of invention." And, again, John was a pragmatist.

Wesley moved cautiously and often contradicted himself on the authority of the lay preacher. As an Anglican, he was committed to a priestly distinction between the role of the laity and the role of the clergy. He could not find scriptural justification for lay preaching. Yet he was committed to a missional vision for the disenfranchised, dispossessed, and ecclesiastically neglected. The struggle of soul was real, pitting John Wesley, Fellow of Lincoln College, against the evangelical pragmatist with mandate for mission. In the end, his pragmatism prevailed.

The person who pushed Wesley to accept lay preaching was his mother. Susanna now lived in the Foundery apartments. To Wesley's sheer delight, she had recently espoused Methodism, celebrating, finally, as an old woman, the assurance of the forgiveness of her sins. While he was in Bristol, he had left a young layman, Thomas Maxwell, in charge of the Foundery in London. Thomas had no formal education. He was to hold prayer meetings, to give spiritual advice, and to exhort (i.e. teach the scriptures), but not to preach. With John on the road and his mother in charge, young Thomas Maxwell began to preach and many people were converted.

This irregularity was reported to Wesley and he made haste to London! "Well, Thomas Maxwell has turned preacher, I find." And his mother replied, "John, you know what my sentiments have been. You cannot suspect me of favoring anything of this kind readily. But take care what you do to that young man, for he is as surely called to preach as you are. First examine the fruits of his preaching, and then, hear him yourself." He did just that and was amazed at what he heard from a "natural." He responded, "It is the Lord; let him do what seemeth to him good."[337]

---

[337] Op. Cit, Heitzenrater, *People Called Methodists,* 115

Wesley heard the echo of Isaiah's experience in the Temple: "Whom shall I send? And who will go for us?" (Isaiah 6:1-8) The result was that he reluctantly licensed "exhorters" who would explain the Scriptures and examine the journeys of new Christians in the emerging societies. The line was fuzzy between "exhorting" and preaching–so fuzzy that the meaning was in the mind of the definer. Soon after the Maxwell incident when his mother set him straight, Wesley ended his struggle with his Anglican heritage conscience. While he continued to license some as exhorters; he began appointing lay preachers to fill the pulpits, even portable pulpits in the open fields. There was one caveat; they could not administer the sacraments.

So it was that exhorters became preachers. A new paradigm of Methodist preacher was recognized—the lay person who had the experience of grace and the gifts of preaching. Wesley designed questions that are still in *The United Methodist Discipline* today for those who wish to be certified as Candidates for Ordained Ministry:

"1. Do they know God as a pardoning God?

2. Have they the gifts as well as evidence of God's grace?

3. Have they fruit?"

"As long as these marks occur in them, we believe they are called of God to serve. These we receive as sufficient proof that they are moved by the Holy Spirit."[338]

He first appointed five lay preachers as his assistants; then a host became itinerants. Wesley the high churchman became a missioner who said, "I durst not refuse their assistance." Indeed, he began calling them his "sons in the Gospel."

Circuits

Wesley's organizational genius made him aware that the lay preachers could not "go rogue." If the "general rules" were to be kept and doctrine was to be taught, Wesley realized he needed a system of supervision. He needed local, assigned leadership. He therefore resolved, "not to strike one stroke in a place where he could not follow up the blow." Following up meant a lay preacher

---

[338] *United Methodist Book of Discipline,* ¶305, 186

who had assigned specific places to preach

Consequently, Wesley, the organizational genius, designed the "circuit plan." To each circuit would be appointed an in-resident "circuit rider." These were not to "ramble, touch and go, "overlapping their efforts and leaving their return unpredictable.

Regarding circuits, Richard Heitzenrater records, "In order to coordinate this program of widespread field preaching, Wesley established circuits, which were regional preaching 'rounds.' Preachers stayed on a circuit only one month; then were rotated to another. However, a local lay person was the "circuit steward" who provided continuity and organized pastoral care. He established seven circuits in 1746—London, Bristol, Cornwall, Evesham, Yorkshire, Newcastle, and Wales. By 1747 there were nine circuits; by 1750, there were seventy with London, Bristol, and Newcastle upon Tyne as the anchor societies. [339]

Conferences

As the circuits expanded, Wesley wanted even more of a connectional, controllable means of missional governance. He became aware of variance in the doctrine being preached, the emotionalism being encouraged, and the lack of discipline. He designed what has become the definitive word and body of connectional Methodism – the Conference.

The first Methodist Annual Conference was convened on June 25, 1744. The London Society alone now had over 3,000 members, but only the preachers could attend Wesley's conferences. There was only one annual conference for the entire British connexion. The preachers from all the circuits and societies were thereby knitted together by an annual conference over which Mr. Wesley presided with total authority. Communion was served to all. Then began a series of questions and discussions that Wesley developed as the annual conference agenda.

Wesley was in total command of the agenda, closing with the "setting of the appointments." The conference provided the venue where Wesley's personality could express itself with the most authoritarianism of the <u>preachers and the societies</u>. The umbrella term for all the conferences became "The Connexion" in Britain and "The Connection" in America.

---

[339] Op. cit., Heitzenrater, *People Called Methodists*, 162

The preachers were licensed, not ordained. Some remained local, but some were licensed to be traveling preachers. These were not to "ramble, touch and go, overlapping their efforts and leaving their return unpredictable." They traveled with a plan, preaching in each place at fixed times, with the regularity and harmony of the solar system itself."

Wesley never ceased being an academician. He identified himself as a "Fellow of Lincoln College" and he wore the gown of the academy. He insisted that the unlettered lay preachers must be students: "Some of you say, 'But I read only the Bible.' If you need no book but the Bible you are above St. Paul. He wanted others too and wrote to Timothy, 'Bring the books when you come, especially the parchments.' (II Timothy 4:13) 'But I have no books.' I will give each of you, as fast as you will read them, books to the value of five pounds."[340]

By the third conference (1746) the question was asked, "Can there be any such thing as a general union of our Societies throughout England?" The answer was affirmative. By this time, the Methodist movement had taken on most of the trappings of a denomination, but John and Charles Wesley still insisted that only the Anglican Church was "the Church."

By 1758, Wesley had preached in every county of Ireland except Sligo. In going there, he discovered a settlement of German Palatinates, Protestants who had escaped from Catholicism in the Alsace-Lorraine Rhine River Valley that divided France and Germany. They had no ministers and were known for drunkenness, cursing, and utter neglect of anything religious. Some were soldiers. Wesley had a great response to his preaching and the earliest Methodist emigrants to America were the Palatinates from Ireland in the early 1760's.

As has been mentioned, the Industrial Revolution had wreaked havoc with the "old order" in Britain. Emigration became widespread. Cultural security had morphed into cultural insecurity which made the Methodist society and class meeting a welcome opportunity for developing some sense of belonging. It was a providential moment in time for a new religious movement that had Anglican roots with a populist accent.

---

[340] Ibid. 227, 228

The Methodist Movement's Place in English Society

By the 1760's most opposition to Wesley had abated; he was by then considered a venerable old man. The mobs gathered to hear him preach rather than throwing rocks. Technically, Methodism was still a movement, but only technically. They were holding annual conferences, gathering in conference owned meeting-houses, and licensing lay preachers, both men and women.

Wesley was facing tremendous pressure at home by the lay preachers who were wanting separation from the Church. "In February, 1766, he wrote to John Fletcher, 'Unity and holiness are the two things I want among the Methodists.'"[341] When Wesley spoke these words to Fletcher, he was almost unaware of what was happening in the American English colonies. Without Anglican clergy or the British parish system, the other side of the Atlantic was a "field white unto harvest." The same Enlightenment philosophy that was read in England was being read by men in the colonies like James Madison, Alexander Hamilton, Benjamin Franklin, and Thomas Jefferson. Parliament, in order to pay off the national debt amassed by the Seven Years War, passed laws to impose a number of new taxes on the colonies, and a resistance movement was becoming rather raucous.

Even as early as 1760, Methodism had spread without missional intent to the American colonies. Philip Embury and his cousin, Barbara Ruckle Heck, moved with other German Palatinates from Ireland to New York. There they were helped by Captain Thomas Webb of the Queen's Navy, a Methodist lay preacher who knew John Wesley personally.

Also, Robert Strawbridge and John King moved from the "River Shannon" in Ireland to Maryland in about 1760 and began laboring in the Baltimore area. Robert Williams who came to America with Wesley's knowledge but not "under appointment" had established preaching points in the Virginia Tidewater and into North Carolina. All these went at their own initiative without being officially appointed.

Finally, through the influence of Captain Webb, Wesley read out to the conference in 1769 a new appointment: "America __________."

---

[341] Ibid., 223

Joseph Pilmore and Richard Boardman volunteered and were the first appointed Methodist missionaries sent by John Wesley to America.[342] Boardman made little impact.

In England and America, the next year, 1770, two pillars of Methodism ceased their ministries. Charles Wesley retired and George Whitefield died. Whitefield was buried in Massachusetts in a Congregational Church cemetery. On November 18, 1770, John Wesley preached at a memorial service in Tottenham Court Tabernacle in London to a massive crowd that flowed into the garden. Whitefield's Calvinist followers were offended that Wesley glossed over the longstanding theological difference between the two by saying at the funeral, "Whitefield proclaimed the same 'grand doctrines" as Wesley himself. To Wesley, though, their friendship from Oxford days prevailed over doctrine. Charles' retirement was at least partially driven by his deepening determination that the Methodists would not become a new denomination.

At the conference in 1771, five lay preachers answered a call from Wesley for missionaries to America. He chose two of them, Richard Wright and Francis Asbury, both in their mid-twenties with minimal education. Wright made no mark while Asbury became the father of American Methodism. At that time, the *Minutes* listed 500 Methodists in America and 46,000 in Britain.

The "times, they were 'achanging." Wesley was about to admit that Anglicanism was an "old wineskin that could not accept the expansion and change of new wine." To his credit, he was still amazingly active, alert, and visionary.

---

[342] Ibid., 244

CHAPTER ELEVEN

Methodism in England in Wesley's Later Years

David Hempton has written, "The movement that Wesley founded flirted with the edge of religious enthusiasm, but had some powerful restraining impulses; it came across to outsiders as fundamentally irrational, but it had deep roots in reason and rationality."[343] As Wesley himself moved into what Richard Heitzenrater calls "the more mature Mr. Wesley," he re-thought some of his earlier positions, partly because the world around him changed and partly because his own perceptions had matured.[344]

Opposition from Calvinists

Calvinism was more a thorny issue for Wesley because George Whitefield, a colleague since Oxford days and Wesley's successor in Georgia, had become a Calvinist. Whitefield's "deep pockets" benefactor was Lady Huntingdon who went so far as to endow a Calvinist college—Trevecca. Another outspoken critic of Wesley was Augustus Toplady, who is known to every Protestant today as the author of the hymn, "Rock of Ages." By 1770, the rupture between Wesley and Whitefield's followers had become acrimonious.

The Calvinists believed that the Elect are saved by God's selective grace, monergistically saving some and leaving the rest to be damned ,"For he is deemed omnipotent ... because, governing heaven and earth by his providence, he so regulates all things that nothing takes place without his deliberation."[345] That is, people

---

[343] Op. cit., Hempton 42

[344] Op. cit., Heitzenrater, *People Called Methodists*, 261

[345] Thorsen, *Don, Calvin vs. Wesley,* Abingdon, 2013, 3

have absolutely no role in their salvation. Wesley, an Arminian, insisted that while we are indeed saved by grace, we have the free will to accept God's initiating grace (mediated through what he called a "spiritual sense" or an "inward impression on the soul"). By the same token, he believed that we can "quench the Spirit" and choose not to receive God's amazing grace.

Secondly, Wesley insisted that, once saved, we are called to good works. Calvinists insisted, "Even people's obedient good works, subsequent to conversion, are the result of divine grace and not of human initiation."[346]

Catholics argued that people are to "cooperate with the assisting grace of God," where "We can spurn God's grace or be obedient to it."[347] Therefore, Calvinists accused Wesley of being a covert Catholic, a "Papist." Calvin insisted, "We falsely think that we have some power of free will, but God does not test us as if we have the will to do the right or wrong thing, rather God tests us to compel us to recognize our nothingness."[348] Wesley did not think that we are saved by good works, but he did think that the saved will do good works.

Professor David Hempton of Boston School of Theology states well Wesley's position's contrast with the Calvinists: "What is distinctive about Methodist spirituality is its emphasis on scriptural holiness through which human beings take control of their spiritual destinies, not as passive respondents to the iron will of God, but as active agents in 'working out our own salvation' or what Randy Maddox calls 'responsible grace.'"[349] Whereas in "monergism," God is the only actor, in "synergism," both God and humankind are free agents. The result was a Methodist emphasis on spiritual zeal, moral earnestness, and serious Christian living. These principles spurred many "deeds of justice and acts of kindness." It also inspired Christian women to use their gifts in Christian service. Methodism was restless, energetic, expansionist, emotional, and earnest about improving the social order.

As a printed confrontation to the Calvinists, Wesley published

---

[346] Ibid., 47

[347] Ibid. 47

[348] Ibid. 47

[349] Op. cit., Hempton, 58

a new edition of his sermons in 1771, making the number of his "standard sermons" to become fifty-two rather than forty-three in his previous editions. In the sermons he often quoted biblical passages that support holy living and biblical books like James who wrote, "Faith without words is dead." (Remarkably, in no sermon of this or later editions did he mention Aldersgate.)

Six years later, he decided to meet the Calvinist controversy head on by producing the *Arminian Magazine* which he would continue until his death. It had four parts:

- writings that defended universal atonement (Jesus died for everyone, not just the Elect)

- biographical vignettes of saints who practiced holy living

- letters from and about contemporaneous Christians known for their "deeds of justice and acts of mercy"

- poetry and hymn lyrics that were Arminian, predominantly by Charles Wesley.

As a movement, Methodism continued to grow but the increases were becoming smaller as the Methodist movement entered its fourth decade. There also were fewer conversions. In 1774, Wesley wrote Edward Perronet, the author of the hymn, "All Hail the Power of Jesus' Name." He confided his concern about the smaller conversion numbers, "If we could once bring all our preachers…uniformly and steadily to insist on those two points, 'Christ dying for us,' and 'Christ reigning in us,' we should shake the trembling gates of hell."[350] Doctrinally, those two messages would be God's saving grace and God's sanctifying or perfecting grace.

Women as Preachers

Women, sometimes called "Mothers of Methodism," found much in Methodism that attracted them. In 1771, the Calvinists published pamphlets quoting Paul's prohibition for women to teach or preach, or even to speak in church. Their fury was spurred by the testimonies of Mary Bosanquet and Sarah Crosby that they were called to preach. Wesley responded with equal

---

[350] Op. cit., Heitzenrater, *People Called Methodists*, 251

passion, "I do not believe that every woman is called to speak publicly, no more than every man to be a Methodist preacher; yet some have an extraordinary call to it, and woe be to them if they obey it not."[351] He went further in explaining that this "extraordinary call" is part and parcel of "the whole work of God termed 'Methodism'" and was an "extraordinary dispensation" of God's providence." Women preachers were euphemistically called "Mothers of Methodism." [352] Wesley was a pragmatist! His orthodoxy has been called "orthopraxy."

Sadly, the more numerous the lay preachers became, the more they were male. "None of the traveling or local preachers were women, however, some were preaching in their societies. Sarah Crosby's class grew to over two hundred people. She stated clearly, 'I do not think it wrong for women to speak in public provided they speak by the Spirit of God.'"[353] In Britain and America, women outnumbered men in all Methodist meetings.

Wesley's Ministry with the Poor

A major dimension of Wesley's "social holiness" was his ministry with the poor. Let us listen to some contemporary voices about this ministry:

Douglas Meeks called Wesley's ministry with the poor "intensely practical:"

"It included feeding, clothing, housing the poor; preparing the unemployed for work and finding it for them; visiting the poor sick and the prisoners; devising new forms of health care; distributing books to the literate poor; and raising structural questions about an economy that produced poverty. Wesley's was not simply service of the poor, but more importantly life with the poor. He even exposed himself to the diseases of the poor by where he stayed and with whom he visited. To be a disciple of Christ, for Wesley, meant to feed his sheep and to serve the least of his sisters and brothers."[354]

---

[351] Ibid. 248

[352] Ibid., 248

[353] Heitzenraer, *People Called Methodists,* 235 - 236

[354] Meeks, Douglas, *The Portion of the Poor,* Kingswood Books, 1995, 10

Ted Runyon's research reveals, "Ministering to the poor and their needs was part of the job description of every Methodist." Wesley applauded entrepreneurism if it were matched by charitable giving. He wrote to one Methodist woman of means:

"Go and see the poor and sick in their poor little hovels. Take up your cross woman. Remember the faith. Jesus went before you, and will go with you. Creep in among these in spite of dirt and a hundred disgusting circumstances.... Do not confine your conversation to genteel and elegant people. I should like this as well as you do; but I cannot discover a precedent for it in the life of our Lord or any of his apostles."[355]

"Lending Stock" was a sum of capital that Wesley raised to be loaned to people as a promissory note. Most people in that time had no access to credit and could buy only what they could pay for in cash. At first the notes were limited to one pound of British sterling. By 1772, the stock had increased sufficiently for the "Steward of the Lending Stock" to make loans of up to five pounds. Money was loaned to "people of the society whose characters were good and who needed temporary relief." Wesley personally gave money away and loaned money, sometimes as much as twenty pounds if the person were a tradesman.

Again, it is Ted Runyon's superb scholarship that lifts up the fact of Wesley's "practicing what he preached:"

"On Friday and Saturday, I visited as many more of the poor as I could. I found some in their cells underground, other in their garrets (attics), half-starved both with cold and hunger, added to their weakness and pain. But I found not one of them unemployed who was able to crawl about the room. So wickedly, devilishly false is that common objection, 'They are poor only because they are idle.' If you saw these things with your own eyes, could you (still) lay out money in ornaments or superfluities?"[356]

Many Methodists practiced the Christian charity that John

---

[355] Op. cit., Heitzenrater, *People Called Methodists*, 252 (copied by Heitzenrater from Wesley's letters

[356] Wesley, John, *Journal,* February 8, 1753, IN Runyon, Theodore, *The New Creation,* Abingdon, 1998,190

Wesley modeled. Oscar Sherwin wrote a fascinating biography of Wesley entitled, *John Wesley, Friend of the Poor.* He insisted, "Wesley brought about a moral enthusiasm which was healthy in its social tone. The real achievement of his movement was in the sphere of philanthropy.... Wesley created a permanent aura of goodness. Methodists felt personally responsible to relieve social need."[357]

Another biographer, John Richard Greene, opined, "The Methodists themselves were the least result of the Methodist revival. A yet nobler result ... was the steady attempt that has never ceased from that day until this to remedy the guilt, the ignorance, the physical suffering, the social degradation of the profligate and the poor."[358] Sherwin follows this with an extravagant accolade, "He was the most powerful and understanding friend the working classes had during the eighteenth century. His ministry proved dominantly and conclusively that the masses were not servile and impotent as believed"[359] The author of an interesting title, *Miscellanies,* wrote in 1902, "No single figure influenced so many minds, no single voice touched so many hearts. No other man did such a life's work for England.... You cannot cut him out of national life."[360]

New Chapel Is Built on City Road, London

Wesley had built the New Room in Bristol and leased and remodeled the Foundery in London, both in 1739. However, he refused to call either a church. In the local towns, he had allowed the building of what he called "preaching houses," but he reserved the word "Church" for Anglican houses of worship, not Methodist. By 1774, he was allowing the Sacrament of the Lord's Supper to be administered in the Foundery, but still did not use the term "church." He learned in 1776 that the City of London was about to raze the old Foundery and would soon cancel his lease.

Bunhill Fields was a graveyard in Moorfields for people who were no longer Anglicans and therefore could not be buried in

---

[357] Op. Citl, Sherwin, 190

[358] Green, John Richard, *History of the English People,* London, 1893, Vol, III, 1278

[359] Op. cit., Sherwin, 191

[360] Birrell, Augustine, *Miscellanies,* 1902, 34-35

what the Anglicans called "holy ground." About 20,000 Quakers were buried there, along with one of their founders, George Fox and notables like Isaac Watts, Daniel Defoe and John Bunyan. Later, in 1742, his mother, Susanna, was buried there. The swampy terrain had been built up by dirt and bones dumped there from graves dug at St. Paul's Cathedral, only two hundred yards west.

When he was seventy-five years old, he finally admitted to himself that Methodism needed something that "looked like a church, had services like a church, and would become the "mother church" of Methodism. He bought property on City Road in London, hired an architect to design what could be called nothing but "a church." Wesley also instructed him, "I want it adequate but not fine." Actually, when it was built, it had the largest unsupported ceiling in London. The balcony was supported by discarded ship masts, given by King George III. It is not a cathedral, but it is "fine." *(In the German Blitz of 1940, every building between St. Paul's and Wesley's Chapel was obliterated, but Wesley's Chapel survived.)*

Wesley, for the first time, appealed to the entire Methodist connexion to contribute toward a new facility on land he had purchased. City code required that only houses face the street. So, he built rooms on the street for lodging and meeting. "Screened from City Road" as code required, he built a "new chapel" at an estimated cost of £6000. The "begging of assistance of all our brethren" was mailed in October. Construction began in April, 1777, when he laid the cornerstone.

"He also used that occasion to preach a sermon outlining the history of Methodism ... as the 'rise and progress' of an 'extraordinary work of God.'" His sermon was from Numbers 23:23: "According to this time, it shall be asked, 'What hath God wrought.'" Wesley confessed, "I am in one respect an improper person to give this information, as it will oblige me to frequently speak of myself, which may give the appearance of ostentation. ... There is no other person who can supply my place, if I decline the task, who has a perfect knowledge of the work in question, from the beginning of it to this day."[361] His major reminder was his favorite definition of Methodism:

---

[361] Outler, ed., Sermon # 112, *On Laying the Cornerstone of the New Chapel, JWW,* Vol 3, 579-580

"What is Methodism? What does this new word mean?
Is it not a new religion? Nothing can be further from the
truth. Methodism, so called, is the old religion.... It is no
other than love: the love of God and of all mankind. It is
loving God with all our heart and strength just as he has
loved us.... It is the loving of every soul which God hath
made, every man on earth, as our own soul. This love is the
medicine of life, the never-failing remedy for all the evils
of a disordered world, for all the miseries and vices of men.
There is humbleness of mind, gentleness, long-suffering, the
whole image of God, and at the same time a peace that passeth all understanding and full of glory.

This religion of love, joy, and peace has its seat in the inmost
soul, but it is ever showing itself by its fruits, continually
springing up in love that worketh no ill to his neighbor, but
in every kind of beneficence, spreading virtue and happiness around it. This is the religion of the Bible, as no one
can deny who reads it with any attention. It is the religion
that runs through the Old and New Testaments: 'Thou shalt
love the Lord thy God with all thy soul," (Deuteronomy
6:5); and thy neighbour as thyself.' (Leviticus 19:34)'" He
concludes with a challenge, "Let our whole soul pant after a
revival of pure religion and undefiled, of the restoration of
the image of God, pure love in every child of man. ... Let us
provoke all not to enmity and contention, but to love and to
good works; always remembering those deep words that God
would engrave on our hearts: 'God is love.'"[362]

There are two striking surprises in this sermon. In a portion
not quoted above, Wesley emphasized that Methodism would never
separate from the Church of England. The second surprise is that
he made no reference to Aldersgate.

English born Professor Frank Baker made an accurate historical footnote about Wesley's Chapel:

"Wesley's New Chapel was not simply another preach-
ing-house. It was seen by him as a special symbol of connexional unity, meriting universal Methodist support.... This
new Methodist headquarters... was from the outset a centre
for sacramental worship as well as for preaching and fellow-

---

[362] Ibid., 591-592

ship and social service premises, in fact, functioned very much like those of a very active Anglican parish church, though without recognizing any allegiance to diocesan authorities."[363]

Just beside the chapel, he built a five-story house that served as his own home, quarters for the visiting preachers, and a "home base" that would survive him. It is very narrow to minimize street frontage, but is five stories high and "three rooms deep." Much of his family was now dead. He did not need apartments for them as he did in the old Foundery. Instead, he had four rooms for visiting preachers. His own bedroom was in the back. A pastor of the chapel, Rev. Birdwhistle, once said to this writer, "From this room, Mr. Wesley kept in touch with the universe." The ground floor was for hospitality and socialization. One room is furnished with artifacts from the old Foundery, including Charles Wesley's organ, and is called "Foundery Chapel." Wesley's study was on the street side of what the British call "first floor." It was designed deliberately so that from his desk, he was in full view of his mother's grave across the street in Bunhill Fields.

Richard Heitzenrater added this to Baker's description: "Wesley built the chapel on City Road on the basilica plan that represented more traditional, if not to say sacramental ecclesiastical architecture."[364] He points out, "Though it had all the features and functions of a church, it was called a 'chapel' and "remained outside the diocesan control of the Church of England and unconsecrated."

The church opened on All Saints Sunday, 1778. The premises became a center of preaching, fellowship and social service as well as of sacramental worship, and thus, with a high level of self-sufficiency, functioned like a parish church (even with a burial ground on the site). It was controlled by twenty-five trustees, a body that included five weavers, a silk broker, three merchants, a gentleman, a banker, and others from a dozen different parishes. The pulpit was restricted to who were ordained clergy. That eliminated all Methodist lay preachers."[365] So it was that Moorfields

---

[363] Op. cit., Baker, 213-214

[364] Op. Cit, Heitzenrater, *Wesley and the People Called Methodists*, 269

[365] Ibid., 269

became his, and Methodism's, *de facto* "parish."

Charles Wesley was the preacher in the "New Chapel" most Sundays. When some preachers complained that he was monopolizing the new chapel, Charles wrote to John:

"My reasons for preaching at the New Chapel (City Road) twice every Sunday are:

    1. Because, after you, I have the best right.

    2. Because I have so short a time to preach anywhere.

    3. Because I am full persuaded I can do more good there than in any other place."[366]

Wesley's Reaction to "a very uncommon train of providences"

All during the "War of Independence" Methodism remained a movement, and its preachers could not baptize or offer the Lord's Supper. Following American independence in 1781 and the signing of the Treaty of Paris in 1783, though Wesley was an Englishman and an Anglican who opposed independence, he came to terms with what he called "a very uncommon train of providence."

He realized that American Independence called for a church that was freed from the authority of the Anglican Church, and free to form themselves into a voluntary association. He knew the theory of government without an Established Church that was defined by John Locke and adopted by people like Thomas Jefferson, James Madison, Thomas Paine, and Benjamin Franklin. His reaction was an historic letter on September 10, 1784, in Bristol, England:

"As our American brethren are now totally disentangled, both from the State and the English hierarchy, we dare not entangle them again either with the one or the other. They are now at full liberty simply to follow the Scriptures and the primitive Church. And we judge it best that they should stand fast in that liberty wherewith God has so strangely made them free."

The American ethos provided the perfect seedbed for Methodism to morph from a movement to a Church. As a free association,

---

[366] Op. cit., Gill,, 220

Methodism had to deal constantly with dissenters who had differing views on such issues as the right to administer the sacraments, the necessity of itinerating, and the restrictive personal discipline imposed by John Wesley back in Britain.

In 1784, to the consternation of his brother, John Wesley ordained Thomas Vasey and Richard Whatcoat, and appointed Dr. Thomas Coke, an Anglican Elder, to be the "superintendent" of the work in America. "Superintendent Coke" was to ordain Francis Asbury upon his arrival in America, and to make Asbury a "joint superintendent" with Coke himself. Dr. Thomas Coke, an ordained Anglican priest, brought Wesley's documents to officially organize The Methodist Episcopal Church in 1784. The "Christmas Conference "was held in Baltimore in 1784, officially establishing The Methodist Episcopal Church.

In the same year that Wesley ordained clergy for American Methodism, he wanted to determine a legal path for Methodist property. Anglican Churches, obviously, were licensed by the Crown as houses of worship. The Act of Toleration, adopted in 1689 allowed the "dissenting churches" to register, with the attached stigma, "Dissenters." Wesley was not eligible for either path to legalization as a denomination. Therefore, Wesley petitioned the Bishop of Lincoln for a "license to worship according to one's own conscience" and it was denied.

He immediately had an attorney draw up the "Deed of Declaration." A rather strange document, it simply identified one hundred of the Methodist preachers (The Legal Hundred), and their successors, to be "The Conference of the People called Methodists." It was registered in the High Court of Chancery on February 28, 1784, and would take effect on the day when the last of the Wesley brothers died.

Charles Wesley's Death

After John Wesley ordained lay preachers for the formation of a Methodist Church in America, Charles lived in fear and dread that the Methodists in England would separate from the Anglican Church. In a letter to his brother, Charles wrote, "I believe ... ordination is separation. Stop here; ordain no more."[367] When Bishop Thomas Coke spoke for such separation at the 1786 Annual Confer-

---

[367] Op. cit., Best, 327

ence, Charles spoke his only word during the entire conference: "NO!" He then said that he would never attend another Methodist annual conference and he did not. His heart was broken. He wrote, "My brother does not see and will not see that he has renounced the principles and practice of his whole life ... I have lived on earth a little too long."[368]

Charles and John preached in rotation their last time in October, 1787 in Bristol. Shortly after his return to their London home, he took to his bed, telling his wife in the words of King David, "I am going the way of all the earth; my night has come." Other than his brother's ordaining lay preachers, his chief life regret was that none of his sons were loyal churchmen. He said, "I have been too little use to all my children, but it is too late to attempt it now."[369]

In mid-March, he had stopped eating. A few days before his death, he called his beloved wife to him and bid her write:

> **"Jesus, my only Hope thou art,**
> **strength of my failing flesh and heart.**
> **O could I catch a smile from thee**
> **and drop into Eternity."**

On March 28, his wife asked if he had any final message for her and the children. He replied weakly, "Only thanks, love, blessing." The next day he held her hand. The next day his daughter Sally heard him whisper three words: "Lord—my heart—my God" and "died so peacefully that we knew not exactly the moment in which his happy spirit died."[370]

Charles was eighty-one when he died on March 29, 1788. His family was disappointed that John did not provide some permanent annuity for his brother who had shared the ministry with him, but had little residual wealth. William Wilberforce wrote that the widow was in "real want" and raised money for her. The Methodist Conference voted her a modest annuity until her death in 1822.

John had set aside plots in the rear of the chapel for graves.

---

[368] Ibid., 328

[369] Ibid. 330

[370] Ibid., 331

He was grieved that Charles directed Sarah to bury him in a "properly consecrated" Anglican cemetery, not at "New Chapel." His written objection was, "I have lived and I will die in the communion of the Church of England, and I will be buried in the yard of my parish church." He died as passionate as ever that the Methodists should not become dissenters."[371]

Charles has been remembered as a superlative hymnwriter, but has not been remembered for his role as a preacher and a partner with his brother in establishing the Methodist movement. His wife wrote, "He not only acknowledged but delighted in the superiority of another, and if there was a human being who dislike power, avoided pre-eminence, and shrank from praise, it was Charles Wesley."[372]

John Wesley's Last Years

When Charles died, John was preaching up in the Midlands, and did not receive notice of his brother's death until a day before the funeral. He kept preaching. He wrote Sally a tender letter, explaining why he had not come.

Two weeks later John was 'lining out' his brother's great hymn, "Come, O Thou Traveler Unknown," but broke down when he came to the words, "My company before is gone and I am left alone with Thee." He burst into tears, and sat down in the pulpit with his face in his hands. The singing abruptly stopped until John could continue."[373]

John Wesley survived his brother by three years. He was now being invited more frequently to preach in an Anglican Church. He had outlived his most influential opposition. He was no longer vilified as a "dangerous enthusiast." He had become known as an ecclesiastical celebrity even among the secular writers. His ministry of unselfish labor and effective organizational leadership had brought widespread appreciation for his character and his abilities.

" Wesley's health was remarkable. He had written in 1782, "I entered into my eightieth year, but, blessed be God, my

---

[371] Ibid., 331

[372] Op. cit., Best, 336-337

[373] Op. cit., Heitzenrater, *People Called Methodists,* 300

time is not 'labour and sorrow.' I find no more pain of bodily infirmities than at five-and-twenty." In addition to the power of God, he attributed "my still traveling four or five thousand miles a year, mostly walking or on horseback; my sleeping day or night whenever I want it; my rising at a set hour; and my constant preaching, particularly in the morning."[374]

Wesley was often guilty of either hyperbole or exaggeration!

- On his eighty-second birthday, June 28, 1785, he declared, "It is now eleven years since I felt such thing as weariness."[375]

- Then, the next winter he trudged all day through ankle deep snow in London begging £200 to augment his inventory of food and fuel for the poor. Result? A high fever, but he survived.

- When he was eighty-four, he wrote that the only effects of another year of aging was greater difficulty in walking uphill, reading by candlelight, and remembering!

- By age eighty-five he could hardly see out of his left eye, and felt much pain in his right shoulder and arm. Still, though, he traveled and preached without weariness, and "feel no decay in writing sermons which I believe as correct as ever." His wonderful strength was, he said, due to "the power of God fitting me for the work to which I am called." He still preached at the factory gates at 5:00.

- That same year, 1787, "he started out at Birmingham at midnight and traveled nineteen hours. By Thursday, he had traveled 240 miles in eighty hours!" Then he "went with a gentleman to hear a famous musician that plays upon the glasses."[376] He continued a trying schedule of many miles until he was eighty-seven. "In 1787 he spent four weeks in the Channel Islands and preached every day to large congregations.

---

[374] Op. cit., Telford, 342

[375] Op. cit., Tomkins, 191

[376] Op. cit., Sherwin, 194

- In 1789, at age eighty-six he preached three and a half months in Ireland. In Limerick, all the gentry came to hear him and the place would not hold the crowd. So, he was obliged to go outside to preach. In England, multitudes thronged to listen to the venerable preacher. The Societies felt their esteemed founder could not be with them much longer and hung eagerly upon every word from his lips."377 Wesley's reception at other places was equally enthusiastic."[378]

- However, age was taking its toll. In 1789, his eighty-sixth year, following his last entry in what he called "his account," he wrote this note: "I have kept my accounts exactly. I will not attempt it any longer. My eyes are so dim that no glasses would help me. I am satisfied with the continual conviction, that I can earn all I can, save all I can, and give all I can – that is all that I have."[379]

- Increasing infirmities did not check his restless itinerancy until he entered a shocking assessment on New Year's Day, 1790:

  "I am now an old man, decayed from head to foot. My eyes are dim, my right-hand shakes much; my mouth is hot and dry every morning; I have a lingering fever most every day; my motion is weak and slow. However, blessed be God, I do not slack my labour; I can preach and write still."[380]

That same year, on his birthday, June 28, his diary entry reviewed his decline since his last birthday:

  "For above eighty-six years, I found none of the infirmities of old age: my eyes did not wax dim, neither was my natural strength abated. But last August, I found almost a sudden change. My eyes were so dim that no glasses would help me. My strength likewise now quite forsook

---

[377] Op. cit., Telford, 339

[378] Ibid., 341

[379] Op. cit., Heitzenrater, *People Called Methodists* 305, Copied from his *Journal*

[380] Ward & Heitzenrater, eds. ̂ Vol. 24, 2003, 164

me and probably will not return in this world. It seems nature is exhausted and, humanly speaking, will sink more and more till 'the weary springs of life stand still at last.'"[381]

Dr. Heitzenrater quotes Henry Moore, "Being in the house with him when he wrote this, I was greatly surprised. He still arose at four o'clock and went through the duties of the day ... without complaint, and with a degree of resolution that was astonishing. He would sometimes remark that he wanted "to do a little for God before he dropped into the dust."[382]

Notwithstanding these entries, he preached and traveled relentlessly, including annual conference in 1790. In one of his last written sermons he noted, "My eyes are now waxed dim; my natural force is abated. However, while I can, I would fain do a little for God before I drop into the dust." A recording secretary wrote that Mr. Wesley was "nearly worn out, his faculties were much impaired, especially his memory."[383]

That same year, in Falmouth, Cornwall, known as "the Methodist county," he wrote, "About forty years ago, I was taken prisoner here by an immense mob. How the tide is turned! High and low now, lining the street from one end of town to the other, they come out of stark love and kindness, gaping and staring as if the King were going by."[384]

Norwich had been a town that rejected him years before, but now he wrote, "How wonderfully the tide has turned! I am become an honourable man in Norwich."[385]

- However, even will power could not keep him going. In October, under a tree in Winchelsea, he preached his last outdoor sermon. Friends had collected money to buy a carriage and he now consented to ride there rather than on horseback.

- By 1791, he was confined to London. His last sermon that

[381] Ward & Heitzenrater, *JWW*, J & D, Vol. 24, 182

[382] Ibid., 164

[383] Op. cit., Heitzenrater, *People Called Methodists*, 305

[384] Op. cit., Tomkins, 192

[385] Ibid., 192

he wrote down was on January 17. It was later titled, "On Faith." The familiar text is Hebrews 11:1, "Faith is being sure of what we hope for and certain of what we do not see." It is an amazing sermon, asking questions repeatedly raised by all who consider their own death or who have lost loved ones. He wonders how we can see or hear without our human organs of eyes and ears A student of science, he wonders where in the universe Hades and Heaven might be. Very importantly to every Christian, he quotes a hymn by his brother Charles who wondered if our departed loved ones ever communicate with us and believes that they:

> **"Sometimes on errands of love**
> **Revisit their brethren below?"**

He calls this "a pleasing thought." He quotes from Bishop Ken, whom most of us know only as the author of *The Doxology* we sing when the offering is taken in church! Ken wrote:

> **'O may thine angels while I sleep around my head their**
> **vigils keep! Their love angelical instill, stop all the con-**
> **sequences of ill:**
> **May their celestial joys rehearse and thought to thought**
> **with me converse;**
> **O, in my stead the whole night long sing to my God a**
> **grateful song.'**

Of our departed loved ones, he wonders, "What can we now know concerning those of a different nature? It seems it will not be possible for us to discern them at all till we are furnished with senses of a different nature, which are not yet opened in our souls." He even asked, "But who knows how we shall be employed after we enter that invisible world? A little of it we may conceive... what God himself has revealed in his Word."

He concludes, "So little could even the most improved reason discover concerning the invisible and eternal world. The greater cause have we to praise the Father of lights who hath opened the eyes of our understanding. These things we have believed upon the testimony of God, the Creator of all things visible and invisible."[386]

---

[386] Outler, Albert, JWW, Sermons, Vol. 4, Sermon #112, 187-200 (selections)

John Wesley's Last Days

First, we review Richard Heizenrater's chronology of Wesley's last days:

"John's diary records another five weeks of fairly normal activity, preaching fairly regularly. In mid-February, he caught a cold … but improved enough to preach on Wednesday, February 23, the day of his last diary entry.

As he rode in his carriage to and from his preaching place, he read the autobiography of an African slave, Gustavus Vassa—a book whose publication Wesley had financed. Motivated by the book, upon returning to his room, he dictated to William Wilberforce, a member of Parliament, the last of his thousands of letters. He wrote about his horror that "it being a law in all our Colonies that the oath of a black against a white goes for nothing. What villainy is this!" The next day, Wesley took a fever and began to decline rapidly."[387]

Dr. Franklin Wilder, wrote a fascinating biography of Wesley entitled, *The Remarkable World of John Wesley*. It purports to be the words of Wesley's sister, Martha, who, according to Wilder, left her diary to Dr. Adam Clarke. Wilder then shares some most fascinating and believable details of Wesley's last days. These seem to be in keeping with scholars like Richard Heitzenrater. Martha is buried in the same tomb as John Wesley, behind Wesley's Chapel.

"Sunday morning, he seemed better, sat up in his chair, looked cheerful, and quoted one of Charles' hymns. Our niece, Sally Wesley and Miss Ritchie prayed with him.

"Monday morning he became weaker. Tuesday, after a restless night, John said he was suffering no pain and began singing. Then he said he wanted to write, but he could not use the pen. His housekeeper and companion, Elizabeth Ritchie, said, "'Let me write for you, sir; tell me what you would say.' 'Nothing,' Wesley murmured, 'but that God is with us.' He tried to speak again, but his friends (around the bed) could not make out what he meant. Then, with a

---

[387] Op. cit., Heitzenrater, *People Called Methodists*, 307

final effort, he said again, while lifting his arm in grateful triumph, "The best of all, God is with us."

"During the night, he kept repeating the words, 'I'll praise, I'll praise,' but could say nothing more." (Apparently trying to complete his brother's hymn):

> **"I'll praise my Maker while I've breath,**
> **And when my voice is lost in death**
> **Praise shall employ my nobler pow'rs.**

"Wednesday, March 2, a few minutes before ten o'clock in the morning, Bradford had just finished praying. Our niece Sarah Wesley was with John, along with other friends. 'Farewell,' John cried—the last word he uttered."[388]

"His body lay in state one day in the chapel at City Road; with an open coffin as thousands filed by in silence, noticing the sweet smile on his face."[389]

In accordance with his will, he was buried behind the chapel at five o'clock in the morning by torchlight to avoid the crowds, but the word leaked and thousands came. His coffin was carried by six poor men, among whom £6 was distributed. He had dictated, "I particularly desire there may be no hearse, no coach, no escutcheon, no pomp except the tears of them who loved me."

Following the funeral on March 9, the black drapings in the Chapel were remade into dresses and distributed to poor women.[390] Profits from his books were to "support Methodism." Once his will was probated, he died as he had promised, with a net wealth of less than ten pounds. He "gave all he could."

---

[388] Op. cit., Wilder, 181-182 (end of quote claimed as Martha Wesley's)

[389] Ibid., 182 (Wilder's own words)

[390] Op. cit., Heitzenrater,

Epilogue to Volume I

In Volume I of *The Methodist Story*, we have included Wesley's ongoing work in England until his death in 1791. I have ended this volume with an account of Wesley's last days and his death. As Francis Asbury's account of Wesley's death rather cryptically indicates, Bishop Thomas Coke left America immediately for England, hoping to receive from his peers there the mantle of Wesley. By contrast, Wesley's death was no cause for Bishop Asbury to interrupt the task at hand. After noting that Coke had boarded a ship to England, Asbury wrote in his *Journal*, 'I was left to make the appointments."

Wesley had lived seven years after he ordained clergy and, in effect, established The Methodist Episcopal Church in America. The formative "Christmas Conference" had been held December 22-30, 1784, at Lovely Lane Methodist Church in Baltimore, and Francis Asbury was ordained Deacon, ordained Elder, and elected Bishop! From that point, *The Methodist Story* as we relate it will be the "American Methodist Story."

Volume II of *The Methodist Story will begin* when missionaries came to America at their own initiative and without Wesley's knowledge. Volume II will necessarily review their lay ministries. These pioneers were Barbara Ruckle Heck and men like Joseph Pilmore, Phillip Embury, Captain Thomas Webb, Robert Strawbridge, and Robert Williams.

Their work began about 1760-1766. In 1769, Wesley included in his list of appointments, "America: __________." Francis Asbury was appointed in 1771 as a lay preacher, unable to administer the sacraments.

The first bona fide General Conference of American Methodism was being shaped and would take place in 1792. Leadership of

the Wesleyan movement in America was the mission of Francis
Asbury whose ministry would dominate and shape the formative
years of American Methodism.

Denominationally, Wesley's ecclesiastical progeny have both
splintered and merged. Volume II will define the issues that
divided and unified, and might divide again Wesley's American
progeny.

Bibliography

Anderson, William K, ed., *Methodism,* The Methodist Publishing House, MCMXLVII

Anonymous, *The Tablets at the New Room,* Andreas Haaf& Sons, 2004

Baker, Frank, *John Wesley and the Church of England,* Abingdon, 1970

Baker, Frank, *The Works of John Wesley, J & D,* Vol. 25, J&D 1991

Best, Gary, *Charles Wesley,* Epworth, 2006

Birrell, Augustine, *Miscellanies,* 1902

Cadman, S. Parkes, *The Three Religious Leaders of Oxford and Their Movements – Wycliffe, Wesley, and Newman,* Macmillan, 1916

Clarke, Adam, *Memoirs of the Wesley Family,* London, 1823

Cowper, William, *Table Talk,* John Sharpe, London: Picadilly, 1782

Cragg, Gerald, ed., *The Works of John Wesley,* Vol. 11, Abingdon, 1989

Collins, Kenneth, *John Wesley, A Theological Journey, Abingdon, 2003*

Cushman, Robert, *John Wesley's Experimental Divinity,* Kingswood, 1989

Dallimore, Arnold, *Susanna Wesley,* Baker Book House, 1993

Davies, Rupert, *Methodism,* Epworth, 1985

Edwards, Maldwyn, *Sons to Samuel,* Epworth, 1961

Ferguson, Charles, *Organizing to Beat the Devil,* Doubleday, 1971

Fraser, Rebecca, *The Story of Britain*, Norton and Company, 2003

Garrison, Webb; Luccock, Halford, *Endless Line of Splendor*, United Methodist Communications, 1950, 12

Gill, Frederick, *Charles Wesley, the First Methodist*, Lutterworth, 1964

Green, John Richard, History of the English People, Vol. III, London, 1893

Hardt, Philipo, *The Soul of Methodism*, University Press of America, 2000

Heitzenrater, Richard, *Mirror and Memory*, Kingswood, 1989

Heitzenrater, Richard, *The The People Called Methodisis*, Abingdon, 1984

Heitzenrater, Richard, *The Elusive Mr. Wesley – as seen by his contemporaries*, Abingdon, 1984

Heitzenrater, Richard, *The Elusive Mr. Wesley– John Wesley his own Biographer*, Abingdon, 1984,220

Hempton, David, *Methodism – Empire of the Spirit, Yale, 2005, 7*

Henderson, Michael, *John Wesley's Class Meeting: A Model for Making Disciples*, Francis Asbury Press, 1997

Hyde, A.B., *The Story of Methodism... to the Present Time*, Willey & Co. 1889

Internet, Wikipedia, "John White, Puritan English Minister"

Lecky, W.E.H. *History of England in the Eighteenth Century*, Vol. III

Luccock, Halford; **Hutchinson, Paul**; **Goodloe, R.**; *The Story of Methodism*, Abingdon, 1926

MacCulloch, Diarmaid, *Christianity—the First Three Thousand Years*, Viking, 2010

Maddox, Randy ed., *Aldersgate Reconsidered*, Kingswood, 1990

Maddox, Randy, *Responsible Grace*, Kingswood, 1994

Maddox, Randy, *The Works of John Wesley, Doctrinal and Controversial Treatises I*, Vol., 12, Abingdon, 2012

Maser, Frederick, *Seven Sisters in Search of Love*, Academy Books, 1988

Meeks, Douglas, *The Portion of the Poor*, Kingswood Books, 1995

Moore, Henry, *The Life of the Rev. John Wesley, London: Kershaw, 1824*

Outler, Albert, *The Works of John Wesley, Sermons Vol. 1,II,III*, Abingdon, 1984

Pellowe, Susan, ed., *A Wesley Family Book of Days*, Renard Productions, 1994

Pollock, John, *John Wesley, the Preacher,* Kingsway, 1989

Rack,Henry, *The Works of John Wesley, Vol. 10*, Abingdon, 2011

Richey, Russell; Campbell, Dennis; Lawrence, William; eds. *Marks of Methodism*, Abingdon, 2005

Rowe, Gilbert, *The Meaning of Methodism*, Cokesbury Press, 1926

Runyon, Theodore ("Ted"), ed. , *Wesleyan Theology Today*, Kingswood, 1985

Runyon, Theodore ("Ted"), ed., *Wesleyan Theology Today*, Kingswood, 1985

Sangster, William, *Methodism: Her Unfinished Task*, London: Epworth, Epworth Press 1947

Schmidt, Martin, *John Wesley, A Theological Biography*, Abingdon, Vol. 1, 1973

Sherwin, Oscar, *John Wesley, Friend of the People*, Twayne Publishers, New York, 1961, 39

Telford, John, *The Life of John Wesley*, Charles Kelly: London, 1906

Thomas, Arthur, *Profiles in Faith—Susanna Wesley*, C.S. Lewis Institute, 2002

Thorsen, Don, *Calvin vs. Wesley*, Abingdon, 2013

Tomkins, Stephen, *John Wesley—a biography,* Eerdmans, 2003

Troeltsch, *The Social Teaching of the Christian Churches,* Harper Torchbooks, 1960

Tyerman, L., *Life and Times of John Wesley, Founder of the Methodists,* Hodder & Stoughton, 2882

United Methodist Book of Discipline, United Methodist Publishing House, 2016

Urlin, R. Denny, *The Churchman's LIfe of John Wesley,* London: SPCK, (no date)

Vickers, Jason; Maddox, Randy, eds. *The Cambridge Companion to John Wesley,* Cambridge, 2010

Wallace, Charles, *Susana Wesley's Complete Writings,* Oxford Press, 1997

Ward, Reginald; Heitzenrater, Richard, *The Works of John Wesley, Journals and Diaries, Volume 18,* Abingdon 1988

Wearmouth, Robert, *Methodism and the Common People of the Eighteenth Century,* Epworth, 1945

Wesley, Charles, "Come Thou Found ot Every Blessing," *United Methodist Hymnal,* Methodist Publishing House, 1989

Whiteley, J.H., *Wesley's England,* London: Epworth Press, 1954

Wilder, Franklin, *The Remarkable World of John Wesley,* Exposition Press, 1978

Winchester, C.T., *Life of Wesley,* McMillan, 1906

Also from Donald Haynes

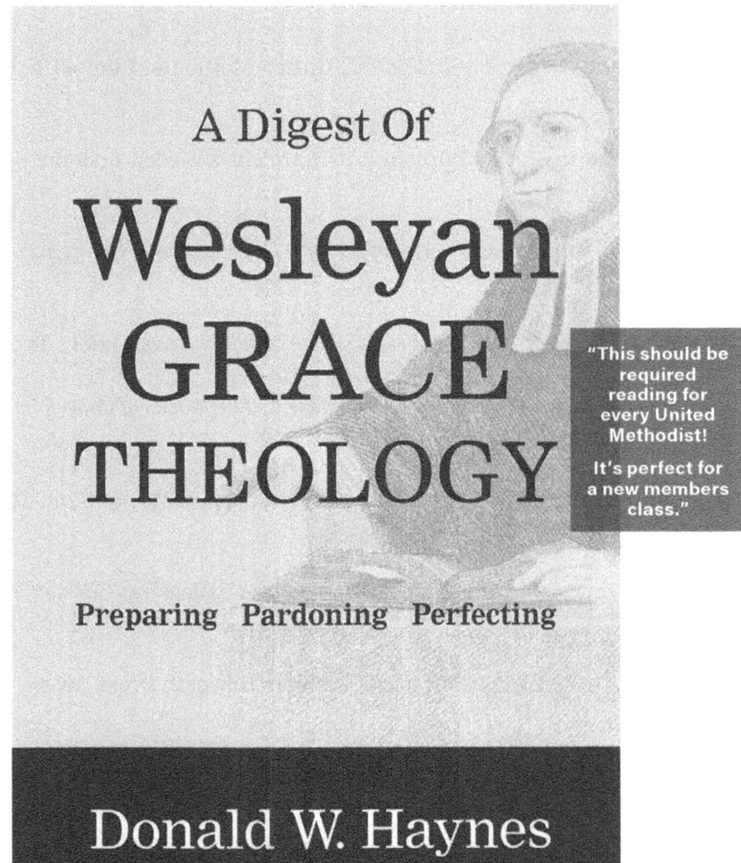

A Digest of
Wesleyan Grace

Preparing Pardoning Perfecting

Other Books

from Market Square

marketsquarebooks.com

IMPACT!
Reclaiming the Call of Lay Ministry

Kay Kotan & Blake Bradford

Where Do We
Go From Here?

20 United Methodist Writers

The Good Folks
of Lennox Valley

Kevin Slimp

The Methodist Story
1792-2019

Dr. Donald Haynes

Grow Your Faith

with these books from Market Square

marketsquarebooks.com

Discipler

Phil Maynard & Eddie Pipkin

Hear It, See It, Risk It

Steve Cordle

A Christian Teenager's Guide
to Surviving High School

Ashley Conner

Understanding Your Call

11 Biblical Figures Understand
Their Calls from God
by 10 United Methodist Leaders

Grow Your Faith

with these books from Market Square

marketsquarebooks.com

Obvious Wisdom

Bishop Bob Farr

Shift 2.0

Phil Maynard

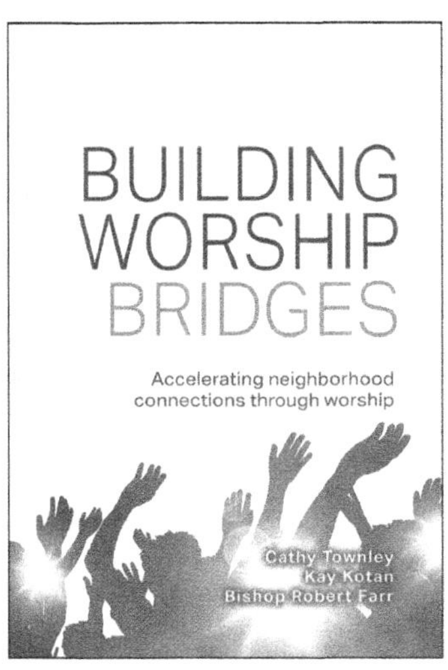

Building Worship Bridges

Cathy Townley

Get Out of that Box!

Anne Bosarge